Stained with the Mud
of Khe Sanh

Stained with the Mud of Khe Sanh

A Marine's Letters from Vietnam, 1966–1967

RODGER JACOBS

McFarland & Company, Inc., Publishers
Jefferson, North Carolina, and London

LIBRARY OF CONGRESS CATALOGUING-IN-PUBLICATION DATA

Jacobs, Rodger, 1946–
[Correspondence. Selections]
    Stained with the mud of Khe Sanh : a Marine's letters
from Vietnam, 1966–1967 / Rodger Jacobs.
        p.   cm.
    Includes bibliographical references and index.

    ISBN 978-0-7864-7215-4
    softcover : acid free paper ∞

    1. Jacobs, Rodger, 1946– —Correspondence.   2. Vietnam
War, 1961–1975—Personal narratives, American.
3. Marines—United States—Correspondence.   I. Title.
DS559.5.J345 2013
959.704'3092—dc23
[B]   2013029582

BRITISH LIBRARY CATALOGUING DATA ARE AVAILABLE

Front cover: Rodger Jacobs showered, shaved, and secure behind
the wire writing the letters in this book, Dong Ha, March 1967

Manufactured in the United States of America

*McFarland & Company, Inc., Publishers
    Box 611, Jefferson, North Carolina 28640
    www.mcfarlandpub.com*

This book is dedicated to all the children, women, and men,
friend or foe, who gave their lives in the Vietnam War
so the rest of us could live.
This book is further dedicated to the Marine grunts listed on this page.
Some of these men were killed through no fault of their own, as they
were just in the wrong place at the wrong time. Some of these men
went knowingly to their deaths to save their brother warriors.
I am alive because of their sacrifice. I sing their praises.

Thomas Kindt	Kim Lin	September 22, 1966
John Freeman	Kim Lin	September 22, 1966
Norman Hoyt	Kim Lin	September 22, 1966
John Jolley	Kim Lin	September 22, 1966
Bryon Highland	Street Without Joy	February 21, 1967
Robert Wade	Street Without Joy	February 25, 1967
Louis Perry	Phu An	March 24, 1967
Walter Singleton*	Phu An	March 24, 1967
Michael Stewart**	Phu An	May 13, 1967
John Avila	Phu An	May 13, 1967
Richard Sarakas	Phu An	May 13, 1967
Michael Amato	Phu An	May 13, 1967
Jerry Gorney***	Phu An	May 13, 1967
James West	Phu An	May 15, 1967
Clyde Clark	Phu An	May 16, 1967
Thomas Chaffin	Phu An	May 16, 1967
George Linder	Phu An	May 16, 1967
Stanley Godwin	Quang Tri	May 18, 1967
Russell Keck**	Quang Tri	May 18, 1967
George Custer	Ouan Nam	May 22, 1967
Doc James Gales	Phu An	May 26, 1967
George Coutrakis	Quang Tri	July 2, 1967
William Rash	Hill 200	August 21, 1968

*Medal of Honor (posthumous)
**Navy Cross (posthumous)
***Silver Star (posthumous)

Acknowledgments

I would like to thank the people who helped this endeavor take wing. Lucy, my defiantly better half, who stood by me during the six years it took to create this work and thanks to all my veteran friends who provided insight and encouragement when I was running out of gas.

Thank you one and all.

Rodger Jacobs
August 2013

Table of Contents

This poem is to honor the Marines in the dedication. They were the best of us.

The Best Are Washed Away

The young march into the killing field
one step in their fate is sealed
fiercely fighting to the fray
and the best are washed away.

Virgin to the breech
God what do old men teach.
Honor, glory, with death young men pay
and the best are washed away.

Bouncing Betty, RPG, tomato can
one misstep will kill a man.
Sail the sea of fate each day
and the best are washed away.

Ignore the death surround
the fight, the fight abound.
Give no quarter night or day
and the best are washed away.

Some survive with body rent
on the field their spirit spent.
Death was the price of life they say
and the best are washed away.

Some returned unscathed home
behind the mask routefoot roam,
anguish, anguish, feet of clay
and the best are washed away.

Those who play know no game,
life of rage, nothing is the same
for when the war tide recedes to day
all the best are washed away.

Preface

I'm a lucky man. Writing the letters in this book saved my life.

When I arrived at Parris Island, South Carolina, United States Marine Corps Boot Camp, one of the first things my drill instructors told me to do was to write at least two letters home a week. Like all recruits I did what my DI told me and I started writing letters. My father, a World War II combat veteran, kept my letters and numbered them as the letters arrived. I continued to write all through my training, through my combat tour in Vietnam and through my hospital stay in Japan while recovering from wounds. My dad saved all the 146 letters and over 250 images that I sent home. Those letters and those images are the framework of this book.

This book does not contain all the letters that I wrote and the photographs that I took and sent home. I have selected and edited my most meaningful correspondence and added a narrative thread so I could tell the full story of my military experience. The letters I have kept are the ones that paint the picture of a high school kid from rural Ohio being transformed into a Marine warrior, a trigger-puller. My letters describe my further transformation into a war-fighting Marine grunt, and finally this volume will take you into my metamorphosis into a war-altered ex–Marine but a Marine still.

The narrative, interspersed between letters, tells the full truth of the story that unfolded beyond the surface of the letters. I describe some of the feelings and events that I couldn't write home about. I just couldn't tell my family that I was playing a daily game of life and death and that I lived in a savage, bloody place without any rules whatsoever. I had to write about what was happening, but I also had to protect them with small lies.

My only escape from the madness of war that surrounded me was the unbroken chain of letters I was writing and the photographs I was taking and sending to my family back in the World. These two things saved my life. A belief if truly believed will manifest itself in reality. My repeating in my letters over and over that I would be coming home safe allowed me to survive when so many of my friends were killed.

My dad gave me back my letters and photographs more than 20 years ago.

Author with M-14 and K-bar on the Street Without Joy, March 1967.

Since that time I have humped this collection of letters, photographs, and memories. I have humped all this every day and every night and everywhere my life led me.

When I made the decision to start putting all these elements into a book I had no idea it would take me the better part of five years. I've had to set everything down and walk away from the manuscript several times as the memories were just too painful to continue. My Marine training kicked in, though, and that training and the duty I feel toward the men I served with allowed me to put one foot in front of another and see this effort finished.

I've had to use some noms de guerre in the narrative text to protect the innocent, as that is my warrior's duty. I was a PFC grunt at the time I wrote these letters. The numbers of killed and wounded and the facts stated in my letters reflect what I knew at the time. I have not altered any of the facts as I knew them then. In Vietnam I did not have the luxury of sitting back and deciding if the war was right or wrong. I and the Marines around me were not fighting for the United States, we were fighting for our very lives. I'm a very, very, lucky man. I survived.

I am bringing my letters to light because of the sacrifice of the men who didn't make it. This book tells our story. I want this book to speak for these men and to teach people what happens to the young we send to war, and I want this book to help heal those young ones when they return to us.

Semper Fidelis
Rodger Jacobs

Abbreviations and Slang Terms

60	60 mm mortar (U.S.)	MOS	Military Operational Specialty
81	81 mm mortar (U.S.)		
AIT	Advanced Infantry Training	NVA	North Vietnamese Army
		PI	Parris Island (South Carolina) Recruit Depot
AK-47	.762 submachine gun, enemy weapon		
AR-15	.223 automatic rifle	R&R	rest and recuperation
ARVN	Army of the Republic of North Vietnam	RPG	rocket-propelled grenade (enemy)
Bouncing Betty	antipersonnel mine (enemy)	rubber lady	air mattress
		short timer	Marine with little time to do before 13-month tour is up
C-4	plastic explosive		
c-rats	c-rations; standard combat meal		
		slop chute	enlisted men's club
DMZ	de-militarized zone	toe popper	anti-personnel mine (enemy)
DI	drill instructor		
Grunt	Marine infantryman	tomato can	anti-personnel mine (enemy)
hootch	self-made shelter		
hump	what a grunt carries	VC	Viet Cong, Victor Charlie
K-BAR	Marine fighting knife		
KIA	killed in action	ville	Vietnamese village
LAW	light anti-tank weapon (U.S.)	WIA	wounded in action
		The World	Continental USA
M-14	.762 automatic rifle	World of Hurt	where a grunt lives
M-60	.762 machine gun		
M-79	40mm grenade launcher (U.S.)		

1

USA: Boot Camp and Training: Letters 1 to 38

Introduction: Boot Camp, March 1st–August 10, 1966

My letters dated March to May 1966 were written during training at Parris Island, South Carolina, USMC boot camp. These letters describe the transformation of an 18-year-old high school kid from Ohio into a warrior, a combat-ready United States Marine.

High school bored me mostly and that was reflected in my grades. After barely graduating in June 1965 I had a couple of dead-end jobs and was drifting. The draft had been reinstated at the time and Vietnam was looming on the horizon. My draft lottery number came up a 3 and that made certain that I would be one of the first to be called. Rather than take a chance with which service would take me I decided to take a look at all of them and make that decision myself. After looking at all the posters, printed material and uniforms, I picked the Marine Corps because I liked their dress blues. Funny how things work; I would serve three years and the only time I was in blues was for five minutes when I got my picture taken for my Parris Island platoon graduation book.

I signed the papers, and then told my parents and my sister Debi. My mom was not happy, but both she and my dad were glad to have me out of the house and on my way somewhere. I was also. My father, a World War II combat veteran, was secretly proud, I think.

I received my orders and in March 1966 was off to see the world on my grand adventure. I got on a train in Cleveland, Ohio, and headed to the United States Marine Recruit Depot, Parris Island, South Carolina. I arrived in Beaufort, South Carolina, and found a group of kids that had been traveling from all over the eastern U.S. and were waiting for a Marine Corps bus to take them to Parris Island. Our bus arrived at 1:00 A.M. and we got aboard and were off to the Marine Corps.

I didn't know what to expect when we pulled up to a well-lit building with three Marines waiting for us at 2:00 A.M. The drill instructors were on us from *the moment the bus doors opened. "Out, out, out, you dirty pigs," was the first thing I heard. Before I knew it I was standing on a pair of yellow footprints along with a big bunch of scared kids all doing the same. It was the start of a very long day. We were given a 30-second haircut and stripped to our shorts, and had a grease pencil number scratched on our chests. Our transformation into Marines had started.*

We learned to move as a unit and to salute and to stand at attention. We ate our chow at attention and we ate as fast as we could.

We were moved into a barracks that was a long room with double-decker bunks along the walls, a shower and bathroom called a "head" on one end, with a DI's office next to the head. The walls were called bulkheads, the floor was the deck and the ceiling was the overhead. The doors were hatches and the drinking fountain was the scuttlebutt. There was lots of stuff to remember. We counted off and the evens got bottom bunks and the odds got top bunks and at 11:00 P.M., which was 23:00 in the new world I was in, the lights went out and sleep came fast.

Precisely at 4:00 the next morning we were awakened by the sound of a large metal trash can crashing down the center of our squad bay followed by two DIs screaming, "Up, up, up, you dirty hogs" and it started all over again.

Washington, D.C. letter 1
March 3, 1966

Mom and Dad.

I am writing from a USO in Washington, D.C. We just spent the night in a Pullman 1st Class. There are seven of us and we played cards throughout the night because the train was swaying back and forth and we couldn't sleep. We ate pretty good so far. We ate in a restaurant that had a cover charge and everyone had dress clothes except us. The USMC paid for it. We are having fun now because when I leave in two hours it will be more of the swaying side-by-side.

I have got to go eat now.

Love,
Rog

Boot Camp

U.S.M.C. Recruit Depot letter 2
Parris Island, South Carolina
March 5, 1966

Dear Mom and Dad

I've been here for two days now and it seems like two weeks. Not that I don't like it but you learn so much (you even sleep at attention). I have been eating good food but I miss your cooking.

This is the first letter I could get away from Boot Camp because of many, many other things to do.

We have been marched and stood at attention and ate and been issued articles for the past two days and I have not even said hello to any of the other privates.

The life looks as if it is going to be tough but I know I can make it. You will be receiving two letters a week instead of one (the D.I. says two — I am not going to argue).

I was told by the drill instructors in no uncertain terms that I would be writing at least two letters home per week. It was at this point that I started writing the letters in this book. It was then that I started stating in the letters "I can make it." I wrote constantly, using every spare moment of my time. The unbroken chain of letters my drill instructors started me writing in boot camp would continue all through training, my Vietnam combat tour and my hospital stay in Japan. I'm convinced that if I had not been ordered to write these letters in boot camp I would not have survived Vietnam.

Say hello and pass my address around as much as possible. It is as follows:

> PVT Jacobs, Rodger E.
> PLT 255 CO "L" 2nd RTBN
> MCRD, Parris Island, South Carolina 22905

> Love and all,
> Rog

P.S. I've got two minutes left. Bye.

Parris Island SC Boot Camp letter 3
Beaufort, SC
March 8, 1966

Dear Mom and Dad,

Today our PLT (No. 255) (The best) took all kinds of tests for classification. The average is about 90 and I got about 115 on all of them.

We had our shots and blood tests yesterday and don't let anyone tell you those guns don't hurt your arm. It feels like a hot cigar pressed against your shoulder.

I haven't smoked since I got here and the only girl I saw was a very ugly woman Marine checking forms.

I am sitting by my footlocker on my bucket and writing out of the Marine book they give us stationery, envelopes, etc....

I hope you can read this writing well because I don't have much time for letters. I have to polish my boots, straighten my foot locker and bounce a silver dollar on the bed like a drum. Whenever the drill instructor talks of the army we all laugh. I am going to come out a regular Marine which is equal to a Green Beret in any person's book. I have been learning my eleven general orders and the chain of commands. President of the US through Drill Instructor by heart.

Well, I have to polish my boots now so take care of yourself and write me back.

Love always,
Rog

Parris Island letter 4
Beaufort, SC
March 10, 1966

Dear Mom & Dad & Debi,

We just finished our first official day of training.

We got up at 1630 hours (4:30) and made our bunks, scrubbed the place from top to bottom, did the windows, got dressed and went to chow.

When we got back we had a class on interior guard duty (sentry). A physical training instructor came into our squad bay (place where we stay) and we did a few exercises for about two hours. We then practiced port arms and all the other things that go with handling a rifle.

We ate lunch chow and it was graduation day for another class so we had chocolate milk in the mess hall. We came out of the mess hall and drilled until physical instruction time, where we exercised for awhile then ran a mile. We got back to our squad bay and showered and took off for chow, we ate, marched back and had a class on sex hygenics. The instructor only hit kids 40 times and cussed 10,000 times today — only kidding.

The DIs would make us stand at attention in our underwear with one hand on our rifles and one hand on our crotch and repeat, "This is my rifle, this is my gun. This is for killing and this is for fun." If we laughed the DI would tell us to hit the deck and give them 25 push-ups. Woe to the recruit who dropped his rifle.

But there is a little guy across the aisle from me called Puss Gut (Drill Instructor's nickname for him) that is entirely uncoordinated and who the DIs are trying to make crack so he will be transferred out of the squad or platoon so that it will be in step. Both marching, eating, getting dressed, etc. He cannot do anything. They get about an inch from the tip of his nose with theirs and scream at the top of their lungs at him at the same time cussing, yelling, ordering and putting him down.

Don't do or write anything about this, Mom. It would just get me in trouble.

> I have got to go along now,
> Rodger

In boot camp, kids' names were important. We had a tall white kid named Smith and a short black kid and a short white kid named Smith. The DIs called them Big Smith and Blacksmith and Little Smith. One of the kids had the same name as an infamous U.S. Army general who suffered a crushing defeat in the 1880s: George Custer. The DIs were always telling him that they were the Indians and they would kill his ass. That recruit did well at Parris Island and graduated with us. In the next year that kid would be killed in action by the North Vietnamese Army.

Parris Island letter 5
Beaufort, SC
March 12, 1966
Part I

Dear Mom and Dad,

I am starting this letter on Thursday night, 9 March. I don't think I will be able to finish it because of all the other things that I have to do first and I don't have much time left.

I got to Parris Island Wednesday morning about 2:00 and got to bed at the regular time of Thursday night at 9:00. What a day! Haircuts, photos, issues and everything. The next day after getting our bunks and everything at 4:30 in the morning we were awakened by the lovely tone of two drill instructors dumping over garbage cans (2) full of glass and plastic in the aisle between our bunks and screaming at the top of their lungs, "Get up you dirty hogs. Move it out, pig. Let's go Puss Gut," and knocking over bunks with the occupants still in them.

> *There were three drill instructors: one senior DI and two junior DIs. One mean DI, one good DI and one neutral DI. I didn't know it then but they were playing roles and the roles changed with every new platoon they trained.*

We get really good food at the mess hall and all we want, but we eat all we take and believe me, we eat it all and more. I must be gaining weight and losing weight at the same time....

I've got to go. I'll finish it tomorrow.

> Rog

Part II

I am back again. I have got a lot of time to write so I think I will finish this letter now....

The boy called Puss Gut who is across from me finally cracked today and begged to be sent to the brig. They had him doing physical instruction so long that he went in his pants and passed out cold. When he came to he said he was crazy and that he would go quietly if he could go soon. (Do not take any action. This is confidential....)

Before any training, certain recruits were singled out and pressure was applied to break them. They were the guys who were always screwing up. The DIs figured to get rid of them right from the start. I learned later in combat that this was ok, as you didn't want to share a fighting hole with a screw-up — we had to depend upon each other for our lives. Our DIs broke two recruits.

We ran a mile today after 1 hour of sit-ups, pull-ups, squat jumps and nearly everything you can think of....

Love always,
Rog

Parris Island letter 6
Beaufort, SC
March 14, 1966

Dear Mom & Dad & Debi:

I just received your letter (the second) and read it. I am not even allowed to smoke or talk yet so I doubt if I could make a phone call. I am not even allowed to receive phone calls. The Drill Instructor takes a message for me.

We had a field meet today. The 1st, 2nd and 3rd battalions competed. I am in the 2nd, as you know, and we lost by one point 43–42. The Drill Instructors took it out on everyone. The weather is about 80 and humid making the sweat come easy and being on a second story doesn't help matters.

I am not sure but I think I will graduate around the 28th of April. After that, for 3 or 4 weeks at Camp Lejeune, NC, and home for 30 days. Then one year without leave....

We ran the obstacle course yesterday and I found it fun passing fat bodies (fat kids) right and left. If you do everything right you have no problem getting over and under all the obstacles.

Well, I have been informed I have 5 minutes free time left so I will sign off.

Write back, Love,
Rog

The no-see-ums were horrible. When in formation we had to stand at attention and just let them eat. One of the kids swatted one and the DIs made him dig a four-foot-deep hole so the kid could bury it. The whole platoon stood at attention during an hour-long memorial service for that Parris Island sand flea. The memorial service took place in the evening and the fleas ate us alive. Nobody swatted one then.

Parris Island letter 7
Beaufort, SC
March 15, 1966

Dear Mom and Dad and Debi:

How are all of you? I listen for my name to be called on mail call nightly. I received two letters tonight and I read them both twice.

Life is what you make it here at Parris Island. If you don't do something right the second or third time you do exercise until you pass out. If your M-14 rifle is not held right the DI will point to the barrel and say, "Look here, private," you will look, and he will bash his hands into the barrel causing it to strike your head and raise a lump. Our DI is God (he told us). If you do everything right and stay in the background nothing is said (no credit). Just no punishment. Discipline is the key they try to brainwash you with here.

We had a rifle drill (exercises) with the 11.34 lb. M-14 rifle followed by a mile run on which you chant dirty phrases. One of the kids is a glutton for punishment. He is doing an average of 500 jumping jacks and 100 squat thrusts every time he makes a mistake. Good thing he is strong as a bull....

Love Rog

P.S. The obstacle course is a bitch. P.P.S. Write back!!!

Boot Camp was the first time for many things for me and it was the first time I interacted with black folks. In my high school there were no people of color. I heard about people that didn't look like me but I had never met anyone but white folks. Under the surface in the Marine Corps I found racism, but that racism would evaporate in combat in Vietnam. I learned that if I had to judge a person I judged them by their actions, not from the way they looked.

Parris Island letter 8
Beaufort, SC
March 16, 1966

Dear Mom & Dad & Debi,

I received your letter, Dad, and will try to answer as many questions as possible.

My DIs are all right except one is the worst. He is the senior DI. Of course, he is only doing his job, but sometimes being called "pig" or saying "Godamm" four times in one sentence is too much. But there is nothing we can do.

Our senior DI was fond of drinking a few beers at the slop chute and coming into our squad bay at midnight. That DI would then hit the lights and get us up and have us march while shouldering our footlockers instead of our rifles. Our senior DI was mean.

We were issued six t-shirts and skivvies. Five we wear and one pair we put away till graduation as with one belt. We were issued 3 utility jackets, 3 utility trousers, 4 pairs of work sox and 2 pairs of athletic sox, 2 pairs of boots, 1 sneakers, 1 shower shoes then health and comfort items — razor, soap, shaving cream, nail clippers, etc. Next were pencils, lead refills, writing paper, books, stamps and that was about it. Of course, I left things out but these are the most important things.

We got issued work uniforms called utilities, boots, shoes, buckets and all sorts of gear. We ran everywhere, with the DIs looking for weakness and kids that were screw-ups. The DIs were three inches from our faces constantly yelling, "scumbags, dirty hogs," and other assorted obscenities. Stress was the game and the drill instructors played it well.

We got a complete physical, eyes, ears, feet, and a series of shots like cattle in an inoculation line. We were up all the first night, the first day, and half the second night. All that time I didn't speak a single word to anyone. It was "Run, run, run, you goddamn fairies!"

We learned to shit, shower, and shave in five minutes or less. We called everyone "sir" and we learned to march. I learned to be part of a unit rather than an individual. All the hours spent on the parade deck called "the Grinder" were about discipline, and when we marched our footfalls sounded like one gigantic boot heel striking the trembling earth. What a feeling of power! We were platoon 255 in the Green Machine and we were the best!

The food is good. I eat so fast I don't even know what I'm eating, but I eat it and I must eat a lot of it. I have no more flab on my stomach (leg lifts and situps) and mile runs.

We work as a team, helping each other in the rough spots and taking pride in our end product. Like a tug-o-war or relay race against other platoons.

I have seconds left to get into bed.
Love, Rog

All the training platoons in Parris Island competed in weekly field events. The Marine Corps is about competition. My jarhead buddy Jim "Strongbear" Smith and I were talking in 2005 and I found he was at Parris Island in platoon 253 at the same time I was in platoon 255. We had competed against each other in field events 46 years ago. Both of our paths led to Vietnam and combat and we both survived to become artists. Strongbear is a painter and I'm a sculptor. Strongbear showed me how to walk the Red Road, which is a Native American spiritual path that emphasizes honoring the natural world. His guidance has allowed me a great amount of healing. Semper Fi, Strongbear.

Parris Island letter 9
Beaufort, SC
March 21, 1966

Dear Mom and Dad and Debi,

It is Saturday night and I am on my free time. We (our platoon) had a very good day. We ran 2 miles after the obstacle course and exercises and our platoon didn't have anyone drop out. The other ones had 15 or 16, maybe one third drop out, but 255 had none. We got a spear head for our guidon. And we got to open the top buttons of our shirts and lay the collar flat (a mark of efficiency and great pride among the Parris Island prisoners). If we keep going as we are going now we can become honor platoon of our series (252, 253, 254, and 255).

Inter-platoon competition is rough and tough but we are leading and keeping the DIs happy.

The losing platoon double-timed it (180 steps a minute) into a wall of their barracks yesterday. Their DI made them hit it 4 times. Sorry I have to use the back of this paper but I only have so many sheets.

Tomorrow we get an extra hour sack time in, we will arise at 0600 instead of 0455. We will also have no physical training (P.T.) on Sunday. I used to hate to go to church but now all I have to say is I get to sit down.

A guy got a large box of candy, cookies, etc., and the DI made him sit there and eat every bit, washed down with a cup of warm shaving cream.

In our platoon there are tall and short and then smart and stupid and negro & white — but what's the difference? We work as a team to help each other. I quit smoking and I am not going to start when he lets us smoke again, Mom! ...

Five minutes left, Rog

I drank Parris Island in like a dry sponge drinks water. Structure, work and reward, being a part of something important, becoming a warrior. I learned to obey orders without hesitation or question, and that kept me alive later on in Vietnam.

We had classes on all manner of military stuff, weapons, combat c-rations, hygiene, and Marine Corps history. In the history class we learned that the Marine Corps never leaves any of their members behind. Wounded or dead Marines take care of each other. I would later inadvertently break this sacred trust in Vietnam.

Our physical training consisted of a three-mile morning run, hand-to-hand combat, the fireman's carry, treading water for 30 minutes and running the confidence course. Of course the DIs added squat thrusts and jumping jacks all the time. We were never idle. I believe I left Parris Island owing one of my drill instructors about 600 squat thrusts.

Parris Island letter 10
Beaufort, SC
March 21, 1966

Part I

Mom and Dad and Debi,

I am in church listening to a Baptist preacher so I though I would write you a letter on the back of the church program. We got up at 0600 this morning and we left for breakfast at 6:15 after changing clothes, making our bunks, and going into the (john) head. [...]

The Army boot camp is a breeze compared to Parris Island. Our DI said he spent one night and was so disgusted at the lack of discipline, sloppiness, laziness that he left before the night was over. He said kids were talking during chow and standing around leaning against the Coke machine and going to the PX after two weeks and smoking and unpolished boots. He said that the sloppiest are the following — Navy, Air Force, Army, Coast Guard. The best are the Marines. Well, I am out of space.

Love, Rog

Part II

I know all about the M-14 rifle. It is a gas-operated, semi-automatic, air-cooled, magazine fed, shoulder weapon. I also know port arms, right & left shoulder arms, trail arms, order arms, present arms, inspection arms and all the steps for drill. We drill about 2 or 3 hours daily and have 2 hours of class and 2 hours of physical training (P.T.) and 1 hour of free time and the rest is eating and standing at attention.

I don't have any blisters yet, but I do have sore legs from running the obstacle course.

[...].

I will finish it tonight on my free time.

Bye, Rog

Part III

I guess we are allowed to write during this period so I will continue.

We will wash our clothes with buckets and brushes in another hour or so and then we drill for 2 hours. Then we have a field meet — platoon against platoon. I am in the tug-o-war and the fireman's carry and 255 will win and bring back a trophy to defend next week.

Well, I will end with a happy vacation to all of you and take care and save some of the chocolate cake with caramel icing for me. But don't send any down here.

Love, Rog

We learned that where there are Marines there is always some Marine assigned watch. The only time that Marines cannot defend themselves is while they sleep. In Vietnam half of us slept while half of us stayed awake on watch. Falling asleep on watch could cost Marines their lives. In combat I would learn this lesson in blood.

Parris Island letter 11
Beaufort, SC
March 23, 1966
Part I

Dear Mom and Dad and Debi,

I already wrote you a letter today, but I am starting another as I now have the time. We washed our clothes and drilled today. That 11.34 lbs. of rifle gets pretty heavy when you run a mile or a mile and a half with it at port arms.

The food here is pretty good. We get enough! I get all the tossed salad I can eat. Supper tonight was — soup, beans, corn, spaghetti and meatballs, salad, garlic bread, butter, pie and milk. I ate every bit so you see my appetite is improving.

In history class I heard that it took 26 days of fighting to take Iwo Jima and of the 20,000 Japanese on the island, only 26 were captured. That's how brutal the battle was. One of the DI's fathers was killed by a Japanese machine gun on Iwo Jima — This DI, Sergeant Good, is a nice guy and he said ever since his father was killed he wanted to be a Marine. The Marines have been to Korea twice and China twice. The things they did early in their history are very interesting.

During this time one of the DIs, Sergeant Good, became our mentor and surrogate father. Good told us about himself. He told us that his father was a Marine and was killed by the Japanese on Iwo Jima and after that all this sergeant ever wanted to do was to become a Marine like his dad. That DI built the desire in our hearts to become Marine warriors. In a painful twist of fate, this good man, our mentor and teacher, would be killed in action in Vietnam while going to the aid of one of his wounded Marines. I discovered this while doing research for this book. Seven of the kids in platoon 255 and our DI Sgt. Good would be killed in action. Forty-five years later I can still remember that sergeant because he made me a Marine. I have traveled to Washington, D.C., where I sat down at the Viet-nam Veterans Memorial — the Wall — and spent some time thanking him for my life. I wonder how many of the recruits that he trained are alive today because of the way he trained them. I am. Semper Fi.

I am going to the PX on Friday and I will try to get a decal of the Corps for your Mustang, Dad. I have to go for now. I will be back Monday night.

Your son,

Rog

Part II

Here I am Monday and I don't have enough time to finish. Some kids were caught with illegal cigarettes and had to eat them and do jumping jacks at the same time. Ha Ha.

Some of the answer periods came up with some strange answers from my fellow prisoners.

Well got to go will see you later

Love Rog

In boot camp I found out where the word jarhead comes from. The name emerged around 1870 when Mason jars were invented. Mason jars were known to all households in those days, as canning was something everyone did before refrigeration. Marines with their dress blues collars and their high and tight hair-cuts looked like a Mason jar. Jarhead.

Parris Island letter 12
Beaufort, SC
March 27, 1966

Part I

Dear Mom and Dad and Debi,

How are all of you? I am fine. Saturday we start one week of mess and clean-up duty, then two weeks to the rifle range and then 12 days til we grad-uate.

Dad — I got a pair of GI glasses for the range and I was given a dental check, but it was OK and I don't think it revealed anything.

Tomorrow we go to the PX for our first PX call. Our second one is the day we graduate. This also ends our P.T. for a while and we will still keep up with our daily exercises in the barracks, but no regular program....

We had two men with unsatisfactory shaves this morning. The senior DI made them shave each other. The kid doing the shaving had to wear his bucket on his head. Blood flowed as they switched off shaving each other. Everyone had real close shaves after that.

Tomorrow I will get all sorts of things. I will talk some more tomorrow. I have to go right now, so good-bye.

Rodg

Part II

It is Saturday night and I just read Mom's letter with the rubber bands. We are now at the range and we have guard duty for the week. I was picked out of the 81 men in our platoon to be Corporal of the Guard on one of the seven shifts. I get 12 midnight — 0300 in the morning every day — no sleep — ugh....

I have got to leave — lots to do.

Your loving son,
Rodg

Parris Island letter 13
Beaufort, SC
March 29, 1966

Dear Mom and Dad and Debi,

Well, today I wore out my first pair of boots. The heels are completely worn out but the uppers are in good condition so I will get new heels.

I am a squad leader (there are four) and Corporal of the Guard when we stand guard. I am always told to do little things for the DIs and I try to organize some team work in the morning cleaning. Today I was in charge of a work detail of 15 men. We worked wherever we were needed around the weapons battalion. I even got to say "Column right and left" and all that bull. If this keeps up I will maybe get my PFC stripe by the end of boot camp, but I may botch it up yet.

As the hours turned into days and the days into weeks we were given small rewards for achievements. When we learned to march as a unit we were allowed to open the top buttons on our utilities, and when we won field events competing with other platoons we were given ribbons for our platoon gridiron. We finally could send our utilities to base laundry instead of washing them with a brush and a bucket. If one man screwed up we were all punished so we helped each other. We found our strengths and weaknesses. We became a unit but we were not Marines yet.

I got issued all my regular uniforms, shoes, belts, coats, raincoats, shirts, trousers, sox, etc., etc., etc. They are being altered free of charge and will be sent to me when ready. I decided to buy dress blues because I know a certain Miss C out in Lakewood that I want to take to dinner and I will go to the E.E. Root graduation ceremony in them....

Well I have to go — lots to do

Love,
Rodg

P.S. Hi Debi.

Parris Island letter 14
Beaufort, SC
April 6, 1966

Part I

Dear Mom and Dad and Debi,

Boy, things have really been in a rush down here for the past few days. We have been getting up at 4:00 to pull targets for other platoons on the firing line.

All of us recruits had to sleep with our rifles while on the rifle range. We learned to wrap our M-14s with a towel to keep the gun oil off our sheets. At the range we learned to shoot and we learned to pull targets. That was the first time I heard rounds breaking the sound barrier close overhead. It would not be the last time I heard bullets snapping past. In Vietnam I once had a bullet pass so close to my face the shock wave gave me a bloody nose. It felt like someone punched me.

Part II

I am back again to finish this letter on Monday night. Today I fired the 45 cal. M1911A1 pistol. I fired a total of 45 rounds just to get the feel and it was a ball! Man, firing a pistol like the '45 heavy cal and recoil is fun! And deadly.

On Tuesday, we fire the M-14 rifle. We have already been given classes on windage and sight adjustment so all we have to do yet is fire. We have been "snapping in" which involves getting into position by the devil himself. Man, do they smart. The blood is cut off from your arms and legs and your tendons are slowly pulled apart. There are a lot of tricks of the trade and I am learning some of them now. A lot are unorthodox and illegal, but the DIs use them so we use them. Like abrasive on the rifle, like steel wool or such.

Every night we turn the light out and lay at attention and sing "Battle Hymn of the Republic" or "Marines' Hymn" and then growl like a tiger until the DIs tell us to stop. Then we say the Lord's Prayer and God bless our Family and the Drill Instructors and the Marines fighting in Vietnam.

Love,
Rodg

Parris Island letter 15
Beaufort, SC
April 9, 1966

Mom and Dad,

I didn't write much this week because I had to catch up on the letters and you were not home. There is so much to do during free time that I only get off one letter if I am lucky. I fired the M-14 yesterday for the first time. Boy! That was fun! We shot at a bulls-eye about the size of a quarter from 900 inches. It looked about this big. "**.**" I got all twelve rounds in the black and was high man in the platoon for score and shot group. It wasn't exactly a group — just a large "**O**" punched out hole where the shots went. We fire 70 rounds a day starting Monday and we qualify on Friday. I will write more about this later. We are doing very well on close order drill and could cop the streamer for our standard pole.

We haven't done anything but snap in the sitting, prone, offhand and kneeling positions for the past week. We use a sling that makes the position very steady. Tomorrow we are getting starched utility clothing instead of just cleaned. It will be starched and pressed and our covers (hats) are also starched and our boots spit-shined.

We really look sharp when we are dressed as above. Quite an honor, too. Means we are doing well to have them so early in training.

Well, I only have 20 days left and then two–three weeks at Lejeune, then home on leave.

Well, got to run (Double time),

Rodg

Parris Island letter 16
Beaufort, SC
April 13, 1966

Part I

Dear Mom and Dad and Debi,

Glad to hear about your nice tans. I have a nice one, too. On my face and neck and hands. That's all that touches the sun....

We fired the able course of fire today I shot a 212. One guy shot a 228 expert.

After firing the M-14 for a while the kick doesn't bother you at all but trying to set your sights on that pin head of a bullseye is the worst thing.

Well, I will continue tomorrow because I don't have much time left.

Part II

Well, here it is and I am unhappy. I shot a qualifying score, but just qualifying. The DI was so mad at the platoon (everybody's scores dropped) that we put all our gear in the sea bag and are living out of that. No sitting on bunks or footlockers or buckets. Sit on the floor.

He got very strict and said he was giving too much slack because he wanted high scores so he made us strip, put 80 of us in the shower room and turned on the cold water and made us do jumping jacks for over an hour non-stop.

Tomorrow we will have to do better on the range or heaven help us....

Dear Dad — When you were in the service did anyone in your barracks get crabs? A kid got them in our platoon and no one knows where he got them from.

Well, I have to leave now

Got to polish brass

Love,
Rodg

～⌒∂

Parris Island letter 17
Beaufort, SC
April 17, 1966

Part I

Dear Mom and Dad,

Well, I shot the P.F.C. stripe down the drain this morning. I am a UNC unqualified rifleman. I qualified with points to spare and almost expert on Thursday but Friday morning it was about 50 and raining and I was chilled and couldn't hold it steady. 190 is a qualifying score and 5,4,3,2 and miss are the values. I shot 189. One lousy point. I shot 43 out of 50 at the 500 yard line at a 20" bulls-eye but I needed a 44. Oh well, it's not the end of the world. I will still try harder and harder but no chance of PFC until I get another chance to qualify with the M-14. (Friday was record day.)

I was a pretty good squirrel hunter and I did well on the rifle range until qualifying day. It was cold, wet, and windy and I screwed up the elevation and windage on my sights. I could not hit anything and did not qualify. I was crestfallen. The top 10 percent of a platoon would graduate with Private First Class stripes. I had been on a PFC track before the range, and I had shot my PFC stripe down the tube. I would remain an unqualified rifleman for my complete stay in the Marine Corps. In the Marine Corps being a good, reliable rifle shot is very important. All Marines are grunts when it comes right down to it. Parris Island teaches recruits how to march and how to shoot. "Every man a rifleman" is a

Marine Corps concept. My failure struck me deeply. Looking back I see that failure is very important to have and to learn from.

I received your letter tonight and was happy to learn you arrived home alright. Well, we are moving back to mainside tomorrow morning on a forced march. We will really look good running in with starched utilities and covers. Next Thursday we go to Elliots Beach. All that proves to be exciting I am told.

Our DI, Sgt Good, who is the best one and raises our morale when he is on duty, has the duty that night. Well, I have to run. Will continue tomorrow.

Part II

Here I am back at my old barracks at mainside. We marched back on a sandy side trail. Our DI said "route step" which means that we didn't have to keep in step and called our own cadence and sang our hymn and sound off and made up cadence counts about our DIs.

Our standard is now a red silk flag with gold fringe — scarlet and gold making colors with a spear head. We marched back in with the packs on our backs chanting and calling "Marines, Marines" louder and louder and you should have seen some of the visitors look. The girls especially and you should have seen us look at the girls especially. Well, I have to polish a little brass so good-bye — for now

I will write soon

Love,
Rodg

We were issued our tailored uniforms just before we graduated. Now we really looked like Marines. We had been torn completely down and rebuilt. All of the recruits in platoon 255 would forever be Marine warriors.

Parris Island letter 18
Beaufort, SC
April 18, 1966

Dear Mom and Dad and Debi,

Will you send me a few articles? Two cans of kiwi black show polish, 2 plastic cigarette cases, the kind that fit together — one for cigarettes and one for a soap dish, some double-edged razor blades and a couple cheap mechanical pencils and a couple of cheap toothbrushes. About four old handkerchiefs in a small sturdy box for shoe polishing, etc. A couple bars of soap. If you think you could find a container such as a small leather kit bag or something that I could keep all my little stuff in — pencils, razor blades, lead, etc.

We must rate. We now get to drink out of the magical waters of the DIs' water fountain. But we must salute it before and after drinking and must have a cover on our head.

Well, only 11 more days to go until I graduate and go on to advanced infantry training at Camp Lejeune. The series before us received their orders and 80% of them are going overseas to one place or another. (Only two are going to Iceland.)

We are getting ready for command inspection and Elliots Beach which is this Thursday. I shouldn't have any problem with any of them. Next week this time we will be getting ready to leave, turning in gear, drawing gear going to cash sales for utilities and extra boots and all that other good garbage.

Well, I have to move out...

Love,

Rodg

The business of the Marine Corps is killing. We are taught early in our lives that killing is wrong. Warriors have to unlearn these early lessons. The world we live in is filled with people that would use violence to take what we have. Most folks do not have a clue what this is about. Warriors willing to kill have always been necessary. I was now and forever a warrior.

Parris Island letter 19
Beaufort, SC
April 25, 1966

Part I

Dear Mom and Dad,

[...]

I received your letter on Saturday night and I am starting this letter on a Saturday night. Boy, the weekends here are really not what they were at home.

Well, we went to Elliots Beach and had a practical application test. We also had three forced marches of only 8 or 9 miles each with packs and rifles, etc. We really held a pace! Out platoon got a streamer for the guidon because everyone passed the application tests.

We only have about 5 more days left. We graduate the 28th and go to Lejeune the 29th of the month. As of yet I haven't found out what I will be doing in the Marine Corps. I will probably go to Vietnam as 80% of the platoon that graduated yesterday went. I will let you know as soon as I receive my orders.

Part II

I am finishing this letter on a Monday night. I just received the news that I am one of the seven men in our platoon of 80 men that are going to make PFC out of boot camp. How does PFC R.E. Jacobs sound? I am happy and surprised that I made it because of going unqualified on the range. I asked the DI about this and he said it doesn't ordinarily happen — just sometimes.

Well, I have to go now. I thought I'd let you in on the news.

Love, Rog

Our Parris Island graduation parade was a grand ceremony. We had the Marine Corps Band, the recruit platoons marching in formation, DIs with swords, flags, and all. When I hear the Marine Corps Hymn today my heart still sings. We were warriors now and we were awarded with the one thing we had been seeking all the time we were at Parris Island: the Marine Corps globe and anchor emblem. We were Marines! We had each earned membership into a 191-year-old exclusive brotherhood of blood. The Marine Corps salutation "Semper Fidelis" is translated as "Always Faithful." I always will use it when I meet another jarhead.

Graduation from Marine Corps Boot Camp was one of the proudest moments of my life. Honor, duty, and integrity are everything in a warrior culture. I thought that I had earned my manhood. I didn't know it then but the test was just beginning. The DIs told us right out that we all would be going to Vietnam and that some of us would live and some of us would die. I didn't know it would be almost 10 percent of us that would die. I wondered how many would be wounded.

The DIs shook our hands and for the first time called us fellow Marines. We thanked them and then we boarded a bus for Camp Lejeune and Advanced Infantry Training. The next group of letters was written from May to June 1966 while undergoing that training. I attacked the AIT with youthful zeal. I learned to use all the tools of war and I felt invincible.

Advanced Infantry Training

Camp Lejeune, NC letter 20
U.S. Navy
May 2, 1966

Dear Mom and Dad and Debi,

I received your letter last night with the stamps. The stamps are something that I needed.

We left on a Greyhound bus from Parris Island and arrived at Camp Geiger about five hours later. The camp Geiger is an outpost of Camp Lejeune but my address is still Camp Lejeune:

> E O PFC Rodger E. Jacobs USMC
> Co "N" 2nd Plt 2nd BN 1st ITR
> MCB Camp Lejeune, NC 28542

Well, I have a lot to do so I will leave now.

We arrived at Lejeune as brand new Marines. We still called everyone sir and we were kind of unsure of how we should interact with men who had been in the Marine Corps longer.

I was a PFC so I got some added responsibility, which translated into me getting less sleep than most of the other new Marines. Nevertheless I plunged right in.

(Letter 21 omitted)

Camp Lejeune letter 22
U.S. Navy
May 10, 1966

Part I

Dear Mom and Dad,

Yesterday and today were the days to top all days. We were out in the field miles from nowhere and all of a sudden a couple of guys fell down and started convulsions. The helicopter came and picked them up and after that everyone had violent cramps and diarrhea. We had to force march back to the trucks that carried us back to mainside and guys had to be carried out. Some passed out cold. We got back and everyone became ill. This all happened about 12:30 at night.

Sick bay had about 2,000 cases of the same thing — dysentery. I had a slight touch that is still lingering today. Some of the guys are still in the hospital.

I hit the rack about 2:30 and got up at 6 and went to chow and came back and slept till 2:30 in the afternoon. Everyone is taking pills and liquid medicine and is feeling crummy.

Tuesday we have a bivouac and we really love to walk. 5 miles to bivouac and 3 to chow, then back 3 times a day and then back to Camp Geiger. None of us are looking forward to it because it is going to be pretty hard on us since the runs are going around and everyone is still pretty sick and we will probably be weak.

I will finish this letter tomorrow.

Part II

I am writing the rest of this letter in pencil because the person I loaned my pen to is not back from the show yet. I just came back from the indoor show. It cost 15 cents to see pretty good movies. Well, I have to hit the rack....

Be home in three ½ weeks or so.

Love,
Rodg

Camp Lejeune, NC letter 23
U.S. Navy
May 12, 1966

Dear Mom and Dad and Debi,

How is everything? I am fine. We have had some classes but we have not had any real training yet. I guess when we start out training the hours are real rough. Maybe two–three hours of sleep a night.

I just received the word that we might have base liberty tonight. It was just confirmed but I will not go. I have too much to do. I am writing this letter sitting on the steps outside our barracks smoking with a helmet on my head and a T-shirt and shower shoes.

Tomorrow we will go out into the field and play around with demolition charges all morning then we will eat chow and march back. The food here is good but you don't get enough of it. I usually go into the laundry on my way back to the barracks and get a candy bar or something. We can listen to radios or write or generally screw around from about 6:00–8:00 and then we hit the rack.

I have no idea when I will be coming home. It may be 4–8 weeks. We weren't told all. We are not going to be told until just before we leave.

I have to get my stripe sewed on my shirts by the base laundry. I also have to get them pressed. Sometime this week we will go to cash sales so we can get some work sox and skivvies. I am also going to buy an extra belt and two extra buckles. I got my hat brim spit-shined and my shoes done also today. There is an awful lot of little stuff to do to your gear in the military services.

[...]

I learned that in the Marine Corps each uniform is the responsibility of the individual Marine. We got issued a complete set of uniforms at Parris Island, but when those uniforms got worn out we had to replace them out of our own pockets. All cleaning costs, shoe polish, brass polish, sewing and tailoring were our responsibility also. It took a lot of money to keep looking sharp. I would beg my parents to contribute to the Clean Marine Fund.

How is everyone? The weather is very cold up here but at least the bugs aren't out. (The rattlesnakes and copperheads stay in, too.)

Love, Rodg

Camp Lejeune letter 24
U.S. Navy
May 14, 1966
Dear Mom and Dad,

...

Today we fired our M-1s. About 75% are so old that we have to hand oper-ate them. We fired tracer rounds and ball rounds during the day. At night we fired all tracer rounds and had night squad tactics. We fired from the hip and shoulder and prone rapid-fire (or as fast as we could get the rounds off).

We haven't been getting much sleep lately and I have to get N.C.O. duty to top it all off. I get relieved at 3:00 and have to get up again at 4:00 for reveille. I don't know when I will be getting home because the training varies for different types of jobs.

We had a class on automatic weapons and we fired the M-60 machine gun, the 60 mm mortar, the bazooka, the 106 recoil-less rifle, flame thrower, rifle grenades, M-14 setup for automatic fire, the new Marine grenade launcher (breech action) and various other weapons. They showed the different types of shells and loads. It was very interesting and exciting. The most interesting part of the training so far has been demolitions, mines and booby traps.

In Vietnam in the very near future I would learn just what the mines I was studying would do to the human body. High-explosive blasts and supersonic bullets explode flesh. Little droplets of blood are scattered over a large area. I have been sprayed with those drops and they smell like copper.

...

We can have base liberty tomorrow and we can go to the slop chute and the laundry and I will try to get in a phone call though seeing that it is Mother's Day and I would very much like to hear your voice again. Calling home is a difficult matter here because we have about a million Marines want-ing to call at the same time and we can only call at certain times, but I know that one of these times I will get on through....

Well, Happy Mother's Day

Love,
Rodg

Camp Lejeune letter 25
U.S. Navy
May 14, 1966
Dear Mom and Dad,

...

Tomorrow night we go on bivouac. During the day we will have patrols and will be using blank ammunition and will assault pill boxes and bunkers. Yesterday we threw hand grenades and fired the flame thrower. Man, does it get hot.

I am writing the reverse side because I am running out of paper. If I have time I will go to the PX and get more....

Now we are coordinating everything we have learned into squad tactics and maneuvers. The Marine fire team consists of a scout, automatic rifleman, rifleman, and fire team leader. I am a squad leader and I have to look over 3 fire teams. What a job, especially in maneuvers....

I starched my utilities and put USMC on the pockets. The emblem comes on an iron decal-type stencil.

I have to put my chevrons on my utilities that I got back from the cleaners. They are all steel stripes that go on the collar.

Well, I have a lot to do now. I've got to go.

Rodg

P.S. Could you send me some t-shirts and boxer-type underwear and cushion sole work sox (black). I really would like to put on some new skivvies every day.

At this time we learned what our Military Occupational Specialty (MOS) was going to be. My MOS was 0311-rifleman. Machine guns, mortars, and so forth all had different numbered MOS's but we were all grunts.

All brand new Marines learned that the basic Marine infantry unit, the fire team, was the start of a much larger command structure. A fire team has four Marines: fire team leader, automatic rifleman, and two riflemen. A squad has three fire teams plus a squad leader and radioman and that totals 14 men. A platoon has three squads of grunts and one squad of weapons like machine guns and mortars plus a platoon leader, platoon sergeant, radioman, and a Navy corpsman, and that would be around 55 men if at full strength. A company is three platoons of grunts and a platoon of weapons plus a commanding officer, radio operator, sergeant major, supply sergeant, three corpsmen, and attached forward observer for around 200 men. A battalion is four companies of grunts plus a company of weapons and a headquarters company that consists of Navy medical unit, multiple radio men, executive officer, forward observers, and various attached men for an ideal total of around 800 men if at full strength. A division is made of multiple battalions. In Vietnam we were always at about half strength because of the men we lost. The command structure worked pretty good and a lot of grunts owe their lives to it.

The First Battalion, Ninth Marines, the Walking Dead, who I served with for the last part of my tour, would spend three years fighting in Vietnam. During those three years of half-strength operations 1/9 would suffer about 800 men killed in action. The total amount of KIA of the Walking Dead is difficult to pin down because of all the attached personnel that were killed. The wounded numbered four times the KIA.

Camp Lejeune letter 26
U.S. Navy
May 19, 1966

Dear Mom and Dad and Debi,

I just got back from calling you. I will try to call again next week and see if I can catch Dad at home....

We have muster at 12:00 today and then we will receive the word on what we do. Base liberty or something else. Maybe slop chute movies or U.S.O. This morning we had liberty. We went to chow and did laundry and maybe squeezed in a phone call like I did. We are not allowed off base at any time. In fact, I haven't seen a girl in two weeks.

Well, muster time. I must go.

Love, Rodg

(Letters 27 and 28 omitted)

Camp Lejeune letter 29
U.S. Navy
June 1, 1966

Dear Mom and Dad,

I haven't written in a few days because we have been out in the field doing squad and platoon tactics. We have been getting, on the average, about four and a half hours of sleep a night. It really tears you down after four or five days.

This would be the start of learning how valuable and how deadly sleep was. I also learned how unprotected Marines are when they sleep. Staying awake on watch would mean life or death in Vietnam. I learned to sleep anywhere at any time in Vietnam. I learned to stay awake anywhere at any time in Vietnam. Sleep was needed but it could cost you your life.

Tuesday we have a two-day war in which we attack and defend positions. We are dropped in vertical envelopment by choppers and from then we eat c-rations and run and fire blanks. I ate 10 meals of c-rations just this week. They are all right if you barter and trade around jelly and bread and peaches, etc.

We have base liberty now but I am going to sit around and catch up on my letter writing and sleep. Today is Saturday and we went into Jacksonville and went to the U.S.O. We watched movies and drank coke, etc. We also checked out records and read magazines. I listened to a couple of Joan Baez albums and even though my outlook has been influenced I still enjoy her music with the message.

I am finishing this letter in pen. Today is Sunday and I laid out in the sun and got a mild sunburn on my legs. I hope we don't have to march as far as we have been doing lately. Usually it is about 2 or 3 miles to class or 1–2 miles to chow or c-rations and then back. We are barred from the slop chute and the PFCs have to stand watch so none of the people slip in and get drunk without permission.

I will be home within two weeks. I can't believe it. Stop writing me about Saturday or Friday because the last week is going to really move and probably, looking at the schedule, I won't be able to read them at all.

Well I have to leave to stand watch.

Love, Rodg

Camp Lejeune letter 30
U.S. Navy
June 3, 1966

Dear Mom and Dad,

Today we fired the 3.5 rocket launchers. Everyone fired five rounds, two practice with no warhead and three high explosive. The high explosives will cut into a 12" thick piece of steel and leave a hole the size of your fist and scatter shrapnel inside the tank or bunker. All of my shots were direct hits and on my last shot I blew the turret completely off the tank. This weapon is commonly called the bazooka. There is little kick in the practice but the H.E. round really tends to knock you for a loop.

I really liked firing all those big weapons. The feeling of power generated by heavy weapons is addictive. When a whole line opens up at night firing all tracers it is quite a show. I had no idea that one day soon I would be on the receiving end of such firepower.

It is Thursday morning and we just came back from an all night bivouac. We had classes and then we shot blanks and moved through a dummy combat village throwing dummy hand grenades, etc.

We marched out with full field packs of 45 lbs. each. The march was six and a half miles through trails and underbrush and we didn't even stop for a rest.

We learned to save our feet by walking on the road shoulder and not on the pavement. We learned to embrace the pain of the hump and move through it. We thought the training was hard, but little did we know that we were just getting a very small glimpse of the hardships that awaited us in Vietnam. We did a lot of nighttime forced marches of 10 to 15 miles. It was hard but I was a Marine warrior so I could do anything. We got to use all manner of implements of destruction. We fired machine guns at night, bazookas, M-79 grenade launchers, and flamethrowers. We threw grenades, set off plastic explosives, popped illumination flares, tear gas and others. We learned tactics, ambushes, listening posts, night approaches, booby traps, compass and map, and combat formations.

Once again I was cranked with all the cool stuff and I soaked it up. It was just like the army games I played as a child only the toys were a lot bigger.

I learned that there are a whole lot of ticks and snakes in coastal North Carolina and spent some time dealing with these critters. I thought the ticks and mosquitoes at Lejeune were bad but they were nothing compared to the insect invasion that awaited us in Southeast Asia.

My name changed to Jake during this time. No more Rodger, I had a warrior name now.

That woman whose son is a doggie (Army) said that he ran a mile in 7 minutes. We walked and ran 3 miles in 25 minutes. We ran infiltration course in which we crawled under barbwire with a machine gun going off over our heads. We also had a class in gas and spent 3 minutes in a tear gas chamber (1 minute without mask).

Last night we crawled through a night infiltration course that was loaded with booby traps, tripwires and mines. It was pitch dark and we had to grope and feel for the wires with our hands. We were in helmet, pack, and rifle. In the 100 yard trail I went first and found 12 booby traps, wire trips and about 6 mines. I crawled under, stepped over and jumped all of them. They had a double apron barbwire fence booby-trapped and the instructors would, every once in a while, throw illumination grenades and everyone had to hit the deck. I got into the wire and one went off. I couldn't get out without setting off a booby trap and things got pretty hairy after a while.

The worst thing at Camp Geiger outpost of Camp Lejeune is the ticks. Every night I might have to burn about 3 or 4 off of my arms, legs, stomach, etc. God, what a bother....

I have to go.

Love you all, Rog

Camp Lejeune letter 31
U.S. Navy
June 9, 1966

Dear Mom and Dad and Debi,

I haven't written in a while because I have been out in the boonies for four days and the average of four hours sleep every night. Twenty hours working, 4 hours sleep.

We had a tactical bivouac (combat day patrols, recon night patrols, combat search and destroy night patrols and set up in ambush). We fire nothing but blanks and it was so dark that you couldn't see anything and we were in the thick brush and trees and vines, etc. Things got pretty hairy at times.

We worked in fire teams and I was in charge of three of them because I was a squad leader. We reconned an objective first and then I made a plan of attack and then we attacked. I turned out outstanding. We drew their fire from the front with one four-man fire team while the other two came on, on line, from the least expected side and firing from the hip overran and destroyed their position. We got to within 10 yards before they saw us and then it was too late. I got commended for the attack and execution because I took them out and brought them back. The instructor was up a tree observing.

We have so far killed fourteen copperheads and four rattlers. We have snake hunts after noon and evening chow for about a half an hour.

I would encounter brilliant iridescent green bamboo vipers, large pythons, and six-foot fer-de-lances in Vietnam.

We fired dispersing and concentration fire at night with tracers. We also fired the M-60 machine gun. I was squad leader so I got to fire about 400 rounds.

Today we fired the M-79 grenade launcher. You know the small shotgun-type they are using at the big rifle range in Vietnam. I hit dead center with all four shots both high explosive and practice.

I will try to call again tomorrow. I don't know though. We might not get base liberty. We might have to train. Talk about tired! Man, the hours are catching up on all of us. I went to sleep standing in formation and standing at chow and about 12 of us went to sleep sitting at the chow table in the morning.

In the field all we eat are c-rations. Some are good and being a squad leader I hand them out so I get my pick. I have found that if I use a little ingenuity I can scrounge anything. I had two chances to bring home a brand-new M-14 rifle but I couldn't fit it into my sea bag. I will see if I can obtain a H5 pistol or maybe a .38....

We fired the John Wayne-Vic Morrow course. You walk along the firing line and the target jumps up and you fire from the hip as fast as you can pump them out. If you do it like I do it and I was timed at eight shots, all hits from the hip at 30 yds. in 3 seconds.

Well, I have to wrap it up.

God Bless,

Love,

Rog

We learned that our hand grenades were of many types. We had regular high explosive fragmentation grenades, burning white phosphorus fragmentation grenades, illumination grenades, tear gas grenades, and various colors of smoke grenades. We could rig up the grenades with trip wires for booby traps. Smoke grenades would signal landing zones.

We also had pop-up flares. These flares were made from an aluminum tube about a foot long and a couple inches in diameter. Pop-up flares were activated by twisting off the top cap and putting the cap on the bottom and smacking the flare with the heel of our hands. The flare would shoot up about 75 yards and burst. These flares were red and green star clusters and parachute illumination flares. In Vietnam red stars were bad as it meant enemy contact. Green stars were popped by the point man when a patrol would enter our lines. Illumination pop-ups would burn about a minute and throw moving false shadows everywhere.

Camp Lejeune letter 32

U.S. Navy

June 12, 1966

Dear Mom and Dad,

I am sitting on my footlocker writing this letter. Tomorrow I will try to call. I may even try to call tonight.

I found out that I will go to Camp Pendleton, California. After my leave. From there who knows where? I may stay or be transferred overseas. I don't know yet but I will tell you as soon as I get my orders.

I must ask you not to write until I get home. I have not the time now even to read your letters let alone answer them. You know that I would rather read and answer your letters than anything else. Our Sergeant said to write our people and tell them because it would just foul things up and we only have a week left anyhow.

Pass the word around, will you?

(just tell Debi)

I'll be home soon,

Rodg

I got a two-week leave and went home a brand new Marine. All this was in mid–1966 before the antiwar protests, so when I was home wearing my uniform

I did not get disrespected. I had only one ribbon on my chest but I wore my Marine Corps uniform proudly. If I remember it right it was girls, cars, beer, in that order. I had a steady girlfriend, Karen, and she gave me a St. Christopher medal with a Globe and Anchor on one side and inscribed "All My Love Forever" that I put on my dog tag chain. I wore that medal all through Vietnam and I still have it with my dog tags today. I never saw Karen again.

I went back to my high school wearing my uniform. I walked the halls between periods and thought back to the time I spent in this building. Teachers treated me with a respect I never felt before. I was not the kid that they had known.

My folks kind of thought I would end up in Vietnam but I didn't confirm that when talking to them. I was different; I was a warrior and not some 19-year-old kid anymore. My two-week leave went by in a blur and I was off to Camp Pendleton, California, for further training before shipping out for overseas.

PFC Rodger Jacobs
Unit # 382 3rd Rep. Co.
Staging Bn.
MCB Camp Pendleton, Calif.
Oceanside, CA 92655 letter 33
July 16, 1966

Part I

Dear Mom and Dad,

How are you? I am fine. I got out to Los Angeles and then San Diego OK. From San Diego I took a bus to Pendleton and got here pretty good.

I got processed and I leave for overseas the 11th of August. I am attached to the 3rd Marine Division. Even if I go to Vietnam I won't have it so bad. The Third is moving out making way for the 5th either at Christmas or early April.

We have 14 training days in front of us and they promise to be tough.

We can smoke in the

I carried this St. Christopher medal on my dog tags. Karen wrote me a couple of times and then the veil of war closed behind me.

barracks and we probably will get liberty for weekends. I want to get some civvies so I can wear them on liberty.

The weather is fine down here. It gets cold in the night and hot in the day and it really is dry but not too bad.

I have met a couple of guys and am sort of palling around.

Well, I will get a longer letter maybe tonight or tomorrow.

Love, Rodg

Part II

I am finishing the letter that I started earlier in the day. It's 6:30 and already starting to get cold and dark. On the plane ride out we flew over the Grand Canyon. It is a heck of a lot bigger than I thought it would be.

Everything on the base is scattered thinly and therefore it is necessary to walk a long ways to chow and so forth. The land is very scenic and there are quite a few hills. As a matter of fact, the land is all hills and mountains that we have to walk up and down. At least there are no ticks in the hills as there was at Lejeune....

The best places to go on liberty here are Disneyland and Mexico. It costs about as much to go to both places. $4.00 round-trip. Although Mexico is wilder, Disneyland has an awful lot of girls (or so I have been told) so I think I will go to Disneyland first.

I did go to Tijuana and had my first experience in a place without many rules. I remember the booze, the strippers, and the hookers doing things onstage that I never had even imagined. Boy, was I surprised.

I found a tattoo parlor in Oceanside, California, and for $20 got a three-color Marine Corps bulldog needled on my right forearm.

All these things were part of my blood rite of passage that started at Parris Island and would end in a hospital in Japan.

I am going to hate all this waiting around for training to start. There is really nothing to do but lay around.

We found a terrific hole-in-the-wall Italian food place in San Diego and the prices are moderate considering hamburgers at Cleveland can cost about 35 cents and tomato juice comes in two sizes — 9 oz. and 12 oz. — 40 cents and 60 cents. The place was called Carolisa's and it featured everything from cheese to sausages.

Well, I have to get ready for the show.

Love,
Rodg

Staging Battalion

Camp Pendleton letter 34
Oceanside, CA
July 19, 1966

Part I

Boy do I miss home cooking! The chow here is better than at Lejeune but it still isn't as good as home cooking.

The prices are very expensive out here and I am almost out of money but I am getting paid in a week and will make do with what I have. I could use some stamps though.

In the last part of training they send us without any food and one canteen of water and we cover a total of about 25 miles. We have no rifle or helmet or anything and guys that are stationed here are out in the woods trying to capture us. If they capture us we don't get an orange at the end of the day.

Everyone around here is playing poker or shooting craps. I got into a game with the stakes of a borrowed quarter and came out with $2.75 ahead. Now I have about 35 cents to last the rest of the week.

We haven't been allowed off base to pick up our sea bags yet (they are still at the bus station) and I am getting sick of living in my tropical uniform with my good dress shoes.

Well, I have to get to chow. I will continue later and then bum a stamp off somebody.

Part II

...

I guess we do some real mountain climbing around here. The names of the mountains are unprintable and they are long and steep.

This morning I will go down to the recreation center and play pool for free. They also have a TV room, a reading room supplied with books, magazines and newspapers.

I have decided to quit smoking because I have no money and I don't want to bum any more. The trouble is that I have a cigarette lighter and I don't have anything to light with it.

You folks may be getting some post cards instead of letters for a few times because I probably won't have a chance to write much during training.

We had a discussion about draft card burners and all that stuff and we decided that when we come back we are going to go out and get our hands on a couple of them and get them drunk enough to enlist in the USMC and then we are going to drink a little more.

Boy I miss North Royalton already but I am not as homesick as some of the guys that got married on their leave and stuff like that.

They are cleaning now and I am not assigned to anything so I had to go outside and sit on the steps. I can see the whole base from the steps here since our barracks are on the hill overlooking most of the base. There are some guys sitting outside on the steps waiting for buses to take them to the airport. They are going to Vietnam. I may be sitting where they are sitting next month. They are playing cards and cussing to try to eliminate part of their nervousness.

Well, I have to clean after all.

Bye,
Love,
Rodg

—◦

Camp Pendleton letter 35
Oceanside, CA
July 21, 1966

Part I

Dear Mom and Dad,

I am writing you letters now because when we get to Las Pulgas I won't be able to write for a week.

Las Pulgas is a camp in the mountains where we sleep on the ground for six days and nights and we take conditioning hikes up mountains that are really something else.

We have some of the guys that I went to Camp Geiger at Lejeune with here. Most of the guys took boot training at San Diego and the only thing I hear is arguing about which is tougher San Diego or Parris Island.

Part II

...

Well, I finally got all my stuff dyed and hung it up to dry. [Camo green t-shirts and underwear.] It only took one hour to dry in the California sun. I always wanted to see California but this is just too much! I don't think this is the proper way.

We were issued green dye to color all our white underwear. I suppose the powers that be thought it a good idea to have everything green, seeing as how we were the Great Green Machine. Grunts on the hump in Vietnam couldn't use underwear—it was too hot.

...

We have liberty and have to be back at 5:30 in the morning but I don't have any $$ so I am staying back. There is nothing to do but work out in the gym and maybe read or write letters.

One of my buddies is getting a discharge. He got married and he has to have a hernia operation. He won't give his consent so they have no choice but to discharge him....,

Well, I have got to *run*.

I miss home (cooking) Rod

Camp Pendleton letter 36
Oceanside, CA
July 24, 1966

Part I

Dear Mom and Dad,

I am standing duty NCO tonight. I answer the telephone and check liberty cards and passes and I have a little "Godlike" power. We had an inspection today and we cleaned the barracks inside and out. We waxed the floors and spit-shined the garbage cans.

A couple of guys are in the office (my own) (Knock before entering) sleeping on the rack I have to the left of my desk.

The captain came in about 15 minutes ago and they were sound asleep and I yelled, "Attention!" and they woke up and fell down on the floor and stood and swayed groggily back and forth. The captain started laughing and couldn't stop and so had to go out of the room.

I borrowed the corporal's iron last night and ironed *all of* my clothes, even my underwear.

Today is our first day of training and I have to stand duty NCO for the day so I won't have to train.

I spit-shined my boots and brass last night like a good Marine while I listened to the radio. Boy, do some of the oldies but goodies bring back memories of school, friends, most of all, home.

When I got out of the hospital and back to duty after being wounded I found I had forgotten how keep up my uniform. In Vietnam I had forgotten how to polish my brass and shine my boots. It all seemed so unimportant. I lost my good conduct ribbon because I told a sergeant that I was not going to obey his lawful bullshit order. What could they do to me, send me to Vietnam? At Quantico, my last duty station, whenever there was an inspection I was just given a two-day pass and told to disappear and I did.

There is a dance this Saturday night at the U.S.O. in Oceanside right off the base. The girls come from different organizations and churches but they will at least be intelligent and someone to talk to.

Part II

I am finishing in pencil because I just found my pens.

There are some girls at the baseball games at night and we go check 'em out. We have P.T. about an hour a day. I ran 2½ miles yesterday and I wasn't even out of breath. Of course we didn't run hard but we ran at a steady pace up and down hills and around the base and passed about 12 girls. When we passed them the sergeant said "Eyes right!" and we chanted "Marine Corps" and then growled loud as we could while looking at them and they got embarrassed and ran behind a building.

Well, I guess I have to go now because an inspection is coming soon. Big Brass

Yours,
Rodg

Camp Pendleton, CA letter 37
Oceanside, CA
Aug. 6, 1966

Dear Mom and Dad,

I haven't written in a week or so because we have been getting in late from the field or should say "Mountains" and I have been too tired to write. We came back from mainside from Las Pulgas yesterday on a forced march of 7½ miles up and down hills so steep and long that you have to lean forward so that you are leaning over the guy in front of you. I took 6 salt pills and I needed them all. It took us an hour and 45 minutes and it was so dry that I chewed two packs of gum and used my Chapstick at least 4 times. Oh yes. To give you an idea of what the march was, they were registering 115 on the thermometer in Las Pulgas. Man, is that heat. And there is no let up, no rain, no wind, no storm, just heat, and there is no shade at all.

In California we were given a lot of conditioning hikes up and down big hills that we gave obscene names. I thought the conditioning hikes were rough but they were nothing compared to what I would encounter on the hump in Vietnam. California was a beautiful place with good weather, lots of pretty girls and a beach culture. Camp Pendleton was a lot different than any place I had ever been and I was having an adventure and enjoying it.

Tomorrow we have a rifle inspection and a personal gear inspection — "junk on the bunk." I cleaned my personal gear — helmet, cartridge belt, etc. today and spent 2½ hours on my rifle.

Next weekend is the last weekend I have in the States for a while so I am going to a Las Pulgas restaurant. I have a date with a doctor's daughter. I met her at a public pier in Oceanside, Calif. I was watching and talking with her while she was fishing with her Dad. He let me use a pole and I caught a barracuda and 2 bonitos and couple of bass. I made a date and am using her father's T-bird and her brother's suit. (He is also a Marine in Vietnam.) She lives in Los Angeles and she knows of a dark, secluded place that serves a terrific array of food and very good coffee. We are going to Malibu Beach to surf during the day and then dinner at night. She is about 5'6" and blonde and terrific looking — nothing serious. We just enjoy each other's company.

Boy, am I glad to get away from Las Pulgas. From the top of the hill I climbed across from the barracks we can see the ocean 10 miles away. We have unique names for the mountains that are unprintable, but the scenery from the top of them is breathtaking.

Well, Taps are going so I have to sign off now. So long, Rodg

Last Letter from the World

Camp Pendleton letter 38
Oceanside, CA
August 9, 1966

Dear Mom, Dad, Debi,

Well I just got all packed up and am ready to go.

I learned I will be stationed in Da Nang, Vietnam with the 3rd Marine Division tonight. It wasn't much of a surprise really. I kind of knew where I was going all along. We have a short stopover in Okie [Okinawa] and then off to Vietnam. I am kind of lucky with Da Nang as all the big fighting is going on in the Chu Lai area.

I will be going on patrol day and night and will probably be on a couple of big operations. When I come home I expect to be a Corporal with a Vietnam service ribbon. I may catch M.P. duty or perimeter guard or any kind of guard duty before going into combat. That is what they usually do with green men. The thing about Da Nang is sniper, booby traps, and ambushes because of the dense jungle and extremely good cover makes it impossible for a large amount of troops to operate in the area.

A couple of guys in the unit are going over for the second time and they said it wasn't bad at all but I noticed that they don't make many friends. I asked about this and they said that the emotional shock of seeing your buddies wounded or killed can last long enough to get yourself killed.

After my first firefight I didn't make any friends. I rolled up a lot of guys in their bloody ponchos and I hardly remember their names. I still remember their faces, though, and I still can hear their death screams.

I notice everyone and myself also smoking more and getting more irritable with each passing day.

Tonight we get our last liberty and I am going to that doctor's daughter's house and sit around and talk and listen to records.

I am going to miss music a lot but I don't suppose I will be thinking of it very much longer.

I stocked up on toothbrushes and socks, soap and foot powder today. I guess keeping your feet dry is a real important problem over there.

Could you send some photos as soon as I send you my confirmed address? I would like one of each of you and one of the house. They would be nice to look at and remember....

Your loving son,
Rodg

As I got ready to leave for overseas I reflected back on all the things that had happened in the past six months — boot camp at Parris Island and all the marching and discipline; the small rewards I received for my hard work. I thought about my failure at the rifle range and my feeling of invincibility and power upon earning the title of United States Marine. I thought of my feeling of power again upon shooting all the different weapons at Infantry Training Regiment (ITR) and the feeling of comradeship upon completing a long forced march with other Marines. I knew now that even though all Marines are individuals, when the going gets tough Marines work together to overcome any obstacle. I also remembered my short stay at home as a brand-new Marine and how longtime friends treated me differently. I reflected on how I seemed older than those friends and how my parents didn't know what to say or do as I prepared to leave for war. My reflection continued to encompass the fact that I was a warrior trained to kill and tested in every aspect except for the killing itself. I would not have to wait long before I carried out my mission. My first kills would come soon.

2

Vietnam: Da Nang Area, A Company, 1st Battalion, 3rd Marines: Letters 39 to 96

"Forte Fortuna Juvat"
"Fortune Favors the Brave"

Introduction: 1st Battalion, 3rd Marines August–December 1966

PFC R E Jacobs 2203876
"A" Co 1st Bn 3rd Marines
FPO San Francisco, CA

My letters dated August 1966 to January 1967 were written during my tour of duty with the Alpha Co., 1st Battalion, 3rd Marines. All my firsts are in these letters. My first patrol, my first time as point, my first fighting hole watch, my first ambush, my first listening post, my first firefight and my first kills. This was the time of my first combat high and this was when I lost my first friends.

I arrived in Vietnam in mid–August 1966 on a commercial airliner complete with stewardesses. I remember the captain announcing over the PA system, "I hope all of you will be ready for me to take you back stateside in one year's time." I didn't think anything of his announcement at the time, but as I look back on it I wonder just how many guys made it back.

I stepped off the plane and the heat and humidity hit me like a hammer, and in short order my uniform was soaked with sweat. I was driven to the 1st Battalion, 3rd Marines battalion command post at Da Nang with some other replacements. We were issued web gear, M-14 rifles, ammo, ponchos, packs, insect repellent, jungle utilities and jungle boots. After a short time we were driven out to Alpha Company's position on Hill 35 B. The company had just returned from Operation Hastings, where they had seen some action. We were cherries, FNGs

43

(fucking new guys) who didn't know anything. I came aboard with two other replacements. We were assigned to the 2nd Squad with four veteran Marines and a sergeant as a squad leader. The two new FNGs whom I came aboard with and half of my squad would soon die.

(Letter 39 omitted)

Da Nang Area

A 1/3 letter 40
New York, NY
August 17, 1966

[Most letters from Vietnam have one date: the day the envelope was postmarked. For those letters with two dates, written on the occasion when I knew the date, the first date is the day of the postmarking, and the second date is the day the letter was written.]

Dear Mom and Dad,

I am sitting outside an office of the 3rd Marines in Da Nang, Vietnam. There are bunkers and sand bags all around but the VC as of yet have not attacked this part of the base.

We arrived here yesterday at about 5:00 and were processed and given chow. We slept on a floor of a one-story barracks. Nothing more than a wooden framework with a tarp on top and screened-in sides. The area I am in now is known as the rear.

This morning we will be issued weapons and our other gear. We will also be assigned a unit so I can get a mailing address.

The weather is very hot and the humidity is up there around 98 or 100 percent.

I remember my senses being assailed by Vietnam. The heat, the woodsmoke, the odor of decay, fermenting fish, human sweat and shit were physical forces. I had never experienced anything like this and I felt like I was on a different planet. Old men and women carried heavy loads of firewood suspended from each end of a long pole laid across their shoulders. The pole would spring up with each step and create a walking rhythm that was centuries old. There weren't any young men. All the young men were fighters, either friends or foes. These folks lived a meager existence without any of the modern comforts I took for granted. It was like stepping back in time 100 years. No electricity and no plumbing. Black and white were the colors that were universally worn. When the women needed to urinate they would just squat down by the side of the road, hike up a leg of their pants and pee. Boys of seven or eight would beg cigarettes, and those kids would try to sell you something all the time. Sometimes they tried to sell their sisters.

There weren't any men in the villages. All the men were fighters, friends or foes. Women and children, Kim Lin Village, September 1966.

Later in my life as I traveled through South America I would meet children like them again. Whenever there is extreme poverty those children exist. We are lucky people to be able to live the way we do.

The scenery is very breathtaking but ominous. There are mountains all around and they are covered with green foliage that is very dense.

The landscape was strange, foreboding, and spectacular from our little hill. Da Nang is in a valley with mountains all around and the South China Sea to the east. We owned the base and the VC owned the mountains. At night we could see and hear firefights and the flashes of artillery in the distance.

Boy I hate this waiting around stuff. People ask what we are going to be doing and where we are going and no one knows the answer.

There is supposed to be a large movement later this month (operation) and we will most likely be in it. The place I do not want to go is Phu Bai. There the action is getting pretty heavy. From what I picked up last night there is a lot of walking and little action.

I am all for that.

I feel we have to beat these people here once and for all. If it comes my turn to kill I will kill. I think I would rather kill a man than a woman or a child. If a woman or a child is a VC I will cut them down just as fast as I would cut down a man.

View of Da Nang, on the South China Sea, from hill 35B. I had never seen the air so clear. September 1966.

I have a funny feeling that I am coming home safe and sound when my tour is up. I am going to have to make that feeling a reality.

This would be the first of many times that I would state in these letters that I had a feeling that I would be coming home safe and sound. I believe that me stating I would be coming home safe and sound over and over manifested itself in reality because I did survive.

See you in a year,
Rog

Da Nang Rear

A 1/3 letter 41
New York, NY
August 21, 1966

Dear Mom and Dad,

For one thing Vietnam is hot as heck. Man, you are sweating all the time. We got issued weapons this morning. We are in the rear and our company got hit pretty hard last night. Not here but on the perimeter that we are guarding.

We have been down at the club yesterday and all today. It is the company club called the "Pungi Pit." Regular pungi pits are traps with sharp bamboo poisonous spikes that impale the foot. They serve beer for 15 cents a can and we got high all day — Can you blame us? We have a lot to forget for a while.

You will probably notice some of my letters stained with brown. It is sweat and dust from my hand and arm. The heat only lets up at night and then it gets cold. I suppose that eventually I will get used to it but for now it is bad.

The letters take about 10 days to get to you and about 10 days back.

After sleeping on the ground for 2 days we finally got a rack. Boy it will be nice to get a decent night's sleep for a change. We move up on the line pretty soon and we will not get much sleep there.

When I think it will be 13 months before I see the States again it strikes me as pretty hard to imagine but it is true. I am going to get some books and read. I plan on getting ahold of some books of math or something I can learn in my spare time. I also want to get a camera....

It rained all day and will probably rain all night by the look of the sky.

The mountains are picture-book variety steep and all green. You can look as I am now all around and see mountains. Some are Charlie's and some are mine, or, I should say, ours.

Well, I will sign off,

> Love all,
> Rog

Da Nang Area

A 1/3 letter 42
New York, NY
August 21, 1966

Dear Mom and Dad,

I plan on sending pictures of Vietnam home regularly. I already took pictures of the I.M. Club called the Pungi Pit.

I guess we have it pretty good because there are no major operations until early January.

I could go on R&R (rest and relaxation) to Bangkok, Hawaii or Okie or a couple of other places. I am allowed 5 days of RR after 3 months here. Some of the guys never get it and some guys get it right away. I could go and spend $1500 and still not have enough. We will have what we call funny money or military payment certificates.

I will send home a dime of that money with this letter. We have to spend that and only that at the PX and everywhere we go. I have a dollar and a quarter that I am saving to look at every once in a while.

That dollar and that quarter would be two of my prize possessions. I carried them between my helmet and helmet liner. Just being able to look at them every now and then raised my spirits.

[...]

The last couple of days we have been stringing barbed wire to slow down any VC attack.

So far Charlie has been pretty quiet around here but he is expected to start any minute so as a precaution we carry rifles and ammo wherever we go. In fact, it is a $25.00 fine if you are caught without a weapon.

Well, showers go at 6:00 so I must close down now because I want a good *cold* shower.

Love, Rog

A 1/3 letter 43
New York, NY
August 24, 1966
Monday, August 21st

Dear Mom and Dad,

I am writing this letter from hole "11." A bunker on top of a very steep hill that has a commanding view of the area Alpha Co. is guarding. I am in a sand-bagged position on top of an old French bunker looking over the Esso plant. The people in the Esso plant pay the VC not to attack it but nevertheless we still guard. I stood watch from this position with three other guys last night and this morning. I am alone because they only need one man for daylight watch. I will be relieved at 12:00 noon and I will return to my bunker and then eat chow and go swimming in the South China Sea.

We stood a lot of watches at the sites of old French concrete bunkers. The French occupation of Vietnam and their ultimate defeat was a foreboding reminder carried by finding these 20-year-old emplacements. Doing the same thing over again and expecting different results doesn't make sense, but we didn't know anything, we were just jarhead grunts.

It rained last night so I fixed a poncho up and kept quite dry. I have been taking snapshots with my camera and I will send the color home to you people to have developed because there is no means of developing it here.

I just had a call on the radio to ask about ship movement on the harbor below me so I took a look through my field glasses and saw nothing but fourteen fishing vessels and two oil ships headed for the Esso plant. I am supplied with 100 rounds of ammo and about half a dozen hand grenades and some flares.

I learned pretty quick. Keep a round in the chamber with the safety on, carry at least six magazines, carry at least three canteens of water. There is never, ever enough water. We learned to rig a load on our backs, to pad our shoulders and waists with towels to prevent saddle sores. We learned to hump. We learned to accept the pain of the hump and to move through it. We learned if you stare at something in the dark it will move. We learned to make sure we didn't hit a tree with a grenade; it will bounce back at you. I learned that my squirrel hunting days back in the World helped me run point position—only these squirrels here would shoot back.

Boy, the view is tremendous from up here. I bet I could see ten miles. When I go swimming I can take out fins and mask from company supply and the water is clear as a bell and there is coral growing all around.

I should be receiving mail within the next week or so. So if my answers don't come right away don't worry. It takes about 9 days for letters (or so I am told). Well, I am going to brew up a cup of hot java.

Love from the fox hole in the sky,

Rog

A 1/3 letter 44
New York, NY
August 26, 1966

Dear Mom and Dad,

Well, here I am in the hospital. I didn't get shot or anything like that I just severely sprained my ankle. Boy, does it hurt! I was getting my bunker squared away and I went to get a mortar ammo box to keep some of my stuff in. I had to go down a hill to get the box and I tripped and fell. I put my foot in a hole and fell on my ankle. They don't think anything is broken but they will take x-rays tomorrow.

As you can imagine, I am back at the rear area. I am sleeping on a cot instead of a cement floor or a pile of sandbags.

I either stand perimeter or go on patrols at night. Patrols last four hours and cover maybe five–seven miles. Perimeter is two men to a hole, one sleeping, one awake. Two hours on, two off, and two on, two off is how it goes. When you are off you sleep on the ground or sandbags or wherever you can curl up and sleep.

My ankle is starting to hurt again. Man, I am going to catch up on some sleep at last. Sometimes you don't get any sleep for three days and nights at a time.

We have watch until 6:00, we go back, eat chow from 7:00–8:00 and then working parties from 8:30–11:30. 12:00 noon to 1:00 chow and we are free to do anything we want unless there is a special working party for something. We can go swimming in the bay — skin-diving, etc., write letters, buy beer and get high. Everyone usually takes a six-pack (ice cold) to his bunker and sits and drinks it and gets high and goes to sleep til dinner and is back in the hole by 7:30. Watch starts at 8:00. All the same routine everyday.

We get better chow than I ever had *in the Marine Corps*. Our mess Sgt., Sgt. Joe, he is kind of weird and likable once you get to know him. Our looy is a nut. He sits and bulls with us just like a PFC or a LCP. He is a good guy.

I may have more rank here pretty fast as soon as I get settled. Along with rank goes responsibility. I am responsible and the only way is to trust me. About half of the company is going back to the States next month and rank will be wide open.

God, this is boring already. I can't get up and walk a little on the darn foot and I am thirsty. I have to dry my clothes at least three or four times a day — more if I work at all. The jacket and trousers are drenched with sweat. I am wearing jungle utilities that are much like parachute cloth — lightweight and very durable and tough. They also dry out fast.

It is getting dark and I am going to hit the rack right now and catch up on some of the lost sleep. Boy, the foot bugs me. I am going out to get my drink. Heck with it.

Love,
Rog

A 1/3 letter 45
New York, NY
August 29

Dear Mom and Dad,

I am writing this letter by candlelight in my bunker. Last night I stood hole watch (perimeter) and it rained for about 2 hours straight. At home we would call it a downpour with sheets of rain coming down, but here they call it a shower. I got soaked in about 15 seconds and stayed wet all night. I got off after 6:00 in the morning (two guys to a hole, 6 hours each watch) and was pretty beat to say the least. I got a cup of coffee at the mess hall and took my gear up to my bunker. I went to chow at 7:00 and came back and fooled around till 9:00 doing little odds and ends. Today in about an hour we have a patrol. We send out daylight patrols only every so often and they are rough. The average patrol is 8 miles but we're going 10 today. There will be twelve of us plus an officer and we will probably have to drag (carry) him back like the last time.— He got tired.

I am carrying an automatic weapon now because I have just installed a selector on my M-14 rifle that lets me fire semi-auto or full-auto. With full-auto you can make them keep their heads down with a burst and flick to semi-auto and have more accurate when they stick their head up.

Well, I am going to hit the sack. I am pretty tired (you don't get much sleep in a fighting hole half full of water).

Goodbye for now

I will try to write in a couple days,

Rog

(Letter 46 omitted)

A 1/3 letter 47
New York, NY
Sept. 4, 1966

Dear Mom and Dad,

We, we moved out of the Esso area. We got the word to pack up last night and when we came back from patrol we came up to a hill called #35B.

Our bunker needs a lot of work. There are six people in it tonight and it is pretty crowded. We had a patrol last night in an area where 20 VC were spotted by air earlier in the day. We went out at 11:00 and came back in at 5:00. I was point and it got pretty hairy at times. I am point this morning but we are only going down to a road to guard it as a convoy passes our position.

One of the guys in machine guns was a pretty good guy. We called him Okie because he was from Oklahoma. Okie was a wizard with his M-60 and I've seen him track fire down the center of a road at 400 yards. Okie quit college and joined the Corps after he broke up with his high school sweetheart. Okie and I sat in many holes at night and talked of home.

As the rainy season approaches it is getting pretty active (VC). The enemy is making frequent raids and is ambushing trucks or trains with mines every week pretty regular. The monsoon is supposed to hit pretty hard next week and will be in full force in the next two weeks.

I have been standing perimeter watch every day or night and going on patrol. This adds up to four hours sleep a night. I have never once slept a full 8 hours since I got here.

Boy, the view from here is terrific. I can see Laos. We are on top of a mountain and I can see a good 50–60 miles. I will take some photos and send them home.

Well, I am point and I have to go get my grenades and stuff.

So long for now. Write you again soon.

Your loving son,
Rog

Nobody ever pulled the pin from a grenade with their teeth. The pins were hard to pull. We would straighten the pins out at night and lay the grenades up on the edge of our fighting holes. We bent them back in the morning. Later in my tour I would pull the pins of all my grenades and reassemble by putting the pins back in on the other side. I would then hold the grenade upside down so the spoon would fly down into my hole when released. If the spoon flew up the NVA were trained to look for it and they would pour fire into your position with you holding a burning grenade. No good, no good at all.

A 1/3 letter 48
New York, NY
Sept. 8, 1966

Dear Mom and Dad,

I am standing perimeter watch tonight and there is just enough moonlight to do some writing.

Tomorrow we have a daylight patrol that will consist of a lot of hill climbing and walking. They are truly a bitch but it has to be done. We had some slack time today and I slept and made some coffee and got some pictures of the hill, the Ontos, a machine with six 105 recoilless rifles, and a 50 cal. machine gun and some of the bunkers and guys in my squad.

From now on we are going to blow out our living bunkers instead of pick and shovel. We take plastic explosives and dig a small hole and blam! A rough foundation.

I would make a ball of C-4 about the size of an egg and mold it around a overhand knot tied in a length of detonation cord. Then I'd tie the det cord (like a branch) to a main length of det cord (like the trunk of a tree) with other branches to form a Christmas tree. Dig some holes, bury the C-4 and hook up a fuse lighter to the det cord trunk of the tree, and blam! You had a foundation that just needed to be shoveled out. I liked C-4 and had four pounds stashed in my seabag that I was going to bring home for the next Fourth of July. My stashed C-4 was found by the company gunny after I was wounded. I never got to play with C-4 after Vietnam.

Building a sandbag bunker on hill 35B. September 1966.

Boy, there was illumination rounds and small arms fire at a place called Namo Bridge a little while ago. I hope we got them. I guess I will hear about it in the morning.

One night while sitting in an ambush position our squad heard a firefight break out about a half mile away. Coming back into the wire in the morning we found that a Marine ambush had opened up on a Marine combat patrol. The ambush squad leader didn't read the map right and it cost two Marines their lives. War is an easy place to die.

I showed the pictures [from home] around to the guys tonight. The guys thought Debi was my girl or something. One is even going to write her as soon as he gets time....

A cloud just covered the moon and it is kind of hard to see.

Well, I have a four-hour watch tonight and it might get a little bad there towards the end. I don't think I can get enough sleep anytime. I can sleep comfortably anywhere, anytime. Seeing as I am tired I can sleep on a floor, concrete, rocks, sandbags, anywhere....

It is 2:00. Only 4 hours to go. Man, I am going to be one tired boy tomorrow.

The 106's are firing tonight and it is enough to drive you out of your mind. It is like being on a bazooka range all day.—Boy, they are loud!!

Well, it is clouding up and I am signing off.

Love,
Rog

A 1/3 letter 49
New York, NY
September 8, 1966

Dear Mom and Dad,

Well, I just finished taking a shower and feel real good. The shower consisted of hauling five gallons of water down a hill to the shower and putting it in a gas drum overhead and pulling a string. It was primitive but it felt really good....

The only things we are lacking are cigarettes. We can't seem to buy any from anyone up on this hill as we are pretty isolated.

We have a patrol going out tonight at 10:00 and coming back at 3:30 and I am going to be humping the radio. There are only a few bad places (terrain) so it shouldn't be too bad.

So far I have received letters about twice a week and they been only from you. I hope to heck that the guys *(childhood friends)* start writing soon because if they don't when I get home I am going to kick a little tail. I am glad to see that you sent me that little Care package. I am going to really enjoy it after some of the stuff we have been eating.

One of my friend's birthday is Sept 9 and we are going to celebrate at the same time. I have about 9 beers and half-a-fifth of Silver Fox brandy (rotgut) and he has a whole fifth and about a half a case of beer. We are going to get drunk first and if there is any left the rest of the guys are going to join us in our celebration.

I wish you could send me only one thing — ice. The beer will be warm and so will the booze but it will still be a party. They are going to let me fire the Ontos also so I guess I will have a good time.

My birthday is September fourteenth. After Vietnam I would always equate my birthday with my first combat and being overrun at Kim Lin. My birthday was the deathday of four fellow Marines. I haven't celebrated my birthday for more than 40 years.

If you send me any booze, and I hope you do, for Christmas or New Year maybe, you could get those ready-made daiquiris or something like that.

It looks like rain tonight so I probably will get wet again. I have slept in a foxhole full of water up to my neck and fell asleep so a little more water will not hurt.

Well, it is just starting to sprinkle so I will close. I will write in a couple days.

Love,
Rog

A 1/3 letter 50
New York, NY
Sept. 8th, 1966

Part I

This paper is a little dirty because I am out in the jungle. I carried the paper out with me for the purpose of writing a few letters. We are set in ambush along Highway 1, one of the many roads in this part of Vietnam.

We went on patrol last night from 10:00 to 3:30. We came in and went out again at 6.00. This ambush will be from 6:00 to 3:00 all day. We came a good five miles and the march back will be hard because we have to go up Hill 35B again.

I carried the radio last night but today I didn't have to carry it.

Man, am I looking forward to some good chow once I get that packet of goodies.

There is a little shade in the elephant grass, which by the way, does cut you all up. We are set in on the slope of a hill looking down on the road. Cutting up hills where there are no paths or trails is pretty bad going because of the thickness and density of the growth. You can't see where to step because it is so thick and the holes and rocks are numerous.

I will get some sleep. Be back later to finish.

Part II

Boy, I just woke up and it is 11:00 already. I slept so good considering I had to move rocks so I wouldn't fall down into the valley.

I am carrying three canteens of water today because it doesn't look like rain and it is very dry when the temperature hits 120. Like the past few days.

We have to burrow into the grass like a mole in order to have some shade,

We have a patrol at about 11:00 or 12:00. I sit on top of our bunker and listen to our radio set to the Armed Forces radio station. They play rock & roll and albums from Broadway hits and movies. I sit up and let the sun go down and drink a couple of beers and smoke and think about home and stuff like that. I hit the rack for about an hour and go on patrol. If my writing is pretty crummy it is because I am writing on my helmet and it is unstable.

Well, I am going to fix up a shade shelter so I can get out of this horrible sun.

Love,
Rog

Our days consisted of long combat patrols, work parties building defensive positions, stringing wire, and digging fighting holes. Our nights were spent on a combat patrol or we stood hole watch, two hours on, two hours off, throughout the night. Sometimes we stayed awake all night lying along a trail in an ambush and sometimes we stayed awake all night on a listening post. Grunts would go for weeks and months on as little as two hours sleep a night and catnaps. Grunts can sleep anywhere. I remember sitting in a mud-filled hole at night in the pouring rain. Me and another Marine kept awake all night by smacking each other in the face with our open hands when we started to drop off. In my first firefight some men were killed because they fell asleep on watch. Sleep was needed and valuable, but sleep could also cost you your life. Close your eyes and you die.

A 1/3 letter 51
New York, NY
Sept. 14, 1966 (My birthday)

Part I

Dear Mom and Dad,

I have a bit of slack so I will tick off a letter or two.

I have another roll of film that I will send as soon as I get a chance. We don't leave to go to the PX and stuff like that. Trucks can't even get up the hill because it is so steep and rocky and during the rainy season the trucks can't even get up the first easy part because it is two feet of mud (or so I am told). Hey, chow is being hauled up so I will eat now. Finish later.

Part II

Well, it is Saturday night and two days later than the start of this letter. It is the first chance that I have had to write because we have been so busy digging bunkers and running patrols and stuff. I was put in charge of building a couple of bunkers so this may be a bit about rank.

I was just called to hold police call again and pick up cigarette butts and trash. When I finished I picked up seven beers and I am going to sit here and drink them all. It is Miller's and it is warm but good after a day's work. It will make me sleepy and I have to get up at 11:00 for an ambush patrol. We will go out only about ½ mile and set in till 5:00 in the morning.

Boy, I wish I had something to keep me dry. If you can get ahold of a cheap hooded jacket that waterproof or pants that can be worn with it send them air mail. Now I don't want you to go whole hog. Something cheap. That would be a good birthday present.

I am finishing this the 12th (first time I have had any time to myself for a week). I received your package yesterday after I came in from a day patrol. It was happily and gladly eaten (at least partly eaten) and boy was it good, I can't wait till the next one.

In the next one, could you put some stuff to liven up the flavor of c-rations like hot sauce, Accent, garlic salt, etc. Mom, you ought to know what I mean.

I am going to close now — will write next time I get a chance but it may not be for a week or it may be tomorrow. I have no way of knowing.
So long for now

> One month gone
> 11 or 12 to go
> Rog

A 1/3 letter 52
New York, NY
Sept. 17, 1966

Part I

Dear Mom and Dad,

I just got off a day patrol called a Ramble and I am beat. It started at 7:00 this morning and we got back at four. We went up a mountain around the top, blew up some caves and came down a stream bed. It took me about 2½ hours to get down the mountain most of the time falling and sliding on my rear.

I am sitting down inside the door of my hootch or bunker as you might call it. We had hole watch last night and will have a patrol tonight.

It is hard to believe that I will be twenty years old tomorrow. Also, no longer a carefree teenager but an old man (only kidding). I will spend my twenty-first birthday at home next year if I am not home sooner.

It has been raining more and more each day. It is pouring outside now and the monsoons are on the way. It is nice to sit inside and watch it rain while you are dry and warm. I think as soon as I finish this I will put some coffee on.

My squad on patrol in the mountains around hill 35B. September 1966.

Part II

Well, it is the 14th and I am now 20 years old and tired as heck. I got four hours sleep last night and we had a day patrol that involved climbing a mountain. We climbed up a waterfall for about 35 feet.

The streambed and waterfall were beautiful. This was the first but would not be the last time I was struck by the beauty of Vietnam. The natural beauty that surrounded us was stunning. War destroys everything it touches.

Well, have to close now. Got a lot of letters today to read.

Love,
Rog

A 1/3 letter 53
New York, NY
Sept. 19, 1966

Part I

Dear Mom and Dad,

We are moving again. We are going down to Kim Lin Village (about 2½ miles from here). We should be there about a week or so and then we will be coming back to the hill. We will not be going on patrol or anything. We will just be guarding the village against any terrorism that might occur.

On my birthday I got bit by something on my elbow and it got infected and turned into a medium-sized boil. It has a lot of pus and stuff in it now and I have my arm in a sling and I am on light duty. I will probably get a couple of shots and it will clear up in a week or so. The infection made me pretty sick yesterday, but I feel better today. I don't think that if I take care of it that it could turn into anything serious. The main problem is keeping it exposed to the air and the flies off. Doing both of these is a problem because the flies are pretty bad over here....

Oh yeh, I have been put up for promotion by a sergeant, my squad leader, and the C.O. I will probably not make it this quarter but I most likely will make Lance Corporal next quarter. (Rank goes four times a year, every three months.) I would like to make it because of the pay and responsibility.

Part II

Well the morning is completed and we are in Kim Lin Village —¾ of the population is VC or VC sympathizers and there are damn few young men around. We check ID cards and are setting up an aid station for the sick.

We can go swimming again as it is only a few minutes walk to the beach.

We have positions to man at night and we work very hard all day. (The digging isn't bad because we are in the lowlands — sand flats.)

The only time we expect VC in this village is when they come down from the hills to visit their families and we will get them when they do.

Well I will close for now. Expect few letters until we get our work here done (oh, the work).

> Love
> Rog

Kim Lin

A 1/3 letter 54
New York, NY
September 20, 1966

Dear Mom and Dad,

Well I have some time now so I think I will sit down and write you a pretty good letter.

Man that guy was right about the things to spice up c-rations with. Things like hot sauce and garlic salt are just the thing to liven up the flavor. I melt cheese in the rations and have devised a way of making both outstanding coffee and excellent cocoa. I add a little powdered cream and sugar to the c-rat cocoa mix.

...

Oh, about my arm tattoo. It is a USMC not a belly dancer and I didn't get a fly because I didn't have the money (kidding).

Our squad will be combined with ARVNs (Army of the Republic of Vietnam) to make a KACK Company. Combined Forces as they are commonly called. This is all bull probably, but by any spare chance, it is true. We would have it made because we would have slack — loads of slack. Beach parties, running water, maybe electricity and stuff. You see our job would be working with the people so we will also be modestly spit-and-polish and the chance of enemy contact would be practically nil. I will go along with whatever happens.

Our squad invited the Kim Lin women and children into our unfinished compound for medical treatment. Our Corpsman treated several villagers. We didn't know it but the village women were counting our weapons and pacing off distances to our defensive positions. The women then carried that information back to their men and the men attacked us two nights later. We hadn't learned that we could not trust anyone.

Last night a platoon of VC attacked the position next to our old position in the hills. There were no Marines K.I.A. but they wiped out the VC.

I saw an air strike from my foxhole the other night and it was something to see. Rockets, bombs, and cannon fire. At night that is really something.

I have carried weapons from an M-79 grenade launcher built like a sawed-off shotgun that shoots a 40 mm shell, a pistol (45), a shotgun, M-60, and my weapon I am carrying now — a fully automatic M-14. I can get 20 rounds off in a little under 3 seconds but the recoil is so great that only 4–6 round bursts are possible to keep it well aimed.

I received your package yesterday and ate a can of sardines and a can of fruit out of it already. Man are they ever looked forward to. That iced tea is great. (Everybody thinks so and anytime anyone gets a package we all share.) I have been getting some strange food from a Jewish guy — sausage from our Italian guy and some homemade stuff like that.

The cellulosis is almost cleared up in my elbow and I can do some light work.

My squad leader is going on R&R so I will be second man in charge of the squad for the next week or so. I am glad we are working instead of running patrols but it gets kind of hairy and stuff in the dark so there is less tension and stuff between everyone....

Love,
Rog

A 1/3 letter 55
New York, NY
Sept 25, 1966
Sept. 19

Dear Mom and Dad and Debi,

I am writing because I have a lot of slack time or, at least, more than I was accustomed to....

I have an issue air mattress which we call a rubber lady. It is a comfort to sleep on and I have been getting some good snatches of sleep lately. We still stand holes at night which means less and less sleep but when we get the chance we have our rubber ladies and we are out in a flash. I actually don't need the rubber lady because I can sleep anytime, anywhere from a 45 degree ambush site on a hill to a flat rock on the flat lands.

[...]

We have a lot to do around here and the little kids can carry astonishing heavy loads. We pay them with cigarettes. We gave them a pack — one at a time — and we still got three fighting holes with sandbags and stuff dug and bagged and set up.

Sept. 20

It is 6:00 and we have just finished a pretty hard day of work. We laid wire all along the perimeter and dug three fighting holes to be manned at night.

Our perimeter was about 70 yards in diameter. We had one run of concertina wire laid around the edge. We dug three fighting holes equally spaced with a wall tent in the center of the compound. The tent had a radio and some cots and was set up as an aid station for our corpsman. We kept weapons and a case of riot gas in the tent. The holes were manned after dark with two Marines in each hole. We stood two hour watches on and off all night. Our sergeant and corpsman and squad leader slept on the cots in the tent.

I am beat and I still have to stand watch tonight. It will be a problem not going to sleep, but I can do it. I have enough willpower. I am a machine gunner for our squad while we are in this position. I have my own gun (M-60 machine gun) and my automatic M-14 rifle. Tonight I will have some cocoa to make in my hole and I will make it when I get real sleepy. It will pass the time. Tomorrow we have the ARVNs coming and we will put them to work and I mean work,

Well, got to sign off now and get my gun out to the hole.

> Only 360 days left in hell,
> Love,
> Rog

The South Vietnamese force that was supposed to reinforce us was delayed, and on our third night at Kim Lin a VC force of about 15 to 20 insurgents attacked us. Working all day building defenses and three hours' sleep at best caused a couple of our Marines to fall asleep on watch, and they paid for it with their lives. I stood watch from sunset till midnight, and about half an hour after I got off watch we got hit. I woke to explosions of grenades and bursts from AK-47's filling the air. I rolled into my hole and came up firing my M-14 at muzzle flashes coming my way. If you fire a rifle at night it blows your night vision away, you can't see shit. Our squad leader ran from the tent and dove into our hole and came up with the machine gun chugging away. He was firing in the wrong direction and he kept the trigger down in a continuous burst. I yelled, "Left front!" and I could see another of our positions swarming with the enemy. I shot at two figures running toward our hole and fired at more muzzle flashes to my left. A large explosion rocked the tent and the riot gas started to blanket our position. We were getting fired on from three directions and the sand was kicking up around us. They wanted our machine gun. I heard the sergeant in the tent call out for help on the radio. I heard a burst from an AK and he cried out and his voice settled into a moan.

We were coughing and gagging from the riot gas, and my squad leader told us that we had to get out of there and go to the Esso plant, down the beach a couple of miles. He had come out of the tent and said, "The others are all dead." I looked towards the tent and it was burning and exploding. I turned to the beach and pegged a couple of grenades that way and set off a Claymore mine to blow a hole through the enemy so we could escape. This was my first firefight. I really didn't know what I was doing—I just used my Marine Corps training to survive. I was trained to follow orders and that's what I did. One thing, though—we made a big mistake and left an unwounded corpsman in that gas-filled, bullet-ridden, burning tent. Marines are supposed take care of their corpsmen. Most Marines agree that Navy corpsmen are entitled to wear the Globe and Anchor because they consistently risk their lives to save us. I was following my squad leader but what I did and what he did was to break a sacred blood trust.

My squad leader took off, and another Marine and I followed him down the beach about two miles to the Esso plant. While we were running, 81 mortars started popping illumination rounds over top of Kim Lin. The parachute flares descended slowly, turning night into day with false shadows everywhere.

We arrived at the Esso plant and immediately turned around. What was left of our squad went back to Kim Lin with the relief column and found four dead Marines, two dead VC's, several blood trails, one live Marine that played dead and one very fucked up corpsman. I think the trauma of the attack and the concentration of the gas in the tent resulted in the corpsman suffering brain damage. Leaving that corpsman behind at Kim Lin has been a burden I have carried all my life. I have been haunted by that memory every day and every night. Leaving the corpsman behind at Kim Lin followed me through the rest my hump in Vietnam. During heavy combat nine months later I met a corpsman who knew about Kim Lin. That corpsman told me I was on my own if I went down, as he would leave me as I left his brother corpsman at Kim Lin. I was a FNG following my squad leader at Kim Lin but it didn't make any difference.

When the sun came up we cleaned up the small battlefield. We rolled up the dead Marines in their ponchos and we dragged the enemy bodies together and picked up the odd bits and chunks of flesh. I'll always remember a blood soaked rubber lady that one of my squad members was sleeping on when a VC walked up and poured a burst from a AK-47 into his chest. The other man, the one on watch, the son of a bitch that was supposed to be awake to guard his comrade, was killed five feet away as he was sitting up asleep on hole watch. I even now have a difficult time sleeping more than four hours a night. In the bottom of my fighting position I picked up a magazine from my M-14 that had a bullet hole through it. I ended up sending that magazine home and I have it today.

In the midmorning after the small battle at Kim Lin, the village women came to claim the bodies of the VC that I killed. I wouldn't give the bodies of their men to them. The bodies were mine! They were my kills! I stood guarding my kills with my M-14 as the women were crying and wailing and beseeching me for relief, and my heart grew hard. The women unleashed a primal force in me. If this event had happened 1,000 years ago the women would have been mine. I would have made them slaves and concubines.

The women's sorrow was transformed into hate when they realized I was not going to give them the bodies of their men. The women's faces became flat except for their eyes. Liquid hate poured from their eyes. Their eyes, oh, their eyes. This was the first time in my life that I felt that intensity of emotion and I found myself a mirror reflecting the hate back. The hate transformed itself into a physical force and the savagery of war almost overtook me. I learned then that sorrow and hate are not bound by language. I learned also that the people of Vietnam didn't want us there. All they wanted to do was make love to their husbands and their wives, raise their families and their food and live in peace. I learned that I didn't want *to be there either. We loaded the dead, both friend and foe, into a truck and they disappeared from everything but our memories.*

A 1/3letter 56
New York, NY
September 23, 1966

Dear Mom and Dad,

Well, I received my baptism of fire last night. We got hit and I fired about sixty rounds of rifle ammo back at the VC. I threw two grenades and set off a Claymore mine. Nevertheless, they started overrunning us. Tear gas inside our CP tent went off and blanketed our hole. Grenades and small arms fire surrounded us as we broke loose from the hole and got out of the gas. We were on our hands and knees gagging and coughing.

My squad leader said "Everyone's dead" and I wanted to stay and fight (we still had our rifles) but I had to follow my squad leader and run to the Esso plant down the beach.

The total count: 4 Marines KIA

4 Marines OK

1 corpsman WIA

I guess it is needless to say I was very lucky to get out without a scratch.

Bullets and grenade fragments filled the air and kicked up sand all around my hole where I was fighting until the gas covered our position. The gas drove the VC away from our hole and we had to pull out. We couldn't fight in that crap.

We got to the Esso plant and fell down exhausted. They treated us like heroes or something. Even the officers brought us hot coffee and we told our tales. They sent a reactionary force down as soon as they could get the guys together and I went with them. When we got there it was just turning daylight and we cleaned up the area. I picked up a arm and face.

One of the Marines was carrying a M-79 grenade launcher. He had a bandoleer of six grenades slung over his head and under his arm. He took a bullet into the grenades and a grenade exploded and took off his arm and skinned his face and scalp. His arm had the same tattoo that I have. I still remember picking up that severed arm and seeing my tattoo.

Well, that had to be told. I wasn't going to say anything for your sake, Mom, but I had to. I am going to a better position with no action for a while now.

Love,
Rog

Da Nang Area

A 1/3 letter 57
New York, NY
Sept. 28, 1966
Sept. 23

Dear Mom and Dad,

Please excuse the dirt on the paper but we can't keep very clean here even though we try.

I haven't had time to write a letter since the night after we got hit at Kim Lin. The firefight reduced our squad by four men and we now have seven men so we don't go on patrol because there have been some large forces of VC reported around here lately. The other squads go on patrol and we do all the work on the hill. We have been getting probes every night. This means a few VC have been throwing rocks at our position and stuff like that. They rattle the tin cans that we have on the barbed wire and everyone gets jumpy so we start heaving grenades.

During the firefight at Kim Lin I threw three grenades and fired about 100 rounds of ammo and set off a Claymore mine.

I killed the one we found a couple of yards away and I definitely killed another and wounded maybe two more. There were blood trails all around where I was firing my M-14 automatic and one of them lead to another VC.

We lost four men — three of the squad and a sergeant. I was scared out of my mind but as soon as I started firing back I calmed down. There were incoming grenades coming in all around us and the flashes of the grenades and muzzle flashes of the VC automatic weapons looked like flashguns going off all around.

Well, the sounds were like explosions and machine guns and yelling and screaming and moaning.

Well, enough said. I will make it through everything coming up. Old-timers say if you make it through your first firefight you will make it through all the others.

Boy, this is the first chance I have had to write for the past few days and they have been keeping us pretty busy.

Well, I have another working party to go on now.

I am back.

I have a patrol tonight. So I have to get ready.

I will write as soon as possible when I have another chance. (Doesn't that make sense?)

Love,
Rog

I've heard death screams from three sources, men, rabbits, and lobsters. The screams are horrible. The screams still ring in my ears. The screams of men have invaded my very soul and I cannot forget them.

New York, NY letter 58
Sept. 29 1966
Dear Mom and Dad,

How are all of you? I am fine. I received two letters with photographs in them and a package with some outstanding chow in it. Man, you don't know how much I look forward to mail and when I receive a package, well, my morale goes up about 1,000%.

We had a pretty long patrol last night and I was point and carried a sawed off shotgun. In fact, it is the same model 12 Winchester that I have at home. We use 00 buck and that will really tear some new holes in the gooks. It got pretty hairy because it was pretty dark and there are VC out there because we have been getting probed all the time. Every night we throw grenades and stuff from our holes.

This will be the first time I start to regularly use the word "gook" to describe the enemy. Before my first action at Kim Lin I used "VC" and "Charlie." After Kim Lin and my first taste of blood I started to demonize my enemies so they would be easier to kill. In my life now I forgo the use of any type of negative slur of anyone. Respect if given is received.

I got a card from Uncle Bill and I have been receiving mail on the average of three or four letters a week. They are gladly received and I almost am caught up with answering the mail. We have hot chow brought up to us both morning and evening. For lunch we eat c-rats. Speaking of rats we have caught quite a few and some are pretty large. They would probably outclass our dogs. About the only way we can counter the rat problem is to keep the place clean. This is a problem when five or six guys are living in a 10 × 20 ft. area with packs and all the gear. It is quite a problem to get clean.

My mom's brother, my uncle Bill, flew as a tail-gunner in a B-17 in World War II. His plane was shot down over France and he bailed out and was expatriated by the French underground back to England. For years Uncle Bill had to have some padding next to his bed because sometimes in his dreams he would bail out of a burning B-17. Semper Fi, Uncle Bill.

As soon as I finish this letter we will go and start a new living bunker. It will be good to live and have some space.

When I get home I will take a bath with hot water and then while I am bathing I will drink a gin and tonic with crushed ice and smoke cigarettes and listen to records....

Well, I have to sign off now because we have some stuff to do.

Love,

Rog

P.S. I am looking forward to the rain jacket with a frenzy. It gets so cold when you are wet and the wind cuts through everything except rubber or rubberized material.

After the fight at Kim Lin our squad moved back to our hilltop outpost for a time. We ran a few patrols but in a couple of weeks our whole battalion saddled up and flew up north to a little airstrip called Khe Sanh. We came into the airstrip a platoon at a time in a C-130 cargo airplane. All of us sat down on the open cargo deck and used several cargo straps as extra long seat belts. The plane hit the short steel mesh and dirt runway hard and our helmets and rifles and grenades came loose and rattled around on the cargo deck. Our platoon dumped the cargo straps and bailed down the back ramp while the plane was still moving.

Humping all that we owned on our backs we left the airstrip and started manning a series of outlying hilltop outposts. From these outposts we ran long-range patrols in the forbidding mountainous country that surrounded the airstrip.

Khe Sanh Outpost

A 1/3 letter 59
New York, NY
October 5, 1966

Dear Mom and Dad,

We arrived at an airbase yesterday and put our belongings on our backs and marched out to our position. We may stay here or we may leave in the next hour. No one knows. Last night we had watch in a fighting hole we dug. Two men to a hole and you didn't get much sleep.

I don't know how I will send this letter and I don't know if I will receive any mail here. We are supposed to be here fifteen days and then move out to where I don't know. Of course, it might be fifty days too so I can't say anything definite....

I am going to be pretty scroungy and dirty when I leave here.

I have one set of utilities, the ones on my back, and a couple of pairs of socks. Do you think you could send me some sweat sox? White would be fine. I only have about three pair left and I would like to be able to change them every other day or so. While we are out here we get everything we need except food and water. We get food and water, but not enough.

I may not have another chance to write for a week or maybe even two weeks so don't get worried. I will write as often as I can hide somewhere and get a short note off.

Well, I have a hole to dig and a rifle to clean and all kinds of stuff to do.

Love,
Rog

The country around Khe Sanh is central highland mountains and dense jungle. Patrolling was constant and it was hard. Sometimes our patrols would last a week or more. The jungle was a dark, living, breathing organism. There were no paths in the jungle so we followed small creeks laden with leeches, snakes and biting ants. Vines would grab your gear and it was hot enough to kill. Radiomen had to wear their radios on their chests because if worn on their backs the thickness of the jungle and the vines would constantly catch on the controls and change the frequencies. The only way to advance was for the point man to fall forward and break down a few feet and then do it again and again until worn out and let another man take over point. Breaking brush going up the mountains was murder. We all carried at least three canteens of water and that was not enough. The chewing gum that came in our c-rats would come apart in our mouths because we were so dehydrated we didn't have enough spit to keep it from crumbling.

The mountains were covered with eight-foot-tall saw-toothed elephant grass. The grass would cut unprotected hands and faces to shreds. We had no gloves so

Author saddled up to head for a hilltop outpost in the mountains outside Khe Sanh. USMC insect repellent bottle in helmet "warband." October 1966.

My squad on patrol along the ridgelines of the mountains that surrounded Khe Sanh. This country was rough elephant grass along the ridges and jungle in the valleys. October 1966.

we wore our extra socks on our hands. I remember squeezing my hands into fists and the pus standing out on my knuckles. The mountains had small footpaths about six inches wide running along the ridgelines. We learned to hump our combat loads leaning forward and pigeon-toed, placing one foot directly in front of the next and our jungle boots wore out where our ankles brushed together. Halfway down the mountain was the jungle. The only water was in the jungle. Everyone was in a constant world of hurt. We saw signs of the North Vietnamese Army but we were spared combat for the time being.

New York, NY letter 60
Oct. 10, 1966

Dear Mom and Dad,

This is the first time I have had a chance to get a letter off in the last couple of days or weeks. I don't even know.

Our position is about 10 miles from North Vietnam and 8 miles from Laos. That puts us in a pretty hot spot but we have not had any contact as of yet.

I have slept for the past three nights in the rain. It has poured down and when I go off watch I curl up in a poncho and find a place that's not too muddy and sleep. My clothes are caked with mud and all I have is what is on my back. We have been drinking rice paddy water with iodine tablets for purification. It is pretty bad because we are dirty all the time and you can't get clean no matter what you do. You hardly have a chance to get clean anyhow because you are so tired.

I am sitting under a banana tree that shields some of the sunlight. It has been raining for the past three days and nights and the sun is out today and we are drying all our gear out.

The thing about humping that is bad is we have to carry about 300–400 rounds of ammo, 6 or 7 grenades, a mortar round, plus all our own gear, poncho, shelter half, blanket, chow, socks, shaving gear, etc. plus rifle belt, rifle, helmet, flack vest, etc.

The flack vest is a useless piece of junk. It weights us down greatly and is in our way most of the time. It keeps us pretty dry and warm but that is about all it does.

Flack vests were our body armor. We hated the damn things. There were several fiberglass plates inserted across the chest and back of the vest and it was damn hot and heavy. The vest would not stop a bullet but would turn aside light shrapnel. I took off my flack vest after returning from a four-hour patrol in the jungle and an eight-inch-long centipede crawled out of it. I carried that bug on patrol.

These days all grunts are wearing new, better body armor. I think the new vests will stop a bullet. I hope the new stuff is lighter.

We have to be packed up and ready to leave on 15 minutes' notice at all times so getting settled at all is a problem.

Boy, when I get home I plan on having hot meals, hot baths, hot coffee, and cold drinks and sleeping on a bed. I might have to sleep on the floor the first couple of days to get used to the idea of being dry and warm instead of cold and wet.

I think of the things that were so common like a hamburger at Manners after a night at the Corral or a Coke at the Dairy Queen and they seem so far off now.

Well, I must be getting goin'.

I will write soon.

Love,

Rog

P.S. I am looking forward to getting that rain jacket.

New York, NY letter 61
October 10, 1966

Dear Mom and Dad,

Godwin got Debi's letter and picture today and I got a letter from you folks.

[...]

Godwin is a pretty good man. He is in our squad and is a good friend and hopes Debi will continue writing because over here letters mean a lot. Letters lift a guy's morale quite a bit when you get a letter after a couple of hard, discouraging days in the mud.

[...]

Could you put a writing tablet in the next package you send me? Also, a couple of freezer bags because all my gear is somewhere with everyone else's gear.

Boy, we have to move again tomorrow and I have a lot to hump (hump is carry). I have bo-koo to hump — a lot of stuff.

We eat bananas and breadfruits and all kinds of weird tropical fruits that grow on trees and bushes. We also have coffee trees by the hundreds around here but we have no way of making fresh coffee.

You will have to excuse the paper because it is all I have left and dirt is everywhere so naturally it is dirty.

I just got some more ammo to hump. Man, I have a lot. My legs don't get tired, my shoulders just hurt in agony.

We all laugh at anything because we are so tired. We look like a bunch of cruddy slobs that are cracking up.

Tonight I am going to throw a couple of grenades to keep awake and I am going to make some cocoa out of c-rations.

We get a pretty complete meal when we eat c-rats even though it needs a lot of spice. We get crackers, cheese, peanut butter, fruit cake, candy, cocoa, coffee, sugar, bread, pound cake, and other good stuff. There are twelve meals in a case and four have fruit, four have cookies and cocoa, and four have crackers and cheese. B-1 has fruit. B-2 has crackers and cheese. B-3 has cookies and cocoa plus assorted white bread and stuff.

Well, I have to go because I have bo-koo to do.

I am looking forward to the raincoat, food, *dried fruit* and stuff. Wait until I give the word to send any more tea mix. It doesn't taste so hot with Halizone tablets in the water and it would be wasted.

Well, bye for now. See you in a little while.

Love,
Rog

We were issued web gear that was pretty much unchanged since World War II. The Army had the Alice pack with an internal frame that shifted the weight onto the humper's hips and took it off the humper's back. The Marine

Corps liked to say that the Marines did the most with the least. The out-of-date equipment we used added another layer to the World of Hurt. We dumped everything we didn't absolutely need. The only personal gear we humped was maybe a bottle of hot sauce, cigarettes, writing paper and pen, and some spare socks.

The Marine Corps of today is quite a contrast. Good modern lightweight gear is the norm. Of course, if the gear is lightweight the grunts of today are expected to carry more stuff. Grunts always have and always will live in the World of Hurt.

A 1/3 letter 62
New York, NY
October 12, 1966

Part I

Dear Mom and Dad and Debi,

How are you all? I received a letter today that said that Debi wrote to that man, Godwin.

I will send some pictures back as soon as I get a hold of my extra gear. You see, I carried all that I have on my back and I couldn't carry all my gear. So I took what I would need and that is all. I have yet to receive a package in these woods out here. I am looking forward to getting that rain jacket and something to spice up the c-rats because they are all I have eaten in the last two weeks. Not to mention that cheese and salami. Oh man, I will chow down. We have been getting bananas and grapefruits from the gooks for c-rats or we take the fruit from the trees with machetes.

We have been getting mail regularly and my name never seems to be left out. I am glad and I want to keep it that way.

Well, I have an ambush tonight. I will finish tomorrow since it is getting dark,

Part II

Well, today is the 14th and today was my day. I received six packages of yours at one time. My rain jacket, oh joy, and chow galore. The salami came through ok but the cheese was a little rotten but good.

When it stays this hot (it hasn't rained in four days) the stuff will come through OK. I think that the delay in receiving packages was the cause of the stuff spoiling a little. Man, can I brew up some Constant Comment tea that is good. I have crackers, but the stateside jobs are pretty good. In fact, they are outstanding. We have a new squad leader and fire team leader and two corporals for fire team leaders and I retained my place as a fire team leader also, so I must be doing something right. Our new squad leader is a real gung-ho man. We are going to steal everything we need from the army, who has better equipment and we are going to travel light and go get some. He has promised a case of beer to our first kill and I am going to get that case.

It may seem as though I am turning into an animal but it may keep me alive. I want to kill the VC and he is the one who can get them killed. He will undoubtedly square us away. We (13 men) are capable of taking on 30 VC and wiping them out, or so he says. Boy, I am probably scaring the *hell* out of you people back at Julia Drive but my job calls and I am going to do it.

Well, I will sign off for tonight and will add a little tomorrow.

Rog

Part III

Man, am I beat — no kidding. We had a 10-mile patrol over some of the roughest country around and we humped. Man, up hill, down hills, and around hills, through bamboo and bananas and grapefruit trees, down rivers, up rivers and streams with slippery black rocks and leeches that attack in tactical movements. Well, I haven't much time to write so I will sign off for now.

Part IV

Well, I am back and bound to finish this time. We have line tonight and I have about 45 minutes to do just this. We spotted a cave today and our team went and blew it out. There wasn't much in it but there were VC signs all around.

Marines on patrol. The sawtoothed elephant grass would cut unprotected hands and faces. Khe Sanh outpost. October 1966.

Man, do those spices liven up the flavor of c-rats. God! I look forward to eating now.

Boy, just trying to get a letter written without interruption around here is hard. I had to get on my men to get everything cleaned up and rifles cleaned and water and chow given out and team leaders meetings and squad tactics and all kind of good horse manure.

Tomorrow we have weather patrol or lines and we will probably have some slack. Well, I will finally close and mail this tomorrow.

Your loving son,
Rog

A 1/3 letter 63
Army & Air Force Postal Service
Oct. 15, 1966

Part I

Dear Mom and Dad and Debi,

[...]

We are staying here permanently or semi-permanently so we will start building defense positions to protect the air strip. We have yet to have a name for this place but you will probably read about it in the papers because the whole 1/3 is moving up and making headquarters at the rear of the airstrip.

It isn't so bad because we have artillery air strikes, med evac, mortars, everything in the order of supporting fire and med evacs. I have seen guys get hit and been on helicopters in less than five minutes.

We caught a scorpion today that was as big as the end of the sentence to the bottom of the paper + two inches (9"). Doc said that one sting could kill you. The thing was coal black and it was found in my old hole. Man, it was ugly looking. We put it in some gook liquor to preserve it. That booze will preserve anything.

We work during the daytime here and stand watch at night, two men to a hole. We usually are working all day and we sleep for an hour at noon instead of eating and we eat in the hole at night. We have compressed fuel tabs that give off little light and a hot blue flame and we make cocoa and coffee in the bottom of the hole at night. The gooks have been probing our defenses every night to see how alert we are and we have been pretty alert because everyone is scared because all we have is a few booby traps and illuminations set up outside our perimeter. No wire or anything like that. We usually spend the day talking about food, home, women, boot camp, and cussing out the Vietnamese....

I have a 40 mm, M-79 grenade launcher, M-14 automatic and a shotgun by my hole at night plus twelve frags so I am ready for anything.

Godwin and I will be standing hole together tonight and we will probably bullshoot until the wee hours of the morning. We haven't been able to sleep at night because it gets so hairy and stuff. Everyone wants to be up when the wad hits the fan so hardly anyone sleeps.

Well, it ought to start raining any second now because the clouds look dark and ominous enough to cause a downpour that will turn everything else into mud and more mud. It's time to break out the ponchos. We are going to get wet anyhow tonight but if we have ponchos we get wet slowly. No ponchos and it takes about fifteen seconds to get soaked to the skin.

Part II

Well, it is morning and we heard sounds out there all night. We are pretty sure it is a rock ape or a gorilla so we are going to catch it tonight with some booby trapped chop-chop (chow).

It was a strange-looking Southeast Asian ring-tailed raccoon-looking critter. We killed it with a booby-trapped grenade, skinned it and ate it with our c-rations. Yum, yum.

I only have this letter left or the paper left for this letter and a couple of envelopes. I will have to start writing on c-rat box tops or something because the mail must go on.

I did write one letter home on a c-ration box top. To get a letter mailed all we had to do was write "free" in the upper right corner of the envelope. We didn't have to use a stamp. Good thing — I cannot imagine having to keep stamps on the hump.

Today I am going down to the rice paddies to wash some of the encrusted dirt off my cruddy body.

I clean my weapons today and they will probably stay clean for the next few hours. I have to police the area around my hole and keep it somewhat squared away and clean.

Boy, will I be glad when we can go to the PX to get some paper, my camera, film and stuff like that. I have plenty of soap and stuff but I hardly have a chance to use it because we have a lot to do.

Well, this is positively the last piece of paper I have and I can't borrow anymore because everyone hasn't any.

I will sign off for now and I am looking forward to driving, if I still retain the skill, a yellow MGTD with black interior that is if Debi doesn't tear out the gearbox.

I wish I were home,
Rog

A 1/3 letter 64
New York, NY
October 18, 1966

Dear Mom and Dad,

How is everything at home? It is raining and I don't have much to do so I decided to get a letter off while I could.

I spent the morning setting up trip flares, claymore mines, and grenade booby traps. We had a hairy moment last night. My squad leader and I were out after dark setting some trip flares and one just set went off. The thing that set it off was a tiger with real stripes. The line opened up but didn't get him but they almost got us. I was hugging the mud and vines and ants trying to scratch a hole with my belt buckle.

I always liked to set booby traps. I was usually the man who carried the blasting caps and detonation cord. When that trip flare popped I looked back and saw the back end of a big yellow cat springing away. Some fool on a machine gun started to shoot at the tiger and we were in the field of fire. The machine gun traversed right over top of us. I was eating dirt. That was the first time I almost got hit by friendly fire.

The Lt. in charge is our platoon commander. He has let me set up defenses, fields of fire. Principal direction of fire for automatic weapons and stuff like that. I think I am getting up there in the world.

The clouds have started coming in over the mountains and it is going to be wet or, I should say, wetter tonight. Oh joy, that means that my green jungle utilities will be very dark chocolate brown by tomorrow and they match my face and arms. We are getting pretty bad. We sit around the fire on our heels because of the mud and grunt and groan and eat with our hands and drop our food. No one gives a damn about anything anymore. All we talk about is catching a gook alive and making him pay for turning us into primitive animals.

We have oil for our weapons but the mud makes them look dirty even though they are fairly clean and will operate smoothly.

I am carrying a "45" pistol and a M-79 grenade launcher. I also have an M-14 automatic with bipod and twelve frag grenades plus 8 mag for the M-14 (20 rounds each) and 300 extra rounds and 48–40mm — M-79 rounds. Let 'em come. I'll blow 'em all to hell.

I have two kills and another most probably and four wounded to my credit. That makes me high man in the squad so I get my choice of c-rats.

I have plenty of cigarettes that I keep in a steel ammo box along with valuables to keep dry. I have a couple of souvenirs already. A magazine that I was wearing at Kim Lin that has an AK round through it plus some odds and ends.

We are hurting for writing gear. This is why I am writing on both sides of the paper, front and back. We have an ammo box of water on our wood fire at all times for coffee. It is usually boiling so it kills all the germs from the rice paddy and we dip our c-rat cans in and presto, hot, strong, muddy coffee that will keep Rip Van Winkle awake....

They should give us some new clothes pretty soon so I can burn the ones I have on. They may not burn because dirt is not flammable. Everyone is in a weird mood and the most intricate practical jokes are happening all over. I caught the Lt. last night in a snare while he was checking lines. Also, to shake him up, we snap our bolts and yell "Halt!" from a position in the bushes about 10 feet from our hole. We also say, "Dung La!" which means halt in Vietnamese. That scares the hell out of him.

I have picked up enough of the language to make out. If a man has bananas or some chop-chop (food) I can usually get some away from him without offending his manliness. All he does is take one look at me and he drops all his load and runs away screaming....

I also have a shotgun at my disposal — Winchester model 12 — the same as at home in my closet but this one is cut off and fires good 00 buckshot.

My dad bought me a Model 12 Winchester for my 14th birthday. I killed a hell of lot of squirrels with that gun as I was learning how to hunt. After Vietnam I found I had to stop hunting with my Model 12 because in the woods I would invariably forget about hunting critters and start hunting other hunters.

Last night the looy and I were bullshooting and some artillery went off and we both picked ourselves out of the mud cussing. That is how we are getting. Even with five hours sleep a night, if that, I can remain alert on watch. I have seen what happens to guys the VC have sneaked up on while they were asleep and it isn't pretty.

Boy, am I tired! Maybe it comes from lack of sleep or being dirty or something but we are all so weary that we sleep in the mud and rain with ponchos that leak and form puddles of water on our rears and shoulders. I have yet to find a Marine who can sleep on his back.

I have learned a lot. I can talk on a radio with correct procedure and call out grid coordinates and all kinds of good stuff. Godwin was by earlier and said he had a letter halfway finished to Debi. He is a good guy and we are pretty good friends. He has a phobia about grenades, you can never find him with less than four on him and sometimes as many as ten.

Well, we received the word that we may be moving north farther even

The author in the elephant grass, torn pants and all. Everybody smoked the butts that came in c-rats. Khe Sanh outpost. November 1966.

though we are about 10 miles from North Vietnam and 8 miles from Laos. We may be going further and the VC aren't going to like it one bit.

Well, I am going to sign off. I have a lot to do.

Love & Stuff

Rog

A 1/3 letter 65
New York, NY
Oct. 26, 1966

Dear Mom and Dad,

Boy! This is the first time that I have had a chance to sit down and write. I bummed the paper off one of the guys in our squad and I have to scrounge up an envelope as of yet.

We built a larger shelter for the squad on the hill and we eat, sleep, and think in it. I wish I could say we drink but we don't have that luxury.

Boy, this raincoat that I have on now is the thing to wear. It keeps me warm and partly dry. My spices are going fast and they really are super. I look forward to c-rats now and I construct all kinds of various dishes from them. That North Carolina Barbecue sauce is great!! Everyone else in my squad plus the looy and Gunny and 1st Sgt. use them. We make a fire and break 'em out and have a feast.

We have had ambushes and patrols and perimeter watch most every night now and it is getting us all down. I bet I have lost about thirty pounds. I am skin and bone. We have a fat guy that eats two meals at a time and he has still trimmed down.

Vietnam shrinks people. The heat, the hump, and the stress make people smaller. Men become condensed. Every Vietnam veteran I know was smaller when he returned. I weighed 137 pounds when I got to the hospital after being wounded.

Man, we dig all day and cut down trees and stuff that is in our fields of fire. Then we do all the night stuff every night. Talk about beat!

Godwin is scout and point of our squad and my fire team brings up the rear. We are still good buddies and he is awaiting a letter from Debi pretty anxiously though he still has three or four girls writing him....

Man, the leeches are a constant pain in the backside. They can get through anything. We are forever burning them off with cigarettes and cigars. Maybe when you send me the writing gear you could devise a way of keeping it dry and enclose some cigarettes in that package also. I can't wait till I get the next package and I can rummage through the goodies.

The leeches were several different types and sizes. The small ones could get through the eyelets of our boots and we couldn't feel them crawling up our legs. The large leeches would get into our clothes when we waded rivers and streams and could definitely be felt. I burned hundreds of leeches off my body with cigarettes in Vietnam and my shins are still a mass of scar tissue created from all the leech bites.

One of the guys got a case of beer and we all sat down in the mud and had a bottle.

Well, we just got chow. C-rats by the cases and I will eat and then continue....

We have had some extra slack time. The only things we have had had is a few LP's (Listening posts) and hole watch for the past few days.

Well, I have to scrounge up an envelope. I am going to look now, so for now I will write as soon as I can get some paper and stuff.

Love,
Rog

The letters back and forth were what I lived for. Reading letters and writing letters took me away from the mud and the blood for a time. The act of escaping into my letters was like opening a window into another reality. It was my time out from the things that surrounded me. My letters kept me sane and my letters kept that spark of hope alive.

I hope that people who read this will understand how important the connection to home is to a grunt. If I hadn't had this connection to home in my letters the savagery of war would have overtaken me right away. I saw this savagery sooner in the men who didn't get mail. Eventually the savagery of war got us all.

A 1/3 letter 66
Oct. 26, 1966

Dear Mom and Dad,

This is the second letter that I am enclosing in this envelope.

The first was written four or five days ago and I didn't have an envelope and now I have one so I will write another letter. We are on five minutes notice around here in case any of our patrols gets hit or anything. It has rained for six days straight and the mud is above our ankles everywhere and all the rice paddies are flooded.

We swept a couple of hills or hamlets yesterday and came up with some crossbows and swords and pungi spikes. We received sniper fire and a couple of guys from another platoon got hit.

We are on Operation Perry and will soon be on Operation North Carolina and our unit is up for the Navy Commendation Medal and we will most probably get it. There have been recon elements from the North Vietnamese Regulars spotted in our area. This isn't good news. Boy, keeping dry is a problem. Even with that rain jacket the humidity seeps in everywhere. Then the wind starts and you might as well hang it up because you are wet and cold and there is no way to stop it.

You can plainly see the ground up here is reddish clay that is slippery, muddy and miserable. If I had a camera I would take a picture because no one will believe how we live. The rain has stopped for a while now and I have my boots off and socks out trying to get dry. Boy, we use a lot of issue foot powder and I can't figure out why.

The mud was ground into my letters. The mud was ground into everything. The mud was in our ears and mouths. Our c-rats tasted like the mud we lived in. We had no way to wash our hands before we ate. The only Marines with halfway clean utilities were the ones just off a patrol. The saw-toothed elephant grass the Marines moved through would scrape the mud off them for a time.

We haven't had any mail for the past week and a half. I hope my letters are building up. I can't read them all. I don't have enough time and sometimes they get wet. Do I wish I could answer all of them! Boy, would I feel better.

So far we haven't gotten paid since we have been out here but what does anyone need money for anyhow.

I could have had $1,000 and I still would have been on the hump eating c-rats and smoking c-rat butts. There was nowhere to buy anything. Cigarettes came five to a meal in our c-rations. The c-rat butts were so old they had little brown spots on them. They were like gold to us.

My spices are gone. Dratt! My hope is still there if you know what I mean, They were a life saver. I regret to tell you this but no more perishables until I can receive packages regularly because if they sit somewhere for a week the stuff will rot.

So the MG is looking better. OK. I hope that I will have some more happy hours in it when I get home. My plans now are a hot shower, hot meal, cold rack in that order and don't wake me if the house burns down.

Love,
Rog

We had a Kit Carson scout with us to teach us what to look for while on patrol. A Kit Carson was an NVA or VC that has seen the light and come over to our side. Most of them were still NVA that reported our movements to their superiors. The Kit Carson we had was a tough little dude. That little guy humped a 21-pound Browning automatic rifle that was as tall as he was. He humped it all day and all night in all kinds of terrain. Watching this guy move tirelessly gave me the first glimpse of the enemy we were facing. He was with us for about a month and then he disappeared one night.

A 1/3 letter 67
Army & Air Force Postal Service
Nov. 1, 1966

Dear Mom and Dad and Debi,

I just came back from a two day patrol on which I was only 2,000 meters from Laos. We patrolled Highway 9, the first Marines to do so in quite a while....

Could you send some more bouillon cubes? We went on a 12,000 meter patrol from our base camp that took 10 hours to get to our present position. We cut through jungle that was so thick with branches and vines that a person couldn't crawl through. Anyhow, about the bouillon cubes. When we got back we were soaking wet with sweat and those really tasted good. We cooked the water with C-4 — (plastic explosives) and those cubes were tremendously wonderful and they gave us strength, too.

We all were so physically taxed that we could actually feel our strength return when we ate. Sugarcane is what we looked for. We had a Puerto Rican Marine in our squad. This guy didn't speak very good English, and he was a draftee from the mountains of central Puerto Rico. We put him last man in our patrols and called him "Tail End Charlie." He learned to walk backwards. That guy could spot sugarcane from a half mile away. Chewing that raw sugarcane gave us a burst of energy. Most of the cane came from the gardens of the native people called Montagnards who lived in the mountains around Khe Sanh. We just stole it.

Well, Stan Godwin and I were on top of our hill at the base camp talking about what we wanted most. We had been without water for about 24 hours and we were really hurting. We decided that what we really wanted was a big pitcher of lemonade and what was in the package when I got back. You put it in there — glorious lemonade. We were so dry that we were talking about everything that was wet, Coke, root beer, everything and we were torturing ourselves.

Godwin is point and I am right behind him in the order of march. I am on the kill and search team, in fact, I am leader of the kill and search team. I drew some more blood on our patrol. I got another gook that had a rifle and wouldn't stop when we halted him. It was a VC confirmed and we captured him after I wounded him.

Well enough of that garbage. I am getting a reputation around here and no one messes with me because they know that I would just as soon hit them

The hump, take ten, expect five, get two saddle up and move it out. On patrol at Khe Sanh. November 1966.

with a shovel or something than look at him. I will stay this way until I get home because it helps quite a deal in this rotten hole.

Boy, are we cruddy. We have soap and stuff but we don't have enough water to use it. We take showers in the rain everyday and rinse our clothes out. Our clothes never seem to dry and one set is already rotted off me.

Debi, Stan says hi and he will start a letter as soon as he gets a chance and that may be today. In fact, he is sitting here right now and he said he would write today.

If Mrs. Wheller wants to send a package to somebody they could send it to Stan Godwin. He hasn't received a letter in two weeks and is pretty down in the dumps. Boy, everyone is cracking up around here. We laugh at the slightest thing and we get mad at the slightest thing. I think that is why Marines fight so good after a couple of weeks or days on this hill — you are p---d off enough to want to kill something and there is nothing like a p---d off Marine.

Boy, those socks were a life saver. When you send packages pad them with Pall Malls or socks. If you could get some that come up higher on my legs it would lessen the chance of leeches. When I was breaking trail my hands got all cut up on that elephant grass and vines and stuff. I am using that ointment that Dad sent with care. I am on light duty now because of my feet and hands. They are waterlogged and cut up.

Well, I have to do some stuff.

Love, Rog

P.S. Thanks for the paper. Could you send me a pen or mechanical pencil, maybe a lighter, flints and fluid?

(Greedy Rog)

I am thinking about Christmas and what I would wish for — envelopes, self-seal tap — large, small, med. plastic bags.

Number 1,
The Best,
I miss home,
Rog

My good friend Stan Godwin would be killed in action seven months later. Stan and I shared a fighting hole and chow and talked of home many a night. We ran patrols together, we sat in ambushes together, and we made plans to raise some hell together when we got out of that place. Stan was writing letters to my sister, Debi. During the process of creating this book I had the good fortune to meet Stan's sister Judy. Judy and I had a long talk about Stan, shared some memories and shed some tears.

In May of 1967 Stan the Man was the first Marine out of a chopper in a hot LZ. His company was going into an NVA bunker complex very near where I had been wounded two days before. He was killed immediately and did not suffer.

My sister Debi wrote Stan a good number of letters and I was going to bring him home with me to meet her. Stan lived in south Florida and had never seen snow. I miss him still. Semper Fi, Stan the Man

A 1/3 letter 68
New York, NY
Nov. 11, 1966

Part I

Dear Mom and Dad,

I am writing this letter even though I have another one to you that I haven't even mailed. Last night would have been Saturday night in the States and I wonder what I would have been doing. Maybe going on a date or something, even staying at home. Tonight I would be home with pizza and the TV and a Coke or something while I would just sit by the fireplace.

Boy, I can't wait to get home....

Those plastic bags that I got with my writing paper are just the thing to

My buddy Stan "the Man" Godwin on point in the elephant grass. Fleeting, illusive as always, but burned into my memory. Khe Sanh outpost. October 1966.

keep it dry and clean. I should have a big plastic bag to keep myself dry and clean. Could you send me a metal mirror and a comb? I want to see what I look like now. Well, I'll finish this later because I have stuff to do.

Rog

Part II

Well, I am back now and Godwin and I just got haircuts Mohican style. I mean straight Indian style. Boy, do we look weird or he does as I don't know how I look because I have no mirror. Well, I have to make up a list of stuff for my stuff if that makes sense and it doesn't.

> *One small story illustrates the morale problem. I hadn't had a haircut in two months and was told to get one. I found some scissors so I approached Stan Godwin, my buddy, and offered to cut his hair if he would cut mine. I asked him if he wanted a Mohican. He said affirmative, so I cut his hair. I told him I wanted a Mohican also, so he cut mine. We were proud of our new haircuts. We walked past the A Company headquarters tent and a voice rang out: "You two sons of bitches get over here." Our company commander was livid. We stood at attention and he commenced to call us names. He asked, "Do you know what you look like?" I guess he was not expecting a reply, but I said, "No, sir, I don't know what I look like. I ain't got no mirror." I thought he was going to have a heart attack, he got so red in the face. It was true, though. I hadn't seen a mirror in three months so I didn't know what I looked like. We had to modify our Mohicans and we were punished by having to dig a six foot by six foot by six foot hole when we could have been sleeping. It was then that I became the focus of the CO's anger. Respect is earned in the Marine Corps and the CO did nothing to earn that respect. Me not giving a shit about respecting him and me leaving the corpsman at Kim Lin provided a focal point for the anger that our living conditions fostered. In a way it was good fortune because when I put in a request for a transfer in December it was granted. I got out of that chickenshit outfit and that probably saved my life later on.*

Well, I am looking forward to mail. Hey, I just got a letter from home and it lifted my spirits quite a deal. I am so really glad to get mail even though I have to burn them after a week or so. (I read them about four or five times and then have to burn them because of the possibility of them falling into enemy hands)....

Boy, I got the screaming diarrhea from something or other but I am almost over it. I felt pretty bad for the past few days but I feel better now even though I am still feeling side effects (weakness, etc.). We have a 24-hour squad-sized patrol that I will probably not go on tomorrow because I am so weak. We are starting the first of this kind in this area. We will carry special long-range rations and set up an ambush at night and patrol during the day.

That ointment that you sent, Dad, did wonders for my small infection cuts.

My dad was a World War II combat vet and a small animal veterinarian. Dad would send a lot of medical stuff that would make my and my squad's life easier. Grunts respond well to an animal doctor.

I have everything planned for when I get home. I have a lot of time during hole watch to think about home and all the things I will do and stuff like that and I have everything planned out to the minute and hour. I plan on wearing dress blues home and I will wear medals instead of regular ribbons. I will rate three medals for over here and three more from the States. I will probably look like a Christmas tree when I get home but I hope I don't have any Purple Hearts if you know what I mean.

Well, I have to run,

Miss you all,
Rog

Happy Halloween!

A 1/3 letter 69
New York, NY
Nov. 1, 1966

Dear Mom and Dad and Debi,

Thought I might as well write you as long as I had a chance. Just finished a letter to you this morning and will write again now.

The Captain almost had diarrhea when he saw our haircuts. Evidently, he doesn't approve of Indians or something. We have twenty-four hours to grow some hair on our Mohican or else. Hell with it — that's what everyone including our staff sergeant said what can they do — make you paste your hair back on? ...

That company commander at Khe Sanh never made the rounds at dusk to check on his Marines. This officer didn't give a shit about us, what we had to eat, or our living conditions. I would later serve with officers who valued and took care of their men. Good officers know the value of honor. Good officers know what Semper Fi means.

We have sighted and called in artillery upon some North Vietnamese Regulars and we think we got them pretty good but we don't know for sure.

...

We caught a wild boar in our traps (we have a trap line, you know) and we feasted last night. That means there are more around and we will get a couple more. Boy was it good chow (chop chop) for a change from c-rats which we eat every day two times a day seven days a week. What I wouldn't give for a green salad with dill and vinegar dressing and onions and tomatoes and stuff like that. We get enough bananas and other weird stuff off of the trees, but a Caesar salad — God! What a delight.

You could send me dehydrated everything — potatoes and gravy, onions, more red kettle soup. *Coffee*— what I wouldn't give for a good cup of stateside coffee black with sugar. Some lemon juice if it would keep in one of those lemon plastic containers. A wire brush or two to get the rust off our weapons — all kinds of stuff you could think of. Dried fruit is so good that it is gone in fifteen minutes after the package has arrived. Prunes, apricots, raisins, everything. Maybe some more socks, high topped so they won't go down to my ankles. Maybe some insect repellent — 6–12 — or something.

The MC has good repellent but not enough of it and we are always getting bit or stung by some pesky weird little devil — a hunting knife — Herter's or something sturdy as heck. For food, maybe apple pie filling or cherry pie filling — dried apples....

Food was all we had. Food was an escape. Cooking was a distraction from the miserable living conditions that we endured. We made little stoves from empty c-rat cans. We brewed coffee in empty c-rat cans. C-4 made into small balls about the size of marbles could be lit and would provide some fast heat. We cooked down in the bottom of our holes. We were not getting shot at, so we had time to cook little meals with c-rats and spices from home.

One of the guys found some little hot peppers in a village garden. This Marine took one bite to check the peppers out and commenced to run in circles. We had no water to give him, and the corpsman looked in his mouth and found blisters. We stayed away from village hot peppers after that. Later on in heavy combat I just ate cold c-rats whenever I could get them.

Boy, there is a million and one things I could use over here but I want you to take it easy and send what you will. Just the way you have been doing. That way everything is all right and I don't have everything all at one time. Just about the time I run out I get another package and everything is smooth and steady. Of course there have been times that I don't receive anything for quite a while but it is the M.C.'s fault, not yours. I know that, what the heck, you can't have everything, can you? ...

We swept a ville a while back and I have some French Indochina coins that I plan on sending home with these letters somehow. The coins are odd and will be good souvenirs to keep. I may bring back a crossbow or something. I have a M-14 magazine that I was wearing at Kim Lin that has an AK round through it and some other assorted VC gear and garbage like that. I hope I will be able to get some captured weapons to bring home. But what I want to bring home is ME so I will concentrate on that right now and let the rest fall into place.

I sent that M-14 magazine home and have it today. I never got a crossbow, but since 2007 my Native American path has led me to build my own wooden bows and arrows. I still collect and am intrigued by weapons, but these days I kill no more.

Sorry to hear about all the guys getting their draft notices but glad in a way, too. Maybe if some of them get into the Marine Corps they will become men instead of "the guys." I would like to see Ricky Brow go into the Marines if he has enough guts.

When I get home I will have more ribbons on my chest than Sgt. Sullivan, my recruiter. Ha! Maybe I will go kick his rear just for self-satisfaction and then we will go have a few drinks. Did you hear that? Drinks, not beer. When I wear my blues into a bar and they ask for my ID they might as well hang it up because I will bust that place wide open. Sounded mean, didn't I? I think I have a right to be, don't you? If a guy can fight over here he can damn sure drink over there — that is my feeling anyhow.

You know once I get out of here if I see another banana tree I will go nuts. The same will happen if I go for a walk in the woods and a vine catches onto my rifle or canteen, or neck or pack. The way we cut trails over here is we take two steps and dive and let our weight break down the grass and vines and stuff and then do it again and again until you can't stand up and then let the next man take over. It is hard work especially when you are going uphill.

I plan on having that ring that you made, Dad, engraved when I get home.

My dad made a ring while recovering from frostbite he suffered in the Battle of the Bulge. The ring was made from part of a downed German airplane. I wore that ring all through my combat tour. The ring now has been lost to the sands of time. The only reason these letters were not lost to those same sands is because my dad held on to them for 25 years before giving them to me.

Boy, I could eat a whole English cut beef roast in soy sauce and garlic chips. I am turning into myself again but I can't help it.

Well, I will finish later. Got to get the holes checked for grenades and stuff.

Rog

A 1/3 letter 70
New York, NY
Nov. 5, 1966

Dear Mom and Dad,

How is everything? I am fine and I just received a package from heaven. It had shrimp cocktail and assorted dried fruit and a couple of cans of wet fruit and it was good. I still have some stuff saved away in my foot locker, ammo can, and I will eat it when the craving starts again.

Boy, do I wish I could buy you some stuff for Christmas but I won't be able to get down to the department store until next September or August....

I found some bean plants and some hot peppers and a guava tree and made some c-ration stew that was really good. All it needed was some garlic salt and some instant gravy or stuff. Remember all the stuff that you send has to be mixed with water.

I have my boots off and the sun, Good Lord, is shining and all my stuff is drying out. Boy, a day like today could end in me getting some mail....

We, Stan Godwin and I, had the same hole last night on the slope of a very steep hill and while I was standing watch Stan rolled over in his sleep and there he went, down the hill. He got banged up and I never heard (such) a string of cuss words in my life. All Stan talks about is oranges and horses. He wants to come up for a couple of days when we get out of here and I said we would be happy to put him up....

Could you send more lemonade mix? Boy, did Stan and I enjoy that.

We had a patrol the other day that went up a stream that was crystal clear and had a white quartz and gravel bottom. It had great twenty foot tall ferns growing on either side and the water was cold and fast moving. There were places in the black smooth rocks that were just like a bath tub and we finally said hell with the patrol, last one in is a rotten banana. We set up security and bathed. We had soap with us and we stopped at a pool about five feet deep and thirty long, twenty wide. Boy, that was the best I felt for a month. We went in clothes and all. You should have seen the dirt that came off my head. This pool was at the base of a beautiful thirty or thirty-five foot waterfall and the current carried the dirt away so fast that the water was always clear as a pane of new glass. We had a ball. We got out and dried in the sun and sat around all afternoon. I went in about three times as I was first team leader and my men stood security and guarded me. I felt *so* secure.

We haven't had any contact or anything for quite a while and there is a little slack time. That is why I am writing you long and close together. I have a chance now and maybe later I won't.

Well, everyone is gone and I am about the only one left. They all went on patrol and have classes and I got some slack because I went last time, I am sitting on the ground in the doorway of my hootch, out of the sun, but yet in the breeze and my feet are getting nice and dry and hardened up again. My rain jacket is a blessing because it keeps out the rain and cold at the same time. It is a little muddy now but it is dry. It looks brown instead of camouflage.

When I get home I will wear my camouflage utilities and jungle boots and hat with a K-bar combat knife on my belt. Boy, will I look weird.

The K-bar Marine combat knife came into use after the Marine Corps adopted the Browning automatic rifle. The BAR was the fire team's automatic rifle. The BAR is a big and heavy weapon and had no place for a bayonet. The Marine Corps needed a knife for the BAR man. A knife was developed, knife-BAR, K-bar. I carry a K-bar under the seat of my truck. I have never been more than 10 feet away from a weapon since Vietnam. Hell, a man isn't dressed unless he has a knife.

A couple of planes have landed at the air strip two miles away and from what I could see it looked as if they unloaded mail. I hope so because I want a couple of letters badly and they are due in right about now or in the next few hours.

Well, in 10 days I will have three months gone over here and nine to go. Getting to be a short-timer,

Your loving son,
Rog

P.S. I could use another tablet or three.

A 1/3 letter 71
New York, NY
Nov. 9, 1966

Dear Mom and Dad,

[.]

Nothing new has been happening here — same old stuff. Rest of the squad went on patrol and left my fire team behind. We are on post and generally just laying around doing nothing.

Boy, it is getting cold and wet up here and we built a new bunker to keep us dry. It will be pretty good when it gets bad. I would like if you could have the Royalton Recorder [*hometown newspaper*] sent to me. I could get the scoop on what is happening back in the old home town....

I think I am running out of ink so I will change pens shortly.

As you can see I did run out of ink and I had to change pens.

The monkeys around here are pesky. They throw things and scream at night and it scares the hell out of a nervous Marine on watch.

Do you think you could send me a couple of recent magazines? I would like to see what's been going on in the world and what new things have popped up....

I have been seriously thinking of waiting till I get out of the Corps and buying a bike or Corvette or an MG or something. I am going to school on the GI Bill. What do you think of that idea? To get what I want and to get what I will get is entirely different but maybe I can find a happy medium.

Boy, will there be some hell-raising when I get home. I plan on going places and doing things and eating pizza and salad on a Sunday night.

I would buy a really fast motorcycle, live the life of a homeless vet for years on the beaches of St. Croix and never go back to school. It took almost 20 years of my life to start to unstick me from Vietnam.

I hope I get a package today. I will eat good and hearty and I am always thinking of who sent it while I eat.

Well, I have quite a bit to do now. Got to clean my old M-14 and magazines.

Your son,
Rog

A 1/3 letter 72
New York, NY
Nov. 17, 1966
Part I
Dear Mom and Dad and Debi,

Hi, how are you? I am fine and still kicking.

It's about six o'clock and we are in our holes for tonight. The patrolling around here isn't frequent. Maybe one every three days but they are long overnight jaunts that leave much to be desired.

I just got through looking at my dollar bill and my quarter. I saved them even though it is forbidden just to take them out every once in a while to look at them and stuff. They bring back memories let me tell you.

The view from this hill is pretty good. We can see Laos clearly and watch about a five mile stretch of Highway 9 plus keep an eye on three or four other hills. It sure is windy though. I am glad I have my rain jacket and blanket and poncho to keep warm and dry. Semi-dry.

I make coffee in the hole at night to give me something to do. It also serves good to keep me awake. Tonight I think I will construct, in my mind, step-by-step what I will do on the way home and what I will do at home. We stand two hours on and two off all night and I have to start from the beginning every watch as this passes the time real good.

On the coffee, c-rat coffee is strong. I usually add two or three small packs to a cup. It tastes like mud and it *will* keep you awake.

Boy, I wish they made luminous ink so I could write letters in the dark on hole watch. That would be something.

We may be getting another squad leader soon. The sergeant we have now is driving everyone crazy. We have shot at more people, blown more caves and stuff than anyone else and the upper echelon thinks this is bad. I hope they get rid of him because he gives us no slack. He is always saying, "Hurry up" when there is no reason whatsoever. Boy, does everyone hate him in our squad. He is making the squad go to pot.

Well, enough of my trouble. Now I have a *bitch!* Debi! Get on the stick and write Stan or I will tan your fanny when I get home> Comprende!???

Well, I will finish this letter tomorrow or the next day.

Part II

Well, we are out on patrol and chowing down. We humped all day and are due back tomorrow night. We just spotted about eight elephants and the VC use elephants to carry their mortars. We are on top of a high hill and it is on the end of a ridge-line that we followed all day. We will move up and set an ambush tonight and set in observing tomorrow. It is really beautiful scenery all around so I really wish I had my camera, 35mm Petri or something that has light meters or shutter settings all over the damn thing. Well, my coffee is ready so I will put the sugar in. Well, it's really good and warm and it makes you pick your rear end off the ground and get moving.

We don't have much bitching anymore because we have been doing all kinds of unauthorized stuff like taking chickens and rice and onions and peppers from the gooks.

Part III

I pulled 24 leeches off my legs today and I look like the iodine kid. Boy, they attacked us in swarms and were really aggressive. There were guys that had more on them than I had and they were hurting. At least we stopped by a stream and had swim call to clean our clothes and stuff like that. It really helped to get into that cold stream after four hours of hacking a trail with a machete down a mountainside.

Well, I will finish now. The chow is hot but alas no spices for it.

Love, Rog

When leeches are burned off your legs with cigarettes, the blood spots left made you look like you got little dots of iodine on you: the iodine kid.

A 1/3 letter 73
NewYork, NY
Nov. 17, 1966

Dear Mom and Dad,

How are you? I am fine. It has started raining again and this time it looks as if it will not stop this time.

I have been pretty busy this week and we are going to be pretty busy for the next few months. Boy, we have a 36-hour patrol coming up that promises

The author in the World of Hurt that is the grunt's life. My pants were rolled up so I could burn the leeches off. Khe Sanh outpost. October 1966.

to be a hump and a half. We had a patrol today but it was canceled because we had to have classes and drills all day.

We blew some trees in front of our position with TNT. It took three charges and a total of over 8 lbs. of TNT to blow one down.

We blew one tree and a very large, very pissed off python crawled out. A whole squad of heavily armed Marines took off running.

I got a package with some crackers, cheese and sardines and it went with the beer and steak we had on Nov. 10, the Corps birthday. I guess the Marine Corps birthday is a pretty big event all over. We had steak and beer brought to us and we were living pretty good there for a couple of hours. Beer — honest-to-God beer! Oh man, we had two apiece and we were really happy and content.

We just rebuilt our hole and now the rain comes in on only one corner and we can stay semi-dry for at least a while anyway. One of our main problems is hot chow and that is why that Sterno will come in so handy. Rust too is a problem. We oil our rifles with a bowl of motor oil and they still come back with rust after a patrol.

After I finish this letter I will make a hot cup of coffee and get some zzz's for an hour or so.

This place is really putrid. Wet rainwater and leeches is all you see. God, I wish I was back in Royalton, but I have a job at the moment and I will come back soon enough. We had a patrol the other day (overnight) and we went to the top of a mountain by traversing the ridge line. Boy, that was some hump let me tell you. I was really tired and we were all sucking wind.

A Marine cleaning his M-14. You can always tell a grunt. He has a clean weapon and a filthy body. Khe Sanh outpost. October 1966.

Khe Sanh is the name of the air field I found out. If it has it on the map you will be able to find out exactly where I am.

Well, so long for now.

Your Son in Vietnam,

Rog

Tail End Charlie, our non–English-speaking Puerto Rican squad member, was playing with his M-14. He and another Marine were screwing around and Tail End Charlie accidentally let loose an automatic burst that hit the other Marine in the upper legs. The three rounds missed bones but one of the bullets cut the Marine's penis in half. We put the Marine on the medevac and Tail End Charlie was brought up on charges and was court-martialed by our bad CO. Things like this happened because of poor leadership.

A 1/3 letter 74
New York, NY
Nov. 17, 1966

Dear Mom Dad and Debi

Well, today is supposed to be a pretty good day on our hill even though we have to leave on a patrol at three o'clock.

Martha Raye is going to appear here at 10:30 — a couple of hours from now and the chow is supposed to be really good. Boy, when I was home I saw Bob Hope and the USO shows on TV. Little did I know I would be seeing them in person one day.

Well, she came and went and she was pretty good. She told a few jokes and had some pictures taken with some of the guys on the hill and then she was gone. She gave us an inspiring speech — you know, patriotism and all that good stuff.

Martha Raye told us that the protesters back in the World weren't good enough to "lick our boots." This time, early 1967, was the first time any of us grunts had heard of anybody protesting anything. As I look back upon that time I recall never reading a newspaper or hearing a radio that was not controlled by the big Green Machine. All grunts really want to know is where their next meal is coming from.

Grunts go to every church service there is. Going to every church service gave us a chance to sit down and maybe write a letter on the back of the church program. You would be surprised at the multi-religious aspect of a grunt's life. Lots of Jewish/Catholic/Protestant grunts, not too many Buddhists though.

Well, we are going to have hot chow again after Catholic church services and that should be in a hour or so and then we will get ready and go on our patrol.

The patrol route isn't long at all but it is up a mountain. Believe it or not I am the cause of the patrol. We had another patrol along the same route and I found three shell casings from a AK-47 in a tree fork. It is a VC trail marker so we will go up and set an ambush tonight and see if we can catch them coming down to mess around with our lines.

There have been VC around our lines almost every night and last night I was on LP (listening post) about 100 yds. out. I didn't hear or see anything because of the rain but we had reports on the radio of movement around us anyway.

I think some crazy person is seeing water buffalo because we heard the bells that the gooks have around their necks tinkling all night. Right now, there are water buffalo out in front of us on our position. There is a herd of about ten or twelve. The high elephant grass makes it kind of hard to determine the exact amount.

Well, the sun finally came out and I am letting my stuff dry. Boy, I got cold and wet last night! That listening post is no fun in the rain. For that matter any time.

I had part of the day off because of the listening post last night and that is why I am having a chance to get a couple of dozen lines off to you. I have a letter that I haven't had a chance to mail yet and when I go over to get some chow I will mail them both....

Listening post usually consisted of going out from the established lines at dusk to set in at an avenue of approach to the lines. LP was usually two Marines and a radio. Contact was maintained and silence was kept by keying the radio handset three times every 15 minutes all night long. Any other combination of handset keys meant an enemy patrol was sighted or the enemy was massing for an attack. We could not move or make any noise whatsoever. We made sure our lines would know where our LP was setting so they wouldn't open up on us if we had to retreat back to the lines. I went on many LPs and never got cut off from our lines by the NVA. I had to run back in twice.

Well, I have to get chow and I have to prepare for patrol right at the moment — I have about one fourth of my tour over with. Hot dog!

Your loving son,
Rog

P.S. Can't wait for them good old packages of goodies.

A 1/3 letter 75
Army & Air Force Postal Service
Nov. 19, 1966

Dear Mom and Dad,

Well, I was taken by surprise when I came off patrol the other day. There were two packages waiting for me....

We'll be moving to a different location on the same hill. Before we had the worst location. We called it our "jungle" of banana trees, vines, and hardwood thickets and we lived on about a 45 degree angle. Everything was ankle deep mud and it was pretty miserable.

We moved over to the elephant grass on the other side of the hill and we made hootches and are taking it pretty easy now. It is a real nice place. We have a bamboo porch that has a bamboo floor and our hootch has a bamboo frame and we used three ponchos and two shelter halves for top and walls. We can sleep in a pinch, six guys but only three of us live in it. We take our boots off on the porch under a poncho and then come inside. We have a foot of grass with ponchos laid over it for the floor and air mattresses for racks.— And to say something else, it doesn't even leak. We are as dry as a bone. The only way we are damp is the moisture in the air....

We let the water buffalo graze around our hootch to keep the grass down but we don't mess with them. One almost ran Godwin down when he was point on one of our patrols. Needless to say he let out a good old Southern cuss and fell down a hill into a wallow and got his rifle full of mud.

Hey, the Marine Corps will be getting a new weapon pretty soon. Next month we are getting the AR-15, a light, high rate of fire weapon. We can carry the weapon loaded (7 lbs.) and a couple of hundred rounds of ammo pretty easy if not easier than the M-14 with 90 rounds (6 mag). It ought to be pretty good.

The new AR-15 would malfunction and cost a lot of 1/9 Marines their lives. I speak more about this later in this book.

Well, how are things going? Sorry to hear that Royalton lost so many football games. Next year I might be home at a time where I can maybe cheer a little and drink hot coffee in the stands. God, what a wonderfully simple thing to do.

Oh hell! We have a patrol tonight. The Lt. just passed the word. Great! Just what we need, a wet muddy patrol in the fog yet. Oh well, we have to go so why complain. We have a rambler and an ambush. We walk and patrol for a couple — four hours and then we sit in and set an ambush for the rest of the night and we come back in the morning. It wouldn't be so bad if it weren't so cold and wet and the visibility so poor. We will probably just circle the lines and set in about 1000 meters off and come in in the morning.

Tomorrow we have a swim call and it will give us a chance to get our clothes cleaned and stuff like that.

Got to go for now. Lots to do.

Love,
Rog

A 1/3 letter 76
New York, NY
Nov. 30, 1966

Dear Mom and Dad and Debi,

Hi, I don't have much to do so I thought I might drop a line and see how you folks back home are doing....

The Army's got some people down at the airstrip and they are living in tents, sleeping on cots, with sheets, and always have clean clothes. The Army does a much better job of supplying their men than the Marine Corps but I guess that's what makes us better. We do more with less and what we don't get issued we steal....

The *fog* has moved in pretty thick now and Charlie is probably playing around outside the wire. They just fool with us to keep us awake all night and get us mad and disgusted. Every once in a while they will throw a grenade and scare the hell out of some half-asleep Marine on watch.

There are so many mountainyards around that pride themselves VC catchers that there are no sizable units reported. Also, we patrol so frequently and thoroughly that they have no jumping off point to attack us. It is the local yokels that are fooling with us.

The Montagnards were part of a caste system that existed in Vietnam. Most Vietnamese lived in the cities and outlying rice-producing areas. The "Yards" were fiercely independent folks who lived in the Central Highlands, much like the folks who have lived for centuries in the U.S. Appalachian Mountains. City folks didn't like the mountain folks. Mountain folks didn't like the city slickers, Same, same, everywhere.

Well, we stole a bunch of long-range rations from the Special Forces and they are really good! Dehydrated everything with all kinds of spices and stuff. You can only eat one at a sitting because there is so much stuff in it. Spaghetti, steak, potatoes and gravy, rice and beef with gravy — all kinds of good stuff that really tastes outstanding.

Well, I have to go now and wake the next watch up. I will jot some more lines down tomorrow maybe if I get a chance.

Love, Rog

Well, here it is about 6:30 in the morning and I am up. Some dufus spilled water on me and woke me up. I think it was that uncoordinated ape we have in our hole that steps on everyone in the dark. He insists on having all his gear in our little hole and making it as cluttered up as a rat's nest. He spent an hour and a half writing his brother a letter in Vietnamese. He had to look up every word and spelling... He is cracking up. Slowly, but surely.

Well, I have to run. I hope I get a few packages or I will be satisfied with a letter today. Anyway I best get some mail.

Love,
Rog

A 1/3 letter 77
New York, NY
Nov. 20, 1966
Thanksgiving Morning

Part I

Dear Mom and Dad,

It is now exactly five minutes to one in the morning and I am on watch in our bunker. We got a couple of candles in the mail today and we are putting them to good use.

I received the film today and also this writing paper. Good, I just ran out of paper about two yesterday afternoon.

We had a little action last night. We heard sounds and I threw a couple of grenades and shot a couple of magazines (40 rounds) full auto. Just like John Wayne — M-14 jumping in my hands. The gooks set our Claymores backwards. They pull them out and turn them around on us so they face us not them. Well, tonight I dreamed up a little plan. I set two out before dark so they would see them and then I sneaked out after dark and put hand grenades under them with the pins pulled. Charlie pulls up a claymore — the spoon flies and boom — heh heh. The Claymore is a very good weapon. It will cover a 170 degree area when completely spread out with 760 ball bearings. It is simply a shaped charge of C-4 high explosive in plastic with ball bearings. It is set off by a ½ volt blasting cap powered by a hand-powered generator. It is a simple, harmless piece of crap without the blasting cap. You can shoot holes in it with tracers and she won't blow — that's how stable the C-4 is. It will burn, but not blow. You need another explosive to set it off. I set the demo charges for the looy and I also set booby traps but I won't touch a VC booby trap because they often booby trap booby traps.

Well, we are now moved to the airstrip and nobody knows how long for sure we will stay. I hope that I will go back to Ohio, but you can hope for the worst and then never be disappointed.

After six weeks it started to rain and rain and rain and it got cold. It rained every day and every night and the cold wind was constant. We moved back to the airstrip for the annual monsoon. It rained from October till January without letup. We lived in the cold rain and we lived in the mud. We were brown men.

Even the black Marines were brown. Our exposed hootches were always blowing down and we were miserable. Our days consisted of patrols or work parties stringing wire and digging holes in the rain and wind. We lived in our ponchos. Our nights were spent in the mud and in the rain on ambushes, listening posts, combat

C-rat chow down. Meatballs and beans cooked with C-4 on a little c-rat can stove between the Marine's legs. Khe Sanh outpost. November 1966.

patrols or on hole watch two men to a hole. Our only chow was two Korean War-era c-ration meals a day and packages of food from home. A bottle of hot sauce was a treasure. A case of c-rats contains 12 different meals, so after six days you've sampled every choice you had. Some of the meals were good and some were really bad. We coveted a mixture of peaches and pound cake and hated ham and lima beans so much that we called them ham and motherfuckers. Sometimes we burned small balls of C-4 plastic explosive or we had heat tabs to warm our c-rats and sometimes we ate them cold. We ate those c-rats for three months straight. The only hot prepared meal was on the Marine Corps' birthday, November 10th; I don't remember what we got but it was hot.

I contracted diarrhea so bad that I stopped wearing pants under my poncho. Our Corpsman passed out weekly malaria pills and had us sprinkle charcoal on our c-rats for the diarrhea.

We visited (three of us) a Frenchman who owns about 300 acres of coffee. He has a mansion with marble floors and the whole works. We stopped to ask directions to a place where we could buy a goose or pig and he took us in. We sat on chairs and drank coffee and rum and he showed us where to buy the best booze.

He was really excited to have us as guests as dirty and scuzzy as we were. It was a luxury to sit in a chair and drink good coffee. He gave us 10 lbs of fresh coffee as we left. Now I know how they pick, dry, shell, and grind coffee. (He showed us his entire process.)

That chair was the first chair I had seen in three months. The Frenchman had killed several tigers and had the skins on the walls of his great house. He told us that he had been paying off the local VC since the French occupation of Vietnam had ended in the '50s. He had created a paradise for himself in these beautiful mountains. With us being there his whole world was crumbling. I hope he survived.

This morning Stan Godwin and I hid and drank a bottle each of Vietnamese rum. The looy had his share too, one or two good pulls off each of our bottles. He really enjoyed them. Well, I hope he didn't get sick because Stan did. It seems as if c-rats have turned my stomach to iron because I didn't get the slightest bit sick.

Well, the candle is burning low and almost ready to go out and I will see if I can get another one somehow. If not, so long for tonight. I will finish when I can. I have a lot of wire stringing to do tomorrow.

Love, Rog

Part II

Well, here it is morning and I have just finished a good cup of wake-up coffee (triple strength), black. It is horrible but it gets you up. I can hardly wait for the Herter's package or the camera. Man, does the time go by slowly when you know that you really have something coming but you don't know when.

There wasn't much fog out last night so Charlie didn't play with the Claymores. Maybe tonight. Well, so much for that. I got my rifle cleaned and the area policed up this morning before chow. You should have seen it after our party last night.

That French man invited us back whenever we could make it and I think we might go today. We will also visit some American missionaries in a ville not too far from here. They are two women that are about 45–50 years old and we met them on one of our long-range patrols. We were walking by and a voice said, "Hi, where ya goin'?" I nearly browned my green camouflage skivvies. We went in and had some tea and they explained their work.

Well, I have that wire to lay now. Will write soon,

Love, Rog

P.S. Still can't wait for all that good stuff. Happy Thanksgiving!

Khe Sanh Airstrip

A 1/3 letter 78
U.S. Navy
Nov 27, 1966
Part I

Dear Mom and Dad,

We have a person who is in charge of getting the men all they need. He is called the Right Guide. He gets chow, ammo, clothes and extra stuff that we need. The only thing wrong with our right guide is that he is eating and living about 100% better than the men. He takes the fruit out of the extra chow that is supposed to go out to the men. He also takes the heat tabs even though he has us chop his wood for his cooking fires. He also takes the special foods like big cans of canned fruit and canned hamburgers and chili. Well, today we got even. While he was gone we raided his tent and ate everything and everything we couldn't eat we took. I imagine he'll blow his top when he gets back (he is a sergeant) but if he says anything to anybody higher than him the truth will come out — heh heh — blackmail. Now we have him where we want him....

I had a picture taken with Martha Raye when she was here and my buddy is going to get it developed and I will send it home if I ever get it. My buddy who lent me this paper just spilled his coffee and it was his last heat tab. I never heard such an oath of speech. My gosh! Now he is throwing things — don't be alarmed. We all do it. It helps let off steam.

The author standing in the mud of Khe Sanh airstrip. We lived, slept, and ate in this mud. We wore our utilities till they rotted off, and it was cold. I forgot how it felt to be clean. November 1966.

Well, tonight we had a crud call in a stream almost a half mile from our hill. I used a whole bar of soap and a half a bar of laundry soap for my clothes. I only washed one set of utilities (I only have two sets) clean. I have one set on. I washed my head and the dirt came out even though I still have my Mohican cut. I feel so clean I don't want to do any work because I will get dirty. Now I watch where I sit and have my trousers rolled up above my boots. I don't know why I am going to all this trouble. My clothes and me will be dirty anyway in the morning. Well, I have to clean all grenades and ammo and stuff so I will sign off for now and continue later.

I remember going to that river to bathe. I got in and the soap I had didn't work. I had to scrape the crust of dirt off my head with my fingernails and then use soap. I would dream about being clean. The leeches and mosquitoes seemed to like clean Marines, though.

Rog

Part II

Well, I am back. We moved out suddenly and we are now in a defense position at the airstrip. We had ½ hour to pack up and put everything on our backs and walk the two and a half miles in the rain and ankle deep mud. We are in mud and we are wet and we are hungry. My raincoat zipper broke and the elbow was torn out. I need another one and the next one could be a little sturdier. I mean in the fastening and stuff like that. The jacket could be shorter and I could have some pants to go along with it, Boy, I stay dry on the top and get wet on the bottom.

The airstrip is okay because we have big pallets to put on the deck to keep dry. We will string wire and stuff around us tomorrow. Today we built hootches and dug holes and my hole was the best on the hill or the Lt. said so. How about that stuff? We can get hot chow once a day and we run no patrols. NO PATROLS!!!! No humping hills, Hot dog----------------

The airpstrip also has some supporting arms like artillery, 106 recoilless rifles, mortars — 81s and 60s and fifty cal. machine guns and other assorted stuff.

They have helicopters that have machine guns that can put out an unbelievable 9,000 rounds per minute and shoot 40mm shells at 250 rounds a minute. Can you imagine how much damage it could do — Wow!

Well, I will sign off now and I will see when I can get this into the mail.

Love, Rog

(Letter 79 omitted)

A 1/3 letter 80
U.S. Navy
Nov. 27, 1966

Dear Mom and Dad,

I have been at the airstrip now for three days and it's really something. At night, it gets so cold that we have on long underwear, utility shirt and blanket wrapped around our necks and crossed over our bodies and field jacket. We are living in the mud — really deep mud. I am brown now. We are living in a five foot hole with a dirt top. More or less a bunker with water at the bottom. The wind at night reaches 70 mph gusts and it is *COLD!*

I received your package yesterday — the socks and hot sauce, and garlic powder. We have hot chow once every two days now and it is pretty good compared to what we have been eating for 7 weeks.

I am mailing three letters to you at the same time because I haven't had a chance to mail the others for a long time.

I am just finishing a good cup of Marine Corps c-rat coffee — double strong and sugar.

When I look at all the stuff that I am going through now I say only one year — but what a year. This pen isn't going to get it. It is getting me mad because I have nothing else to write with as of yet. [*Change of ink color*] One of the guys is cracking up — we call him "Period Rag." Whenever he drops his rifle he goes in fits of yelling and hitting our dirt walls. As he was state champion wrestler (college style) he does some damage to our walls. It is funny. I have a phobia for throwing frag grenades at night. I throw them just to keep awake sometimes. At other times I throw them when I hear noises. I never thought I would be so cold in Vietnam but I guess there are a lot of things that I am doing now that I never thought I would be doing. Well, I heard the straight scoop. In Feb. we are going to Okie for retraining and regrouping. That means that I will be back here for a while in the summer but only three or four months at the most.

While at Okie we have liberty only a couple of times and all we do is the same thing that we do here. Sit on a hill and eat c-rats — only we won't get shot at....

Period Rag has some pictures of his girl in a bathing suit. All he does is look at her and moan. Wow — what a shape. Then we start with our stories and there is when it really gets deep....

Period Rag was in our makeshift hooch with three of us one night. Our hooch was made of four shelter halves snapped together with bamboo for tent

The hootch that "Period Rag" tore down one night in the rain. My fire team lived, ate, and slept in this hootch for two months. Note the two c-rats in foreground. Khe Sanh outpost. Early November 1966.

poles. It was raining hard and there was a drip that kept following him around. He moved three or four times and the drip kept hitting him in the face. We were all trying to sleep and he lost it and grabbed the hooch seam that was dripping on him and tore it apart and stood up screaming and yelling. We were all wet in an instant and we got him down on the ground and dragged him over to a tree. We made him sit on his helmet to keep his ass out of the mud and we each just rolled up in the rain in the mud in our shelter halves. We rebuilt the hooch the next day but we would not let him in it. He lived and slept in the rain for a couple of weeks, sitting on his helmet with his shelter half wrapped around him.

Well, I have to go now. I have a whole lot to do.

I have 9 months, some odd days to go.

Love,
Rog

A 1/3 letter 81
New York, NY
Nov. 30, 1966

Part I

Dear Mom and Dad,

I just received a whole bunch of packages from you. They included that Christmas tree — swell idea. Makes one wish all the more that I could be home for Christmas. It's really great to have a Mom and Dad who care so much. Next I got a package of food — cans and a pen and pencil and salt and Constant Comment tea, and bouillon cubes — oh joy. The next was also food — shrimp cocktail, really a treat to a dirty Marine. Next came a sketch pad with pencil and a package of paper and envelopes.

What a day. One of the happiest I have had in a long time over here. I will eat creamed corn and save my sauerkraut for some rainy day. (It rains every day.) Those plastic bags also will help keep things clean and dry. I put all my writing gear, envelopes, socks, etc. in them. I will save four or five for my camera and it will also be stored in an ammo can with a rubber seal around the lid.

This is important because there is a river running right through our bunker at the moment and when we take the ponchos off of the aperture, the rain will blow in and everything will be wet and I mean wet. Soaking wet and muddy.

Boy when I think of some of the things back home what I could do — hot water at your fingertips, being clean and dry all the time. God. What luxuries.

They seem a million miles away. When I get home sit me down with a pot of extra strong coffee and a couple dozen glazed donuts and the television and I will be all set. If I act kind of funny when I get home don't be alarmed or anything. After a year in this place I might be a little batty. Tonight I will sleep in the mud because there is no place that isn't mud / Remember that small bottle of English Leather that I kept in that black shaving kit? You sent me one while I was in boot camp. I still have them both. When I get a chance to take a bath in a stream I always put some English Leather on and the smell brings back a whole load of memories. Getting ready for a date or going out to the Corral — football games and such. The best years of my life but I didn't know it then and I do know it now.

We just lit our candle and I am finishing this letter by candlelight.

It's good to write home and receive letters in return. It makes a guy feel warm inside even though the wind is driving the rain into his skin. To know he has people back home to look forward to seeing and stuff again. I will probably be a changed person when I come home. Not changed too much I hope. Maybe changed for the better because you have a lot of time to think over here.

Well, I will finish tonight later on my watch maybe or maybe tomorrow morning.

Part II

Well, here I am at night again. We had a patrol during the first part of the day from 9:00 to 1:30 and we worked out in 50 mph wind with rain all the rest of the day. I was colder before but never so cold for so long. I nearly froze. We had to work all day out in the driving rain. The rain rains horizontally not vertically like we have back at home.

We ran out of candles so I am using a small can of oil with some paper for a wick and it gives off enough heat for a guy to dry himself out — semi-dry — and get warmer than he was. Of course we come out black from the smoke, but warm, dry, and happy.

Those little stoves really put out quite a bit of heat and enough light to write a letter by.

We really were miserable today although everyone was. We had to do all kinds of work like stringing wire, make the looy a tent to keep dry in. The only thing that got us real mad was the fact that we had to work on our own places and we were so busy we didn't have time to do it until dark and when it gets dark we man our holes and all activity ends.

God! The wind sure is blowing outside. Our poncho just blew in and it carried 10 gallons of rain with it.

Well, it looks as if we are wet for another four hours. Actually, we don't have anything else to do.

My fire team stood watch in a bunker that faced into the wind and rain. We had a poncho rigged across the aperture to keep the rain off the man standing watch. I slept sitting on an empty five-gallon gas can with my feet in the 10 inches of water that had collected in the bottom of the bunker. When it was my watch I took my gas can over by the aperture and set up, looking into the wind and rain. There was no use bailing out the hole since the rain would just fill it up again. Hole watch was two men to a hole, one man awake, two hours on, two off all night. The only good thing was the NVA wasn't trying to kill us then. Combat would come later.

Well, I heard that Charlie took our old hill back at Da Nang. Old 35B got completely overrun and they also took Kim Lin away from the Army. Army said the hell with it and pulled out and they now have a company guarding the Esso plant. I took most of those slides at 35B and some are of our patrols. Funny we didn't have all that trouble. Seems like the Army is always screwing up something even though they always have the best equipment, arms, chow, etc. Speaking of chow, excuse me for a second.

Found some chow I am going to trade to the gooks tomorrow for a hat or jacket made out of a shelter half or something. The chow consists of the worst extra c-rats possible to have. The gooks seem to eat anything anyhow. Soup will be good fair trade.

Well, I have to wake the next man up for watch. I will keep writing as often as possible.

Love, Rog

A 1/3 letter 82
Army & Air Force Postal Service
Dec. 12, 1966

Part I

Dear Mom and Dad and Debi,

We are on patrol called escort. We are setting in at the water hole and protecting or guarding it for the time being which will be all day today. We are listening to the radio and one of our squads from 2nd PLT is getting a medevac. One of their guys fell off a cliff or something and screwed up his leg. 2nd PLT is out on a four-day patrol way out in the boonies.

I wish I had my camera now because we started a fire and everyone got along by the fire and we are all cooking our chow and making coffee. The sun is out and we washed all our clothes and everyone's feeling clean and pretty good.

I just pulled a couple of leeches off of my legs. They get pretty big around here and you would swear they set ambushes for you when you walk through the grass. The only thing bad about leeches is that you have clean clothes on and the damn things get blood stains all over them. Well, I have some clothes and stuff to clean so I will sign off for now. (The water is cold!)

Part II

Well, everything's clean and I can continue with my letter.

Godwin left yesterday for R&R in Tokyo and is due back in about 8–10 days....

If I get back the first of May I will have just over a hundred days left and that will be fine. I will make a short-timer's calendar counting off the days that I have left until the last week or so. Then I will go back to the rear and be off to North Royalton, Ohio — long way off, but good to look forward to.

Well. I put some coffee water on the fire and I have some coffee waiting to be mixed right at hand. I ran out of stateside coffee already and I really miss it. (Hint.)

Since the sky is clear today we probably will have some mail coming in. Bo-koo I hope because we haven't had any mail for the past week or so. I hope we get some because I want that package from Herter's pretty bad. I'll take anything from anyone at all.

We have it pretty good right at the moment. We have seen tiger tracks and wild boar tracks all over the place. I know a corpsman that almost got it by a tiger. It took twelve shots to stop it. I have seen a machine gunner take four hits to stop a water buffalo. They are almost impossible to kill once they get a mind to run down a Marine.

Boy, the coffee is good. It really tastes good with a cigarette.

Well have to run off a couple of gooks, so bye for now. They were rice pickers so no problem but we don't like to have any of them around because as always you can't tell who is who in this green rot hole.

I hope I get a little sunburn tonight because it will keep me warm when the cold comes crawling around.

Well, I have a lot of stuff to do right now so I have to go right now.

Love,
Rog

P.S. Hope there is mail waiting back on the hill.

A 1/3 letter 83
Army & Air Force Postal Service
Dec. 12, 1966

Dear Mom and Dad,

How are you? I am fine and really happy. Yesterday after patrol I received three packages. Two from you and one from Herter's. I have my camera, knife, penlight, bug dope, and pocket knife. I also got that fruit cake — wow. Plus all kinds of good goodies. We are supposed to pull back on the 29th and move out of the field so I probably won't be needing any more spices or anything but keep the stuff coming. You can send the film right away because I am going shutter crazy. The camera is swell, just the thing and compact enough so I can take it on patrol and stuff.

I will be living pretty high for the next week or so with all the packages and stuff— gravy — Sterno — creamed corn — wow! I got a letter from Jerry, Steve, Carol, Karen, home and a couple of girls in Illinois.

Wow! Wow! Wow! Wow! Wow!

I don't know what to say!

When we got back from patrol we marched up the hill and there were stacks of letters and packages! We opened them in the dark inside our hootch with a candle for light and today I had a chance to really see what I had.

We will not get another chance to write today and will continue tomorrow.

Love,

Rog

Just knowing that there was a place called home took me away from Vietnam for a moment. Keeping contact with the World kept the hope alive that I would get out of that place. I was so fortunate to have the support from home. I shared all my packages from home with my squad mates, and sometimes I would read my letters to guys who had no mail. I then had to burn them.

A 1/3 letter 84
New York, NY
Dec. 12, 1966

Part I

Dear Mom and Dad,

How are things back at the old homestead? Fine, I hope. Things here are pretty good considering all the bull we have to put up with from our Right Guide. The sergeant will have working parties and we have to move our tents every day because they change their minds. They just can't seem to leave things alone at all for a minute and I am hiding and eating chow.

Well, I can hear the sergeant coming so I better hide the tablet because he doesn't believe we should be laying around writing letters. Well, he didn't come so I will continue my letter. Could you send me a couple of cheap pens? The last one didn't quite make the trip I guess because it stopped working after about a letter and a half.

We have a new guy over here in our squad and he is jumpy as hell. He woke me up about eight times last night and said he saw something in the lines. I finally said "Shoot the son of a _____ and don't wake me up yourself. Let your rifle do it." He turned pale and sort of shuddered and went back to the hole. He didn't wake me anymore until my watch (I stood two–two and a half hour watches like I stand every night we aren't on patrol). We have a patrol tonight that will only take three hours and we can come in and hit the sack for the rest of the night. Only five men are going on the patrol and I am one of the five. I will finally get some sleep! We won't carry helmets and flack jackets. Just weapons, ammo, and grenades. Move light and without noise and have a lot of firepower — we all are carrying automatics.

Well, I will continue later on. I have to dig another hole, the fifth one in two weeks — six foot deep and six foot long and four foot wide. Oh joy! I dug three in one day. Well, bye for now — being a team leader is great, you still have to work hard.

Part II

Well, the hole is finished and our hootch is moved and built a little better than it was before

We are hearing all kinds of scoop going around. We are hearing that we are going to Phu Bai to get M-16s, that we are going back to Da Nang to rest for about fifteen days before going on liberty so when we hit Okinawa we won't tear the place apart....

I have been on Operation Perry and North Carolina and all it was humping and shooting and that ain't exactly a barrel of cherries or was it a bowl?

No mail again today. That makes five days straight. The weather better get better so we can get some in and I really hope there is some for "Jake" in those big red sacks....

We had a five-man patrol last night. We went out about 700 meters and made a semi-circle of our lines. It was so dark that I couldn't see below my waist and I was point. Did you ever try to find and stay on a six-inch wide path that has branches, elephant grass, and vines grown over it? We crossed three streams by feeling our way and that path was something else. I was point and I had to find it and stay on it. We just carried our weapons, ammo, and grenades so weren't very heavy laden.

I took my right boot off and felt the path with my bare foot. I could hold my hand up in front of my face and even with good night vision I couldn't see that hand. Don't ask me why we were out when it was so dark, the NVA couldn't see shit either.

Today's Marine Corps has night vision equipment, but so do the bad guys.

Excuse me while I light up a Pall Mall (Stateside brand).

When I came back from the airport I snuck into my tent and no one knows I am here. That is why I have a chance to write this letter.

Well, they just found me so I will have to sign off. My fire team has to police the area and I have to supervise the job.

Only two months in R.V.N. left before Okie — maybe.

Republic of Vietnam

Love,
Rog

A 1/3 letter 85
New York, NY
Dec. 20, 1966

Part I

Dear Mom and Dad,

We just returned from a four night and five day patrol. It took us two days of steady mountain humping to get where we were going and the same two days coming back. The middle day we humped up and down mountains in the area of our objective

Tomorrow we are moving to the airstrip and we will probably be humping all our gear. Ugh! ...

I took a roll of film on the patrol and used it all up. A few pictures are of the hill and there are a few of myself, so you people will know what a jungle-fighting Marine looks like.

Well, I will continue tomorrow. I have got much to do.

Rog

Part II

Well, here I am back. I just drank Steve's Christmas present, the whole thing at once — Smirnoff's 100 proof and it was very good. I am forgetting Vietnam for a while at least. Over here you have to get high or drunk or something to forget your troubles and remember how good you had it at home. We have a battalion sweep coming up that is going to be a humdinger. If we run into VC we will probably have to stay in R.V.N. for a while and not go to Okie. I hope to God we don't find VC because getting out of here means a lot to me, even for a while.

Once I am back in the States I will calm down, but before I will really be a terror of the bars and girls in Ohio. You will have to excuse this because you can realize the situation I'm in.

Boy, I am feeling great. I can understand your not wanting to send me a bottle and all that. But take it from me I drank after my watch and there have been no gooks the past week or so. I know that we will not get hit tonight. Well, I will finish tomorrow. So long for now.

Rog

Part III

Boy, I feel great this morning. Sorry the above writing was so hurriedly done but the candle was going out and I save my penlight for emergencies only, so there was little light. We are on our letter writing time now and I really enjoy this time. Well, I will eat now, continue later.

Part IV

Boy, that was good. We have long-range rations that have rice, meat, dried vegetables, candy, spices, soup, tea and a dehydrated orange in each package. I took the rice and soup and spices and mixed in the onion gravy that you sent plus the dried vegetables that were onions or leeks. I then put some of my own seasonings into it and let it simmer. I made a whole canteen cup full of outstanding chow and I ate really good. Of course, I had coffee also — satisfied with a Pall Mall and a letter....

Well, today is Dec. 16th, eight more shopping days until Christmas. I wish I could be home but that is how the cookie crumbles or something like that.

Hey! I received the photos of the house, Debi, and the MGTD — great! Everything is just as I pictured it. I can even pick out the smallest details and remember some good times....

Well, I have to be going. I have a lot of letters to catch up on.

Love,
Rog

A 1/3 letter 86
New York, NY
Dec. 23, 1966

Dear Mom and Dad and Debi,

Well, today is the 20th of December, a Tuesday, over here. We ran a patrol today and found our own private little banana grove. We brought back some and are going to be in bananas till we leave the airstrip.

Boy, do I use that gravy mix. I use rice and dried vegetables and sauces and make some good hot chow. If they have any dehydrated vegetables back home in the wonder store called supermarkets, send some along with the gravy mix and maybe a small package of rice. I could really chow down. When I get home I want to go to Costas with you and start to look and drool. We bought some rum and whiskey from the gooks again plus the ever popular candles and we now make Coffee Royal with a shot of booze. Boy, is it rot gut....

I got some shots of a beautiful waterfall that must go down a hundred feet just like Angel Falls in Africa. It is beautiful as hell! Well, time to light the candle because I can hardly see the paper. We got ahold of a radio (9-band) from one of the Special Forces guys for about four hours and we listened to Armed Forces Radio and they had oldies and goodies on. God, I remember dancing and just memories connected with just about every song played. Really made me want to come home in a big way.

When I get R&R I plan on calling and talking to you. I am also going to send a bunch of belated Christmas presents, too. God! Only five days till Christmas. I suppose you will receive this after the big day. Anyway, I hope yours is as good as you have made it for me....

Well, artillery is really raising hell over the next ridge line. There are two battalions of NVAs over there somewhere and they found a training camp about two and a half hours walking distance from here. The camp was teaching booby traps so now the point (me) steps a little more lightly.

I am sleeping comfortable these days. A couple of days ago we were reissued rubber ladies — air mattresses — oh, how they smooth out the rocks and grass stubble. I received a letter from home today — a pretty long one. Had chow and a cup of coffee and read it and started this one. I will save it for a while

Our fire team's new hootch at the airstrip. We stole these bananas from the Montagnards who lived around Khe Sanh. The bananas were small and sweet and they were pretty good after two months of c-rats. Khe Sanh airstrip. December 1966.

and read it a couple more times before getting rid of it. I wish I could keep them but orders are orders, especially when they check you regularly.

I have stayed clean for a couple of days and it really feels good — no mud — outstanding. I use that comb and brush the dirt away. I look a lot better. My hair is growing out and I will let it grow medium length and try to keep it that way....

Well, I have to get some sleep tonight before my watch so I will end this masterpiece of literature right now by saying — bye!

Your son,
Rog

~~~

(Letter 87 omitted)

A 1/3 letter 88
New York, NY
Dec. 27, 1966

Dear Mom and Dad,

I have just made a marvelous invention. It is called a candleholder, light shielder, write letters on watch by box.

It is a c-ration case (empty) stood up on end in the corner of our bunker. On top goes a sleeve from the box. Place a candle inside and it forms a lantern with light coming out only the front as candles are sometimes too bright.

It is about twelve o'clock midnight and I have been on watch long enough to make myself a cup of extra strength mule kick coffee. The Corps coffee is pretty strong and a hot cup of mule kick will keep you awake indefinitely. Boy, did I sleep while my buddy stood 1st watch. Out like a light, mainly because we ran a patrol, strung barbed-wire and beat down fields of fire today and I was pretty tired. I will stay up until four o'clock and then my buddy will wake me at six for another hour. Four hours isn't a long watch. We started at 9 o'clock and stand till seven. Five hours on, five off. Would be great to have more than two men to a hole tonight.

I am back, thought I heard something so I put out the light for an hour or so and finally went out and checked it out. Just grass blowing in the wind. Never can tell, you know.

Well, another hour another thirteen cents. Isn't so bad because I get paid while I sleep. The only thing is I only get to sleep a little at weird times. Oh well.

We ran a patrol today. It was less than 500 meters and they gave us five hours. We had it just to keep us from laying around the area. We went out, found a nice shady spot and everyone brought books and sat there for four hours and we were a little early getting back. Sometimes the Corps does the weirdest things.

We were issued blankets and wool shirts just a few days ago. Well, the cold and wet is past now and we have to hump all that stuff plus an extra poncho. It doesn't make sense.

Well, at least we don't have rats yet. They can be quite a problem around our living area. In the last position on the hill we finally acquired them. They seem to come out of nowhere and they were a pest at night. They ran all over the area raising general hell until we were issued rat traps to try to stop them. We finally got most of them and were able to sleep without the fear of getting munched on. Tomorrow we will go down to the stream and take a shower. We have a little bamboo plumbing system hooked up that allows for the taking of a real honest-to-goodness shower and it really feels good.

I hope my candle lasts for my whole watch because I would like nothing to do but sit and write letters. I have so many to catch up on it isn't funny.

I listened to that guy's radio again for a couple of minutes today and it was really good to hear some Stateside music.

Godwin came back from R&R with all kind of stories and stuff. He really liked Japan, I guess. He plans on trying to get a duty station there after he gets out of this place. I might try also because with more than a year and a half left in, they could try to send me back and I won't come.

The latest word on Okie is no dice but you never can tell what is bound to happen. It will be a long war, I guess and I count on the worst and I have never been disappointed yet.

If only we had known that the Vietnam War would last 12 years, our longest war. In 1969 when I got out of the Corps I went to the Virgin Islands and commenced to live on the beach. I would be down there for almost eight years and the war would end but I didn't know it. Hell, for a grunt the war once started, never ever ends.

It is common practice among Corpsmen to let short timers — (less than two months to go) get a medical reason for not going on operations. I know our Corpsman really well and he has a non-combat pill which makes the user modestly ill and therefore unable to go on any hazardous jobs. This pill he will issue only to those who have less than sixty days left and who deserve it. Good idea if I do say so myself ...

We just got issued some more long-range good rations today. Just for extra chow. If you have enough water and heat you can really make some good stuff and we have all the water and heat we need here on the airstrip.

[...]

Love,
Rog

A 1/3 letter 89
Army & Air Force Postal Service
Dec. 31, 1966

Dear Mom and Dad,

How's life in the civilized world? Well, the monsoon is back again in full force. We had a guy almost beaten unconscious by a tent that he was trying to put up in this wind.

I am on light duty for the next few days because of an upset stomach. I can't seem to keep anything down and I had hot chills all last night mainly because I was wet. It rains sideways over here and the wind can take down a tent in a matter of seconds if you don't know how to put it up. Take me, for instance. We put sandbags all around our tent and we crawl in and hope for the worst, that way we are not disappointed.

Everyone is out laying wire or digging holes and I am inside writing letters. Outstanding is the only word for it. I am using a candle even though it is day time because the clouds are doing a pretty good job of blotting out the sun. It has rained for the past three days without letup. It isn't so bad if you aren't out in it, but they have had us up and out policing the area, digging holes and messing around with that wire again.

I got to sleep all night last night. I undressed completely and crawled between *two* blankets. Well, I vomited last night. I had to run out of the tent into that cold driving rain stark naked. Talk about cold! Wow!

Had some mail yesterday. A letter from home postmarked the 19th and a church bulletin. This was the only mail we have had for five days. Can't wait till the weather breaks and they start coming in with mail regularly again. I will probably have so many letters to answer I will go nuts.

We have nothing to do but sleep, eat, and write letters while we are sick. Wow, such slack time. We have been drinking coffee for the past few hours and just plain loafing. The wind is blowing the tent around like a piece of paper in a wind storm. It will hold up because after last night when I just laid there with a blanket over my head hoping that it would not come down on me it will take almost anything that the monsoon has to offer. I

Well, I must bring this to a close now because I have to go get some more water for coffee.

Happy New Year,
Rog

P.S. After January I will have only seven months of this _____ to go. Outstanding.

Love,
Rog

A 1/3 letter 90
Army & Air Force Postal Service
Dec. 31, 1966

Part I

Well, here it is Christmas morning. We had a small tape recorder one of the guy's wives (Pops) sent him and a tape of Christmas songs by the big bands. They had chimes and stuff and they really made me homesick. This guy with the recorder and I went to every hole and played songs for the guys on watch. It really made me feel like Santa a little bit.

We called him Pops because he was 24 and had two kids. Pops was older than most of our officers. Pops' wife worked in a Chuckles candy factory in Illinois. She sent us a 144-box case of that candy and I ate so much of it that just thinking about it today makes me sick.

I would meet Pops again by chance in an elevator at Great Lakes Naval Hospital in September 1967. Pops was recovering from a bullet wound just like me. We went and had a beer and he told me how Stan Godwin, Machine Gun Okie and the other men from 1/3 were killed. They had a hard fight and Pops was lucky to have survived. Semper Fi.

We worked all day yesterday and stood watch last night. That tape recorder really was the only thing that brought Christmas spirit to our tents and holes. It's hard to believe that it really is Christmas without you people. What would I be doing right now if I were home is what everyone asked himself over here.

We are going on an 8-day patrol. The twelve top men in the platoon are going and I am going. We will probably make contact and of course there will be no time for letters so you may not receive one for a week and a half so don't be worried.

Last night at twelve o'clock I shot a white star cluster. It is a hand flare that shoots up a good 300 meters and comes down on a parachute. The captain came over to my hole and asked me why I shot it. "Merry Christmas, Sir" was my answer.— He didn't say a word to me at all — he just left. Outstanding, Jacobs, I said to myself.

I put in for a transfer at this time as I had found myself the focus of the general feeling of anger that permeated company headquarters. Leaving the corpsman at Kim Lin played a part in that focus of anger. No one had been promoted in the time we were at Khe Sanh, and the weather, the food, and the general primitive conditions affected everyone. Our officers seemed powerless to do anything but constantly show their ass to the men. The shit rolls down the hill.

We have church services today at 9:30 and it should be coming up pretty soon. A plane came in a few minutes ago and I hope it held mail because I haven't got any for the past three days and I would like some before that patrol.

Well, everyone was sure in the spirit last night. Some were sober, some were drunk and some were about half-pissed. I fixed a good dinner of rice, onions, leeks, bouillon cubes, and spices. It was good. I have to go now because church is coming up in the next few moments.

Bye, Rog — I will continue later

Part II

Well, I have heard the very end. We have one hour to write letters, eat chow and clean our weapons before we start on the wire-laying again — on Christmas Day. We had the Marine Corps birthday off but not Christmas. I don't know what the heck is going on because word was passed that we are not expecting gooks or anything. We just found out why we are working — the battalion commander told the Captain (A-Co.) we had laid the wire in the wrong place. Well, everyone got mad because the crap rolls down the hill and stops at the men. So we are getting screwed because the brass is mad. (ON CHRISTMAS.) I wished the C.O. a Merry Christmas this morning and he gave me a dirty look. I couldn't care less. Those people really know how to monkey around with the troops.

We got worn out. The c-rats, living in our ponchos, the cold, being wet, catching catnaps in the mud and rain, no rest, constantly working and patrolling. We were not even given time to eat our c-rats. We worked stringing wire in the rain every day including Christmas. We started work when it got light and ended work when it got dark and then we stayed up most of the night on hole watch. If we didn't have hole watch we went on listening post, combat patrol or ambush. During this time our morale hit rock bottom. We were literally worked out, slave labor, no breaks, no sleep, always wet, muddy, and miserable. Our weapons rusted and we had no oil. My boots stayed on for six weeks and my utilities rotted off. When I finally took my boots off the skin came off my feet with my socks. Our officers did not look out for or respect their men. We were treated terribly. I developed an attitude problem with authority that I have to this day. The only good thing was that we were not being shot at. That would come later.

Boy, I wish I were home. Tonight over here it is Christmas, in the States tomorrow is Christmas. I will celebrate twice. New Year's I will probably be out on patrol near Laos so I won't be able to celebrate that very much. 1967. Boy, what a long time and I will be home in August. As long as it is in the same year it will seem like a downhill grade — or at least it will sound good.

Well, I scarfed (stole) up some looy's rations — chile con carne, it is a new Army type and is dried. All you do is add hot water, let it sit for about 20 minutes or so and eat. It makes a big helping and is light and easy to pack. All you need is water, hot or cold, but hot is better. Best chow I have had over here in a long time. He won't miss them because he has so much stuff all over his tent and I am tired of seeing him and the sergeants eating good and us eating rotten c-rats.

Well, I have to sign off. I want to get this mailed today.

Love,
Rog

A 1/3 letter 91
New York, NY
Jan. 6, 1967

Dear Mom and Dad,

Well, here it is at the end of another day. We dug holes all day today and they were a job because they had to be 18 inches wide, 15 feet long, and 6 feet deep. That's a hole! Let me tell you. We had three guys working on one and we completed three of them — top made of sandbags and all.

No mail today either. I am wondering how long it will be. The wind has quit but heavy fog came in and made it almost impossible to see for twenty yards. I am burning a Santa Claus candle one of the guys got in the mail. It is funny to look at it and think a few short days ago it was Christmas seems like only yesterday I was home and I can pick out very small details of my room, the house, the cars and all the other stuff I haven't seen for so long.

[...]

We are standing two watches tonight. Three hours on, three hours off and then three hours on again. It isn't bad since we can stay inside the holes without the rain blowing in on us and getting everything drenched.

I hope tomorrow we get a chance to rebuild our hootches. Everyone's hootch needs rebuilding and we only got about a half hour off during the day.

I hope you don't mind me writing on both sides of the paper. It conserves paper a little because I don't have a whole lot left and I hate to borrow from the other guys because no one has much of anything they can spare.

Well, New Year's Eve is coming up and we have a party planned. I have a bottle of Vietnamese rum that is pure rotgut and everyone else has a bottle or a share in one. Might be a gasser.

Well, I must sign off for now. I have to get some sleep.

Thinking of you a lot,
Love,
Rog

A 1/3 letter 92
New York, NY
Jan. 6, 1967
Part I
Dec. 26
Dear Mom and Dad,

Hi, how's everything back at home? Well, what did you do for Christmas? Sure wish I could have been home to enjoy the holidays with you. Next year will be different. You can bet on it.

Well, yesterday was Christmas. I laid wire all day with the other guys. Today I hauled sandbags and cut wire and worked really hard. We got fifteen minutes for lunch and we ate chow for evening in our holes. God, they have really been working us hard and tonight it is raining and we have to stand outside the holes. It is really pouring down rain. We haven't had any mail for four days so I think when it comes it will come in quantity as always.

I have second, fourth and sixth watch tonight so I am in my hootch with a candle burning writing some letters. It is really nice to have letters to write and now is the only time I can write them.

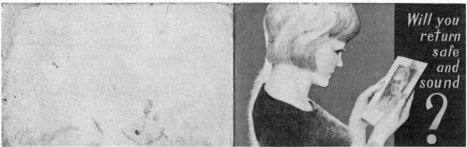

Enemy Christmas card to us. Author found this card on the ground along a patrol route. Khe Sanh airstrip, December 1966.

I couldn't go on that patrol because I had a small infection in the finger of my right hand (trigger finger) and the Doc said all the wet and stuff would just make it worse. They gave me a shot of some powerful stuff for it and it really hurt. Ouch! That was yesterday after barbwire-laying was secured (because of the lack of light), the sun went down.

I just like to write home to feel as though I am talking with you — really gives me an incentive, something to look for, a goal. Like coming home never to be wet, cold, hungry, miserable, homesick and plain fed up again.

Well, I have to get some sleep even though it will be in a wet rack before watch. I will continue tomorrow after we finish laying wire.

Love, Rog

Part II

Well, here I am again (January 1) Happy New Year. I haven't had a chance to write until now. Boy, have I been busy lately. Well, I have a patrol and I will finish this letter by candlelight when we get in at midnight.

Part III

January 2

Well, here I am again. It has really been hard to get anything off for a while lately. I have second watch tonight so I will stay up until I go to the hole. The sun is just starting to go down and I have a candle burning and a cup of coffee brewing. Coffee from home that is.

[...]

Hope that rain suit appears soon. It is getting wet and pretty cold here and it would keep me dry and warm. Outstanding.

We had a pretty good Christmas even though the C.O. Played Scrooge. New Year's was better. Had booze and song. Too bad about the women. We had two out of three.

Well, the word was just passed that a platoon of NVAs are less than 1500 meters from us and they are carrying mortars and we might get hit tonight. Great — just what we need. It is colder than hell, darker than hell, and the wind is blowing at about 40mph. Outstanding, isn't it? — Oh, it is raining also as if it makes that much difference.

I think I will make another cup of coffee. I am using a Sterno and it really heats it up good'n'hot. Starting to boil already — Good, no kidding — real good. Sorry you haven't received a letter in so long but I haven't had time to write at all. I hope you won't have to go so long without hearing from me again.

Well, I have to get about an hour's sleep before I go on watch so I will sign off.

Thanks for your letters and packages. They keep me going when all else fails.

Love,
Rog

P.S. Mail tomorrow I hope.

A 1/3 letter 93
New York, NY
Jan. 6, 1967
Dec. 26, 1966

Dear Mom and Dad,

I received a package from Herter's today and that rain suit was just what I needed for patrol tonight. Right now I am writing with a pen that you sent, using paper that you sent, writing by candlelight from my lantern and eating vegetable beef soup heated by Sterno — You sent me everything. I am wearing socks and a t-shirt that you sent. Boy, I don't know what I would do without packages from home. That soup is really good. I cut down a gook candle and it fits perfectly into the lantern. One of the sergeants after seeing the lantern offered to trade it for a bottle of scotch — not on your life. I have to have light to write letters by.

We laid wire and dug holes all day today again. Boy, this work never seems to end. They dreamed up some more stuff to do after we get the wire completed.

Does it get cold! Last night if it wasn't for coffee I would have froze my rear off. Boy, this lantern is neat, no kidding, it is perfect for my kind of use. It folds up and is light and gives off all kinds of light. We also warm our hands on the top.

We have hole watch tonight I guess. They haven't told us yet what we have. If they don't tell us we will sleep all night. I have accustomed myself to sleep in a ball to keep warm and I can sleep in the oddest places and positions.

That rain suit will keep me warm. Boy, that will feel good on these cold nights.

Well, we should be getting some slack time soon because they are beginning to realize that we can't work all day and stand watch all night and still be doing any good. Although we have been doing it for three months.

Boy, I can't wait to get home, no kidding, I want to come back so bad I can taste it.

Well, in one month I will have half of my tour over and I will be going downhill. Nice feeling if I do say so myself

Well, we have hole watch again tonight instead of patrol. We are eating now, time to chow down on some boned chicken and creamed corn — pretty decent if I do say so. Also coffee or hot chocolate to wash it down. Great!

One of the sergeants somehow secured half a five-gallon gas can of white lightning. This sergeant would traverse the lines at dusk and hump that can along with him from hole to hole. We would be given the password and countersign and get half a canteen cup of booze. Ended up calling the liquor "password." I think that sergeant stayed drunk.

That lantern really throws off some pretty good light and let me tell you a lot better than a regular candle that the wind creeps in and blows down sometimes....

Boy, our hootch is really blowing around but it hasn't gone down yet. (Thank God.) It is pretty sturdy even though we have no bamboo around here. Boy, we have four men in the hole tonight. Only three hours watch each maybe I will get some sleep tonight. We are supposed to get some slack tomorrow. Work is supposed to secure right after noon chow and then we can lay on our butts all day or so they say.

Well, the password tonight is sugar-cube and coffee and cake.

I must go.

Love and always thinking of home,
Rog

A 1/3 letter 94
New York, NY
Jan. 11, 1967
Jan. 7

Dear Mom and Dad,

Hi, how are you? I am pretty good I guess. Just finished cooking up some rice with gravy mix and dehydrated vegetables. Was pretty good. I used C-4, a plastic explosive that burns good for the heat and it really put forth some hot flames.

We have another patrol tonight. We had one last night and it was so dark you couldn't see past your rifle barrel. In fact, you couldn't see past your receiver group. Man, it was like walking inside a black velvet bag. I was point and I had to find an intricate path that we made through our barbed-wire fence. It's like a maze and in that dark it was a real pain. I cut my legs all up and really got mad but I didn't lose my temper. We finally got in and got back to our hootches and had a stiff drink before hitting the rack for a couple hours sleep before we had to get up and go to work.

As point man I had to memorize the pathway through the maze of barbed wire. Going out and coming back in, it was up to point to lead the patrol. When it was real dark this was a bitch. The wire had trip flares, Claymores, and c-rat cans with pebbles in them. If the point man fucked up, it could get people killed. I would always talk to the guys manning the hole opposite the pathway on the way out. I would shoot a green star cluster flare before starting to come back in and I always knew the password. I liked running point because it made me feel alive.

We worked all day today and had 15 minutes for noon chow—then back to work, We were tired of the petty _____ but they kept us working until 15 minutes to go into the holes for watch. Then they let us off "secures." Well, we had to get back to our hootches, eat chow, draw grenades and Claymore mines and illumination pop-ups before 6:00 to go into the holes. They let us off at 5:45. We also had to draw chow and have a briefing. Well, that meant the guy that has first watch had to eat out in the hole or go hungry again. We are getting tired of this stuff and we made up some songs to let the platoon commander and platoon sergeant know how the troops feel. They could let us have an hour a day if they wanted but they won't for some strange reason. They tried to take our candles away so we wouldn't have any lights at night. We couldn't write letters at any other time. Common sense tells us that we button up our hootches tight so no light goes out. This _____ is something else.

Oh, about those songs. They heard them one night and they took my buddy's guitar away from him and told us not to play them anymore. A guitar may not seem much but it us a godsend over here. He was playing Christmas carols softly on it and we were in one of the bunkers singing softly and they told us to cut the bull_____, it's only the 25th and that's just another day like yesterday.

The men are at the point of killing the troop leaders. We have an intricate way worked out. Back in the States I was never messed around with so much. They must take pleasure out of it. They make us wait on them hand and foot and even then they take and never give.

Well, enough of that. On our patrol in the fog on the blackest night of the year tonight we have to go cut about 1000 meters and come back in. Fan patrol they call it because you usually send out a lot of patrols at a time and they resemble a fan pattern.

If you are in an entirely unknown area you usually send out the fan patrols in a 360.

Well, we have our poncho over the door and our candle burning. If they want it out they will have to put it out and they first have to get past me and then one of my buddys and whoever else is coming over for a drink and a bit of letter writing. (We keep a bottle of gook whiskey on hand at all times for morale purposes only.)

We are living pretty good even though we work all day and stand watch all night. Had to change pens because I don't have any more cartridges for the other job.

I received your letter from everyone Christmas Day and I am keeping it in my wallet until next Christmas, then burning it while everyone sits around the fireplace.

Well, the patrol goes in about a half hour so I must pack my gear.

So long for now. I will write whenever I get a spare moment.

Love,
Rog

A 1/3 letter 95
US Navy
Jan. 18, 1967

Dear Mom and Dad,

We have a patrol tonight. It goes out at 01:00 and comes in at 06:00 with the wind and the little but noticeable rain it will be pretty cold, dark and damp. It gets so dark you have to feel the ground with your feet in order to find the foxholes.

We are going on a five-day patrol starting tomorrow. Wow, it promises to really be a hump and a half. It will be pretty good to get away from the C.O. For a while anyways. We really don't have it bad out there. We are cold and wet, yes, but we can sort of get away from it all. Check out areas — recon — do what we want. We are on our own on this type of patrol. We can put out booby traps, etc. and we usually find a lot of VC signs like pungi spikes and filled in dugout positions and mortar pits.

The gooks have a 120mm mortar. It weighs about 120 lbs. and takes two elephants to carry it with ammo. One elephant for the tube and one for the baseplate. We have found mortar pits with elephant dung spread around it. This means you know what and we are usually commended on out patrols. I am usually point because I know my stuff (modest, aren't I?). The only really bad part in point is that you usually have to bust brush and it is exhausting work and I mean it. Jump again and again five feet, fall down on the grass that sometimes bears the weight of two men with 50 lb. packs, before bending and breaking — and the vines. God! The vines grabbing everything you have attached to your body plus your legs, feet, head and rifle. Makes you tired mentally and physically. Radio has to be carried on your chest because the vines constantly change the frequency by spinning the knobs of the radio top.

Well, enough of that. Good news. We are taking Army-type long-range rations for patrol rations instead of c-rats. You pour boiling water in them and let them reconstitute for about 20 minutes. Presto, you have one of twelve meals. Spaghetti and meat balls, meatballs and beans, beef hash, chicken, rice, chicken stew, chili con carne, beef stew, beef with gravy, etc. I mean pretty good stuff.

One fills a person up and you can eat two a day and that is all. Perfect, compact, light, easy to make, perfect.

We have a candle burning now and we are chowing down and writing letters. Well, I have to get some sleep before one o'clock in the morning.

We have a guy so raunchy that he sits down in the middle of his hootch while everyone is there, uses a heat tab which, if not given enough air, produces a teargas-like odor. Well, he puts on his gas mask which he scrounged up somewhere and everyone runs out coughing and he laughs. Raunchy is the word for him.

Got to go out. Out of room.

Love,
Rog

A 1/3 letter 96
Jan. 26, 1967

Dear Mom and Dad,

Well, I finally got my transfer approved and so did four of my friends including one whom I came over with. We are probably going to somewhere in the 9th Marines but I don't know for sure. They had to transfer me a couple of weeks before our outfit moved to Okinawa but I really don't mind. Where I am going I will get the M-16 plus a lot of targets to shoot at only these shoot back. We are happy to leave this battalion even though we like the men in it. The leaders are OK I guess, but scared stiff of the gooks and the men. They seem to get their cookies by making us do all this anal petty stuff. Well, the 9th Marines won't do this. Did you know that our platoon dug holes for the entire company, policed the entire company front, cut grass and laid barbed-wire in from of the other platoon lines? This is the stuff we are getting away from. Happy? Yes!

I was put up for Lance again — my name was first on the list. We are being transferred so I will have to start all over again. No matter. I will make it somehow.

I got your letter with the photos yesterday, good old home. Man, does it look good. Everyone laughed at the way Trixie [our dog] was sitting. I guess they have a point there,

Not much around here but they did spot a hundred or so NVAs and called in Artillery on them — only 700 meters short. Today Charlie and Delta Co. made contact and received three W.I.A.s. Old Alpha moved out on a sweep about an hour ago after we left. Oh, by the way, I am in a tent on the inside perimeter of the strip awaiting a plane to take me to Da Nang to get our papers and all the bull straightened out. Beer and floor shows at the Enlisted Men's Club — Wow! At least one night....

I I have read the books that you sent, Dad, and they are pretty good. They have cost me an hour of sleep a night or so but they are really enjoyable. Received a package last night with Sterno, soup, socks, the book "Andersonville" and some of the Mandarin oranges — Wow! Also corn.

[...]

Well, I must sign off now. I hear a plane coming in.

> Bye,
> Rog

P.S. I will send my new address whenever I can.

As luck would have it 1/3 went back to Okinawa for rest and retraining right after my transfer and I missed that. The 1/3 battle name is "Forte Fortuna Juvat," which means "fortune favors the brave." Really it was strangely ironic for me because later in May 1967, 1/3 would return to Vietnam and be thrown into heavy combat with the NVA that I was fighting at the time. Most of the brave men of Alpha Company that I lived with in the mud of Khe Sanh would be killed or wounded during that action.

I saw the names of the guys I served with in 1/3 on the KIA list in the military newspaper The Stars and Stripes *while recovering from a gunshot wound in the hospital in Japan. I'm convinced that I would have been killed if I hadn't got that Mohican haircut.*

3

Vietnam: Phu Bai, CoCo Beach, H & S Company, 2nd Battalion, 9th Marines: Letters 97 to 104

"HELL IN A HELMET"

Introduction

PFC R.E. Jacobs
H&S Co. 81st PLT
2nd Bn 9th Marines
c/o FPO San Francisco, Cal

In these letters from January to February 1967 I describe my short tour with 81 mm mortars in 2nd Battalion, 9th Marines in mid–January 1967.

I was relieved to get a transfer out of 1/3 and was looking forward to something new. I remember getting a C-130 hop out of Khe Sanh and landing at Da Nang. Two of us grunts stepped out of the plane and looked around. We saw guys with clean utilities, polished boots and shined brass. We were a contrast with our filthy and ragged utilities, torn boots and loaded weapons and grenades. The other guy and I automatically stood back to back. We got stares and I overheard someone say, "Who in the hell are those guys?"

Our orders said 9th Marines so we found the 9th Marines headquarters and I was assigned to H&S Company, 2nd battalion. The H stands for headquarters and the S stands for support in the form of machine guns and mortars. I was assigned to 81 mm mortars. I went to the company area at Phu Bai first, then to CoCo Beach and found heaven. There was a large tent with real cots and an electric light and a large radio. I hadn't even seen a bed in the past four months. The only place I had slept was a fighting hole in the mud. The 81's even had hot chow prepared for them. I took a shower with hot water and soap. It was wonderful to use the shower instead of jumping into a river to bathe.

I started to get back all those things that made me human. I got back hot chow, I got back hot showers, I got back sleep, I got back electric lights, I got back all the water I wanted to drink, I got back clean clothes, I got back a place to buy stuff like cigarettes and a new camera. I got back all these things. Hell, I even had a chair to sit on. The only thing that was hard was the fact that my mail took forever to catch up with me.

My short time spent with this outfit was the easiest duty I had in Vietnam. My World of Hurt went away but I still couldn't sleep more than an hour or two at a time. I was still on the hump.

Our days were spent filling sandbags, constructing bunkers, going on short patrols and learning to operate the mortar tube. I scribbled a few letters during slack time.

We had one two-hour radio watch a night waiting for a fire mission to be called. Our rounds were illumination and high explosive charges. I started to learn to set up and fire the mortar. I got pretty good at it and learned to read map coordinates.

Phu Bai

H & S 2/9 letter 97
U.S. Navy
Jan. 18, 1967
Jan. 14

Dear Mom and Dad,

Well, as you can see from my new address I am in 2nd Battalion 9th Marines. I am also in mortars. How about that? I'm in mortars now, Dad, just like you were in WWII. No more standing holes and going out on every-day patrols for this bird. No, Sir. I stand an hour gun watch a night in a tent with *electricity* and a *stove* and *cots*. I eat *hot chow* and live in a *hard-floored* screened-in sided wood framed tent-like affair, and have *showers*.

We will start having gun drills pretty soon and the guys say it is pretty easy to learn.

I don't know how my name was picked out of the list of grunts [infantry] but I am pretty happy. We have a club that serves beer not more than 100 yards from our hut. Wow!!

I guess that I will miss patrolling and getting out into the woods but it might be worth it.

We are stationed here at Phu Bai which was a pretty bad spot until last year. It has cooled down considerably though and it looks as though the rest of my tour *could* be easy. We spent part of our time in Da Nang in the 1/3 rear getting our papers to 2/9. I went to a club that had a real American floor show with a band and girls. Wow!!! I got kind of happy and got up on the stage and danced with them. Dirty and scuzzy from four months in the field. We had a great time, music, booze and women and all that rot. After I finish writing this letter I will go and get some sleep on my *rack*, rubber lady, blanket, ahhh ... the luxuries of life.

The only bad thing is we have to hump a lot of weight once we get going on patrol and stuff. But we don't go that often so it isn't so bad.

We have *showers* and places to put all of our stuff — I feel almost like a civilian — almost.

I knew some of the guys in the 81s back at our old position and I always wanted to be in 81s and see how and what made the gun function. I may be a gunner sometime in the future....

Well, there is a friendly card game starting and I will get into it.

Got to go,
Love,
Rog

Will write when I can.

H & S 2/9 letter 98
Jan. 19, 1967
Dear Mom and Dad,

Well, here I am again. I am on watch in a large tent, on a cot, with heaters and plenty of coffee, etc. We started watches at 10:00 so everyone stands 1 hour and a half. I stand from 2:30–4:00. Our section has gun watch every fourth night and this is the most sleep I will get while standing watch.

We have been having daily drills with the gun and my teacher, the gunner, says I am catching on really fast. I have been going at it for about two days now and he says if I progress I might make gunner pretty soon. I can set her on any target and understand the sight, etc. Now it is only a matter of shaving valuable seconds off of my technique. Some of the guys have the gun set on a target and leveled and the first round on the way in ten seconds or so. The average is about 20 and I, after two days, am taking about 30–45 seconds which isn't bad at all. The only bad thing about being gunner is that when going on a hump the gunner has the heaviest load of all — 40 lbs. of bipods and the sight. Wow.

It is interesting working with mortars and I am awaiting our first fire mission. As it turns out H&S Company is a pretty good duty. We eat hot chow, sleep on cots, have plenty of slack time, etc. so we are pretty happy. We have a treasured light bulb that we burn all night down here at the gun pit. When we are on watch we can read, write letters, make coffee or chow, just about anything we please as long as we don't leave the radio. I have a January issue of *Playboy* over here that I will continue reading after I complete this letter.

We don't have to go to chow if we don't want to. Usually we do because they serve pretty good chow. Included in the menu is salad — dressing — God, did I miss that. In fact, the meager salad and passable dressing makes me long for one of Mom's masterpieces. It has been rainy steadily since I arrived here in Phu Bai and it looks like there is no letting up in sight. It is always raining a little. Not enough to matter much but always a little.

We are supposed to go out to a place called CoCo Beach. We will stay there approximately thirty days before returning to the rear. No hot spot mind you. Just an observation point with a company of grunts guarding us. Pretty slack duty over here I am told. Navy chow also which is the best of all the services.

My watch is about up so I will wake up the next man and hit the rack. It's surprising how time goes by when you have something to do like read or write a letter.

Well, I will sign off now and get some sleep. I have to get up at 6.30 for *hot* chow.

Your Son,
Love,
Rog

H & S 2/9 letter 99
U.S. Navy
Jan. 21, 1967

Dear Mom and Dad,

How are you? I am fine and feeling great. We have a pretty good unit here in 2/9 hardly any of the people in the battalion get messed with by the higher echelon. Even the grunts [infantry] have it good.

I am working the gun now with no difficulty and am already cutting my time down getting on target. The platoon Sgt. says I have caught on faster than anyone he has ever seen. In three days I can give coordinates, get the gun on any target and a round in the air in less than thirty seconds. The mortar is a simple instrument of destruction. Sight it, level, drop in a round and boom. Loads of fun.

Well, we are going to go to the flick tonight "Nevada Smith" starring Steve McQueen. Pretty recent for this neck of the woods.

I have no watch tonight so I just might hit the rack early and sleep till 6:30 tomorrow morning. I seem to be catching up on my lost sleep in the past few days.

I have had a few classes on the new M-16 or the AR-15 as the Army calls it. Pretty fine weapon. It shoots faster, has less recoil for automatic bursts. Pretty good on accuracy, too. Easy to take down, completely rustless, you can wash it off like a play toy in a puddle. It looks and feels as if it should be stamped — "Made by Mattel Toy Inc."

Well, I am going to put some coffee on. Ah, water heated with plastic explosive (innards of a Claymore mine) and Maxwell House (the only kind they sell at the PX). The PX is a large place but they don't have much to buy. Couple this and that — soap, cigarettes, etc. Nothing spectacular but every little bit helps us exist over here. It hasn't rained all day but it just started now. Light almost drizzle that continues for weeks at a time is the monsoon.

We have a Club a few doors down and there is two beers per man per day limit. Price is 15 cents each. All Stateside brands and *COLD* — brrrr. We gather there on nights sometimes to view the CO's stag movies. This was a first for me. And I was somewhat amazed — Wow! Enough of that bull.

That coffee is pretty good. I have a pretty bad head cold and it clears my head for a while at least. Tomorrow we will go on a search for a light bulb....

Well, I have to leave for the flick if I want to get a seat.

Love,
Rog

CoCo Beach Jet Fuel Dump

H & S 2/9 letter 100
Jan. 25, 1967

Well, here I am at a little spot called CoCo Beach. — Grid Coor 321 408 if that means anything. It is about a two and a half hour ride from Phu Bai. Pretty safe here also. We are on an island of some sort and there are supposed to be no VC for miles, but they always say that. There are a lot of villes surrounding us and there is a lot of stuff I would like to buy, but alas, no leaving the compound. Oh well. We can do without. Most of the girls have V.D. for sale if you know what I mean. Don't worry about me catching it. No chance. We might have a fire mission tonight. Someone passed the word that there were VC within range — 4500 meters. Well, we are sitting around waiting — probably won't come off until we are in the rack. I have watch from 3:30 till 6 which isn't bad at all.

Little boys trying to sell their sisters. Note the shape the boys are making with their fingers. CoCo Beach. February 1967.

I guess I was kind of an innocent kid. I never pursued the chance to get laid in Vietnam. I heard stories about the places called dog-patches just outside the wire of every main firebase but I never sought them out. I spent most of my time sitting in a hole out in the boonies.

Well, I will continue tomorrow. I have to get some sleep.

It is 10:00 and I have just come off watch. I stood from 7:30–10. Not a bad watch at all considering we had two men on watch. We sit up and shoot the breeze and the time passes faster.

I haven't had any mail for two weeks now and I am getting pretty anxious for some mail. It should be another week or so before it comes through. I hope it gets here soon.

Well, lights just went out so I am finishing this one in good old candlelight.

Now that I can look back on what I lived like and how I lived I can say it wasn't so bad at the time. Our officers in 1/3 didn't take care of their men whatsoever.

Well, I'm starting to get organized and to feel half-way squared away again and being clean is wonderful. I can take a shower everyday now and take my boots off every night (kind of hectic when we have a midnight fire mission).

Well, it is dark and wet and getting cold so I guess I will retreat under a blanket.

Love, Rog

P.S. I will write a longer letter later when I get a chance, that is.

H & S 2/9 letter 101
Feb. 3, 1967

Part I

Dear Mom and Dad,

Well, things are moving along pretty smoothly at this end. How goes it on the other side of the globe?

I am writing this on a little box-type table affair. Works pretty fair and is homemade like most of our furniture.

The rain has stopped and the sun came out and dried up everything. Pretty nice out.

We are on the Gulf of Tonkin and we have a nice mild breeze. We are going to move our position down the road about 200 yards and then we will be well inside the perimeter. This battalion treats men so differently than 1/3. They treat the men like people instead of our old platoon commander's phrase "warm bodies." The morale and spirit is always soaring and when they get into battle they come out on top. They always kick tail or should I say we always kick tail.

Had a fire mission last night, illumination type. I was sleeping one second and the next I was out the door waiting to fire with a 13 lb. round in my hand. We will fire about five rounds a night from now on.

Well, it is pretty hot in the tent, with my pen in my hand I made my bird to the great outdoors. The beach is only 25 yards from the gun pit and 50 yards from our tent. Last night we couldn't find one of the guys after we fired. Well, we finally found him. In the 50 yard dash from the tent to the pit there are a number of trees. Well, it was dark and our boy ran headlong into one and knocked himself out for about ten minutes. Today he has a black eye and a doozy of a goose-egg.

Part II

Sorry I haven't written you in the past few days but a lot has been going on. We moved our gun position down the road that runs through the compound about 200 yards. We sat and watched as a gun pit, bunker, and tent was put up for us to live and work in. We didn't do any construction. Maybe what they say is true. 81s *do* rate.

Well, we moved all that ammo down plus the gun and our personal gear. We are now set up and we have had fire missions almost every night (illumination). We are sitting around and over the phone comes in — "Fire Mission" — mad scramble for the door and out to the pit.

They say I will be gunner pretty soon if I continue the way I am doing.

The author learning 81 mm mortar. CoCo Beach. February 1967.

Fishing ville on the South China Sea. This ville was built on a beautiful stone jetty. No men were present; there were only women and children. CoCo Beach. February 1967.

We have hot chow but never enough so keep canned stuff coming because it is great to snack on in the middle of the night. Remember (my snacks). When you get hungry around here it is tough until chow time — no c-rats at all.

Hey! I received first mail since I left 1/3 yesterday. Five or six letters and film, batteries, and a package containing rice, curry powder, stewed tomatoes, apple sauce, tea, hot chocolate, etc. How in the world do you fit it into such a small box? Every time I unpack one I cannot for the life of me get it packed up again. There are always cans sticking out.

I have read your books, Dad, and I will have more time to read them now. Send a couple of grungy Marine war tales, OK, just for the hell of it. (No, I haven't reverted back to comic books yet.)

I am going to make that rice up tonight along with the tomatoes and curry powder and a couple of secret added ingredients. So I must go. Will write again soon

Love, Rog

1. Bipod	42lbs.	Gunner
2. Tube	37lbs.	A- Gunner
3. Inner baseplate	20 lbs.	First ammo humper
4. Outer baseplate	20 lbs.	Second ammo humper
5. Mortar round	12 lbs.	

I am ammo humper. I hump 3 rounds x 13lbs each for 39 lbs + 20 lbs. of baseplate + all my gear and a rifle.

~~~

H & S 2/9 letter 102
Feb. 4, 1967

Dear Mom and Dad,

Well, I got as far as the heading on this letter before I was called out on a fire mission. Some guy shot himself with a .45 and he had to get med-evacced by a helicopter. We fired two rounds illumination. One almost blew up on the island and the other was a dud. The one that blew up on the island (almost) the round was still burning and it almost landed in a jet fuel dump.

We man the main gate, have one man per day mess duty, have a man on watch on the phone from the gun pit. We send one man into Phu Bai for mail, etc., and we have a forward observer (F.O.). So this leaves the squad not many men left so there isn't a whole lot of slack but we only stand one hour 10 minutes for the whole night through — a vacation after Khe Sanh....

I have a patrol (F.O.) tomorrow — we just fired another illumination mission. Fired about ten rounds and there I was breaking open boxes inside the ammo bunker and handing out rounds — ugh —13 lbs each +. Well, we have a couple of dozen rounds broken out for tomorrow or tonight. Well, I have to get some sleep before my watch and it is 10:00 already.

P.S. Will write soon.

Rog

~~~

H & S 2/9 letter 103
Feb. 6, 1967

Dear Mom and Dad,

I am on watch right now — gun watch. I sit in a bunker with electric lights and a stove and plotting board, etc. It is called F D.C. Fire Directional Center. I have last watch tonight from five to six. Reveille goes at six o'clock.

I am F.O.ing our patrol this morning at 7:30 and I have to go and eat chow early today. We have our choice of how many eggs and how we want them, pancakes, etc. After four months of c-rats at Khe Sanh this is a *treat* let me tell you. The packages from home still fill in mornings and afternoons and evenings. We have a still set up and are awaiting the amber colored nectar.

I have been firing a lot of different weapons including various hand guns. I fired the Thompson sub, grease gun, .357 Mag revolver, German luger, and a Chinese machine pistol plus a .38 and a .32 and the good old .45. Also an

M-2 automatic carbine. The Navy has all of these and we have been having a ball firing them out to sea. The beach on the Gulf of Tonkin is about 50 yards from our hootch — sandbags filled with sand. Amazing.

We liberated a few tomatoes and spuds from the mess hall and are going to make a stew tomorrow that will be a work of art. CHEF JAKE, of course, is the top cookie in the event.

Soon as the weather clears up (that rain suit is a life saver) I will get some decent photos. I will take some flicks of a very old and rare Buddhist temple and a lot of shots of various Mama-San (girls) that I know. They call me Jacques. Don't worry when I see them the Corpsman (good buddy) goes along to see his girlfriend also. Well, this is my last piece of paper out here in the bunker so I have to be going. Take care of yourselves.

Love, Rog

P.S. Could you send me some books that might be enriching to my mind? Something to prepare me for college if you know what I mean.

Places I have been:

Da Nang	Laos	Kim Lin
Chu Lia	DMZ	Dong Ha
Phu Bai	Tokyo	CoCo Beach
Khe Sanh	Okinawa	Quang Tri
Hue	Esso Plant	Phu An

H & S 2/9 letter 103
Feb. 11, 1967

Dear Mom and Dad,

Hey Folks,

[...]

To answer some of your questions — I get five days and four nights or five nights and four days R&R. I am now on the Gulf of Tonkin on a large highway the other side of Hue from Phu Bai. It is an island so you will be able to pick it out pretty good on the map. No, I didn't see Bob Hope while he was at Da Nang. He stuck close to the rear on most of his stops and us front line troops never even knew he was here until he left.

[...]

I received a few letters today mostly back mail but anything is great. I got some from Caroline, Jerry, Joyce and a couple of girls I am writing in different states. I can never seem to run out of people to write to and I am glad because it keeps me busy....

The author at an old Buddhist temple. This temple and others were in a state of disrepair. The communists were taking over slowly but surely. CoCo Beach. February 1967.

The letters from home really meant everything me. The letters triggered strong memories that pushed aside Vietnam for a time. I had my letters from home, hot chow, a cot to sleep on, and all the water I wanted to drink. I was in fat city.

We have it pretty good here. The only thing I have to sweat is a mortar attack or being completely overrun. Nice to be out of the *grunts*.

In the way of packages — you can stop sending me soups and spices now and I will let you know when you can start up again. I will use all I have and then write you a letter. I received a package yesterday. It had that MAD paperback in it and it is the best! Those stewed tomatoes were pretty good with some hobo stew we cooked up. I have enough "Heat Tabs" at the moment and will tell you when I need more. You are portioning out the socks about right....

Well, I have loads of stuff to do and I must get it done.

Love,
Rog

P.S. This letter was written on Feb. 9 — as of Feb. 14 I will have six months in Vietnam left.

Downhill...

All these three weeks we stayed in place and we didn't hump. It was a good thing too because if we had gone out I would have had to hump three mortar rounds and part of the base plate for a total of 59 pounds plus grunt gear and personal weapons.

I got my new camera and was taking shots every day and sending the exposed film home to my Dad. I was actually clean and had new utilities and new boots, and a haircut. I was getting four continuous hours of wonderful sleep a night. This would all change in a heartbeat as I would be back in the grunts and my hump would intensify. I learned that there is no such thing as a safe place, in a war.

Vietnam: Phu Bai, Dong Ha, Quang Tri: "A" Company, 1st Platoon, 1st Battalion, 9th Marines: Letters 105 to 133

Introduction: The Walking Dead

Well, I had it made for three weeks. The electric lightbulb, all the water I wanted and the restful sleep evaporated in the blink of an eye and I was back on the hump in the grunts again.

My letters from mid–February 1967 to mid–May describe my tour with Alpha Company 1st Battalion, 9th Marines. This battalion got its battle name of "The Walking Dead" because of a political speech made by the leader of North Vietnam, Ho Chi Minh, in 1966. The Unit 1/9 was killing a disproportionate number of his NVA troops, so he called us "Di Bo Chet" or "Dead Men Walking," referring to the fact that he was assigning special troops to wipe out 1/9. Uncle Ho almost succeeded, as 1/9 ended up having the highest casualty rate in Marine Corps history. It was said that if you got assigned to 1/9 the first thing issued to you was a body bag. I went out of the frying pan and into the fire.

PFC R. E. Jacobs
"A" Co. 1st Plt 1st Bn 9th Marines
c/o FPO San Francisco, Cal.

Phu Bai

A 1/9 letter 105
Feb. 15, 1967

Part I

Dear Mom and Dad,

Well, here I go again. 1st BN 9th Marines needed men like crazy. Well, they took all of the new arrivals out of 2/9 including me out of 81s and into the grunts again. I am also awaiting my warrant for Lance Corporal. I was told I made it. Don't put on your letters "L. Cpl" until I let you know if I have my warrant in my hands. How about that — one month in 81s and I was A-Gunner, up for Gunner, and I made Lance. My section leader told me he wouldn't have let them transfer me if he had known. He had no control. I can't go up the chain of command either. About 100 guys have tried and it didn't do any good.

Well, the new outfit seems pretty good. I am in a pretty good fire team and squad.

Now the latest news — we are moving out today or tomorrow. Well, I will finish tomorrow, lights are going out.

Part II

We are moving out tomorrow and it may be quite a while before I can write again. Maybe as long as a month or six weeks.

The operation is called Chinook and it is being held around the Hue area. It is being pulled off in an area never before operated in and we will most likely run up against some Charlies. 1/9 really looks out for its men. I got issued all the stuff I would usually have to wait weeks to get. All of it good or new and modern gear.

I was on my third pair of jungle boots by this time and I stole a pack frame somewhere that eased some of the strain from my back. I treasured and protected that pack frame.

I miss 81s but I miss the grunts also. We will have to see what we shall see once we get back from the operation.

Well, there isn't much more to say because I haven't much time to prepare. I will write first chance I get.

Love, Rog

Dong Ha

A 1/9 letter 106
Feb. 18, 1967

Dear Mom and Dad,

Well, I found some more time to write before we go out on Chinook II (the name of that salmon). This is going to be a pretty long operation from what I have heard so don't be alarmed if you don't hear from me for quite a while. I only hope I come out OK because we will stay out until we get them or so says our Bn. CO. As you can expect most of us are on edge and a little nervous.

We are going to be hel-lifted in tomorrow morning. I don't know when we are coming out and nobody does. I am taking my camera with six rolls of film. I also have a yellow and a transparent filter so I should be OK as long as I have film in. The film should last quite a while. Most of the guys have seen a bit of action so we are not an untried unit. We should be pretty successful in this operation and it would mean another Campaign star for my Vietnamese medal.

Well, I have Operation Prairie under my belt and should have about three or four more by the time my rotation date comes up.

We are supposed to be able to get med-evac in 8 minutes and our positions for resupply and air support and artillery are going to be good. We are also taking 81s and 60s mortars along so we should have plenty of support. I am demo man for the operation (of our squad) and I get to carry *blasting caps* and fuse. Oh joy.

It is amazing how many times a guy can go over his gear just to pass the time.

Well, no word of my warrant yet. I hope that it comes in while we are out. We might be out for a couple of months or longer.

I am carrying:

1 M-14 automatic	1 camera
6 mags	spices — salt, season pepper
240 rounds for M-14	1 carton butts
3 frags	2 pair socks
1 LAW — light anti-tank weapon	1 poncho
3 meals c-rat	1 shelter half
12 fuse lighters	1 rubber lady
20' fuse	1 field jacket
3 canteens	100 rounds machine gun ammo
1 first aid pack	1 radio battery

I could go on and on but here are the main things — heavy — God!

We are supposed to get a resupply also. Darn!! Lots of stuff to hump.

We are going to be moving kind of slow anyway. It won't be bad, I hope. We have to do a lot of humping in sand and it will get hot!!!

I should have a decent tan when I get back.

I will keep taking flicks and send a bunch when I get home. Well, it's getting late and I will need my rest.

Your Son,
Love,
Rog

The first thing that I got rid of was the rubber lady. The second thing I dumped was the shelter half. When we started to really hump there was a trail of discarded gear behind us. First thing we shot was the LAW so we didn't have to hump it. The most important things were water, ammo, and food, in that order.

(Letter 107 omitted)

Chu Lai

A 1/9 letter 108
Feb 20, 1967

Dear Mom and Dad,

Well, the weather was so bad that the choppers couldn't take us in today and seeing as how I won't be able to write while I am out in the field I will get off another short one to you.

I am in good spirits, good shape and good frame of mind and that is what counts. I should be or I will be ok on this operation and all to come.

Here I say again that I will be OK. I was really trying to remain upbeat and find the positive in each situation. The members of my squad never, ever mentioned the future. It was all about what was going on right then. All we wanted to do was to survive.

Good news — If you have a month or six weeks left to serve in Vietnam this battalion doesn't send you out on operations. They keep you in the rear to clean up and stuff. This is fine with all us grunts especially short-timers because it saves them a lot of gray hairs.

We have to swim a couple of rivers if the helo doesn't take us tomorrow. God help us. We are carrying so much we can hardly make it on foot much less swim.

Well, my camera will not get wet, that's for sure. There are war correspondents going with us with their cameras and garbage. We are supposed to get a bit of action.

Well, I must go, have to repack my gear.

Love,
Rog

I will write whenever I can even if it isn't a letter of length. A couple of words to set you at ease on how I am.

I would carry three different cameras in Vietnam. I had to keep them hidden as they were not allowed. Crossing rivers, the monsoon, the mud of Khe Sanh, and the hump on the Street Without Joy would destroy them one by one.

1/9 saddling up for a search and destroy operation. We seldom went into our operations by air. We boarded trucks to a jumping-off place and then we humped. Phu Bai. February 1967.

The Street Without Joy

A 1/9 letter 109
U.S. Navy
Feb. 24, 1967

Dear Mom and Dad,

Well, here I am out on Operation Chinook II. We are doing pretty well by now and have had only a few casualties. We are sweeping and making contact every day and are really kicking Charlie's tail. I haven't had any mail for a while but when I get it I will most likely get a bunch because I have to get it reworked by 2/9 to 1/9.

The area is mostly open sand with scattered villes. We hit a large force yesterday and knocked the hell out of them with fifty cal. machine guns and air strikes. I have some pretty good flicks of guys under fire. Bunch of cameramen and war correspondents got blown away when one of them stepped on a mine. — They were bunched up.

In late February 1967 our first action took place on a piece of land the French grunts in their war called La Rue Sans Joie. We kept the name and called it the

Street Without Joy. The "street" was 100 square kilometers of sand, hills, tidal flats, swamps, rice paddies, rivers, and fortified villages. It was bordered on the east by the South China Sea, on the south by the city of Hue, on the west by Highway 1, and on the north by Quang Tri City. A French photojournalist named Bernard Fall who was there in the 50s wrote a book about it titled The Street Without Joy. *Fall came back to the "street" in 1967 and was killed while on maneuvers with us. Fall triggered a Bouncing Betty land mine about 90 yards from where I was standing. The blast knocked me to my knees and killed another Marine. I can still hear the death screams.*

Boy, am I glad I'm not humping 81s now. Those guys are in a World of Hurt if you know what I mean. I must be cracking but I really get my cookies in a fire fight. Rounds zinging all around and stuff exploding. I know we are pouring it into Charlie and I really enjoy doing it.

There is no feeling on earth that compares to the rush of adrenalin that happens in a fight to the death. Being in the middle of screams, explosions, and blood makes things slow down and become crystal clear. The rush that comes from killing humans in battle is addictive, and once you experience it you are forever changed. It is the hump. Some people hunt animals for this feeling. Grunts hunt men. To walk among the dead and the dying and have lightning bolts shoot from your fingertips and have the earth tremble from your boot heels is an ancient feeling. The power to give life and the power to take life away is something only the gods should possess.

Some men survive only to go back and dare death in the war they love. Some combat vets choose to end their lives by their own hands to make the longing stop.

I survived and didn't want to go back to war, but I spent many years trying to get that combat high in other ways. I would go free diving alone and go so deep I would black out on the way back to the surface. I would crank my motorcycle up to 100 miles per hour just to feel alive again. I was driven to risk my life over and over just for the rush. I tried large doses of sex, drugs, and rock and roll. Nothing came close, but I was driven to keep trying.

My breakthrough to some sense of normalcy came when I became aware that I had to deal with the physical, intellectual and spiritual parts of myself to start my withdrawal. I still am in awe of the power to give and take life but I don't let it rule me as it did in the past. I still like my thunderstorms but I don't go out in them now.

Our squad has been lucky. No one has been hit yet. Other squads are not so fortunate. I can mail letters every day now — or whenever the helo's come in for resupply and it looks like they will be coming in every day because the weather is hot and dry. The only thing that would prevent them coming in would be Charlie and his rifle fire.

I really got mad yesterday. We had some guys shot up and Charlie kept the med-evac from landing. We plastered Charlie with mortars and jets came in with napalm. Anyway the choppers came in and we got everyone out.

We have been moving out pretty early and humping all day until today. I guess it is going to be a day of rest for the troops seeing as how we are pretty tired from lack of sleep and stuff. Well, I got loads of stuff to do and there is a sniper that is dinging at us now. (I am in the bottom of my hole.)

I have to go — will write whenever I can.

Love, Rog

The "street" was full of mines, booby traps, Vietcong Main Force battalions, and NVA regular troops. The NVA were so good at moving mines around that they would put the minefield out at dusk along a patrol route and take it in before dawn. You could clear one area and there would be mines there the next night. I remember watching a Marine with a machine gun across his shoulders step on a pressure release mine. The mine went click *when he stepped on it, and he stood on it for 45 minutes while our engineers dug it out and put a pin in the trigger. We piled our flak jackets around the mine and it didn't go up when he stepped away. There was a TNT booby trap charge under the mine when we dug it up. I had bet another Marine some money that it wouldn't blow. We had become hard men. The machine gunner was evacuated and became the chaplain's assistant in the rear with the gear.*

A 1/9 letter 110
Feb. 26, 1967
Feb. 22

Dear Mom and Dad,

Well, here I am again. We were issued these post cards so we can get some words home. Well, we got our four prisoners today and killed three. Our squad captured two during a brief firefight. Yesterday we killed about twenty in an hour-long firefight. Boy, did we bust some chops. We got KIAs and a bunch of WIA by mines, Bouncing Bettys. We won't go tromping down any trails that we aren't sure of. We were mortared last night but a counter mortar strike ended that quickly.

The face of the enemy: a captured Viet Cong. The Street Without Joy. March 1967.

Blindfolded prisoner on the Street Without Joy. March 1967.

We have been running into some stuff. Well, we have been OK, our squad and I are fine. We will probably go out after the gooks tomorrow and get into a couple of hairy firefights. We haven't had hardly any guys hit by rounds, mostly mines and mortars. Well, it should calm down for a while because we kicked their butt the first time we got into it. They will have to regroup before they stand again.

Will write soon,
Rog

On the "street," Bouncing Betty land mines would pop up around four to ten feet before exploding. Those mines had a kill radius of about 35 feet. I once saw five Marines get fucked up by one Bouncing Betty. The Bouncing Bettys were made in the good old USA.

Some of the other mines were command detonated, some had multiple triggers and some were daisy-chained. I saw Marines going to take a crap get blown into the trees. Little red spots on green leaves just like Christmas.

I remember seeing a prisoner break away from one of our sergeants. The sergeant was a good man, married with two kids and respected by all. The VC ran straight away from us and the sergeant went after him. I tried to get a shot at the prisoner but the sergeant was in my sight picture. I saw the VC step sideways off the trail and then the sergeant ran over the area the VC avoided. I yelled out but

Sometimes the enemy were just children, but they could kill you just as dead as a man could. The Marine has a .30 caliber carbine. The Street Without Joy. March 1967.

I was too late and the sergeant triggered a Bouncing Betty. I was looking down my rifle barrel at the sergeant when this all happened. He was carried 10 feet into the air by the force of the explosion and he came down, hit the ground and started his death scream. His legs were gone, his right hand was gone, and his genitals were gone. That respected Marine started to beg us to kill him. The fire and heat from blast wounds cauterize amputated limbs so the wounded don't bleed out; they linger and suffer. That good sergeant was alive 20 minutes later when we put him on a medevac chopper, but he died en route to an aid station. We recaptured the VC that had caused all this, and our grief turned into rage. The savagery of war overtook us. Several of us beat the VC to death. I don't remember taking part but I do remember cleaning blood and gore from my rifle's butt plate.

A 1/9 letter 111
U.S.Navy
Feb. 28, 1967
Feb. 23

Dear Mom and Dad,

I am doing fine — whoops excuse me — had a little firefight break out down the line a bit. Got one VC and nobody got hit.

Today makes the fourth day of the operation and things are going along pretty smooth. We are finished with the 1st phase of a 4-phase operation. We will most likely be out quite a while yet so I will write when I can and scoop you on what's happening. There are a lot of VC where we are going and we will not have an easy job completing the other phases as we have had with the first phase.

Helicopters come in every day now and bring us ammo, chow, mail, water, etc. They sure are a welcome sight. We have called in air strikes, artillery, mortars and rockets on gooks as of yet. They really help quite a bit and make the gooks more and more afraid of us. We captured a bunch of gooks and sent them out by helos yesterday.

I have that seasoned salt-pepper-garlic powder and that is plenty to use and to hump. You see we move every day and we have to carry helmet, flack jacket, 300 rifle rounds, 100 machine gun rounds, 4 grenades, a mortar round, 25 lbs of demo plus chow, 3 full canteens, LAWs and packs — heavy!!! Heavy isn't quite the word for it. I can think of a couple of adjectives that aren't worth mentioning here.

Time is going by pretty fast now and I hope before we get back to the rear that my time over here will be shortened considerably. Well, I got here in August so I leave in September. Marines serve 13 months!!!!! Did you know that Army and Air Force has it like kings over here. Their PXs have all kinds of stuff where ours has soap, cigarettes, etc. We do the most with the least.

I guess the operation Chinook II is mostly all Marines. You will find Marine units participating in nearly all operations but hardly ever doing it without the Army. Simple reasoning — Gooks like to hit the Army more than hit Marines, so we let them and Marines step in to save the day. Did you know that half if not most of the Marines K.I.A. are done trying to get the Army out of a mess? ...

Boy, they are raising hell with a 50 cal. machine gun outside the perimeter now!

Send me pictures — photos of house, family, anything....

I have some good flicks of the operation already and I have six more rolls to shoot. Two B&W, one color prints and the rest color slides.

Dad, make sure you see them before showing them to Debi and Mom. Might be some gory sights.

Well, I must sign off — ran out of paper. I will write tomorrow if I can.

Love,
Rog

There were people shooting at me again. Alpha Company did combat oper-
ation after combat operation, never spending more than a day or at best two days
behind the wire in a month's time. We were always searching out the NVA, always

Set in for a day on dry rice paddies. A Marine is taking care of his blisters. This was a dangerous place as there were mines everywhere. Street Without Joy. March 1967.

Dr. Sylvester McIntosh cutting hootch poles. At his feet is a case of c-rats and a rubber lady. McIntosh was WIA later at Phu An in May 1967. Picture taken on Street Without Joy. March 1967.

Sylvester McIntosh guarding Viet Cong prisoners, who were blindfolded and staged in a ditch. Street Without Joy. March 1967.

on the hump. I hated mines and booby traps and I hated getting mortared. At least in firefights we could pour it on them, get some feel-good payback.

I remember making FNGs carry the grotesquely arrayed, stiff nude bodies of Marines that were untouched except by the concussion of the mines. The force of the mine explosions stripped them of all their gear and clothing. Their only visible wounds were blood flowing from their eyes, ears, and mouths. Rigor mortis comes quick in the heat of Vietnam and bodies would bloat and turn black in a matter of hours. We sat and ate our c-rats and ignored the death that surrounded us. It didn't mean anything.

A 1/9 letter 112
March 8, 1967
Feb. 28

Dear Mom and Dad,

Well, I have time and a chance to write you a longer letter. We are back from Operation Chinook II first phase. We are embarking on the 2nd phase tomorrow. We are going into the mountains around Hue. I have taken over the radio and it is a pretty good job of the most importance. As you can imagine the radio is the only link of communication between us supporting arms, med evac, etc. The only thing bad about humping it is it weighs 29 lbs. and that adds some to the shoulder strain.

Well, we had 39 casualties for Alpha Co. for the first week. Most of these came from mines. Bernard B. Fall, the author, was also killed by a Bouncing Betty. He was about 90 yards away from me when he got blown away. We had some pretty hairy firefights and some pretty bad times.

I have flicks of a lot of the operation but when the stuff hit the fan I was too busy shooting my rifle to shoot my camera. I do have some flicks of VC prisoners and wounded. I could tell you a number of specific incidents but I won't. Dad, you know how it is. Well, it is cold, wet and unbearable, but remember Jake, you are a Marine and you just go through kicking ass with the Charlies.

I humped the radio day before yesterday for four solid hours without a rest. Through rice paddies and knee-deep mud. I was hurting to say the least and I was so glad when we got to our objective that I almost dropped.

Well, we are getting ready for tomorrow. The helos will drop us in and we will work our way around and out. Where we are going is nicknamed "Valley of Death." We will prove it by killing every VC around.

Well, I must go now. I will write when I can but don't expect mail for a while.

Love, Rog

By this time I had insulated myself from any kind of feelings, so when a man went down he was just a hunk of meat. I didn't care about anything. We lost guys every day, and I still dream of explosions of fire and red mist and bodies flying through the air and coming down smoking and screaming. I didn't want to know the members of my squad; I didn't want to know anybody. In four days on the Street Without Joy we had 37 casualties by mines. I stopped mentioning Marines' names in my letters. I was operating in full survival mode. My world got smaller and smaller. Sometimes I would forget to eat.

Grunts exist between a rock and a hard place. The rock is in front and the rock is the enemy, sworn to kill the grunt, and the grunt is sworn to kill the rock. The hard place is behind the grunt. The hard place is the command structure ordering the grunt to kill the rock. The hard place pushes the grunt to kill the rock, and if the hard place screws up the rock kills the grunt. Surrounded by death the grunt exists between the rock and the hard place.

Dong Ha

A 1/9 letter 113
March 4

The prisoner with the white hat. Street Without Joy. March 1967.

Dear Mom and Dad,

I am at Dong Ha Air Base. Well, I just came out of the field for a day and a night and we are going back again and we will hump the hills a lot.

At this time we treated our enemy wounded. Street Without Joy. March 1967.

We called the new Alpha Company commander, Captain Al Slater, Captain Contact. Slater got this name because of his aggressive nature. At times I was more scared of Captain Slater than the NVA. Slater was one of the good ones, though. He actually cared for and took care of his grunts. This small story illustrates the role of a good officer. Alpha Company was humping back to Dong Ha after being in the field for three weeks and we were worn out. I was carrying the radio and I heard some arguing on battalion net. Captain Slater had called ahead so we could have hot chow when we arrived at the firebase. We had started humping at around midafternoon and humped all the rest of that day. We had humped all night and humped the next morning and came into Dong Ha around midafternoon. We had humped more than 25 hours straight. Eight-one mortars were sucking wind big time. We entered the firebase, went into a mess hall and found hot steaks and potatoes waiting for us. Someone asked for two steaks and he was told no. Wrong answer to a bunch of heavily armed war-faced grunts. We took over that mess hall, ran out the cooks and cooked every steak they had. We stole all the big cans of fruit and anything else we could get our hands on. We then went out by the wire, dug some holes, crawled in and slept.

We have been getting into some pretty thick stuff with main force VC battalions. Body counts for yesterday was 24 with five captured. We had artillery, air strikes, mortars, and then us. We really tore up the gooks. We captured mortars, carbines, machine guns, and all kinds of good stuff. I have a few souvenirs.

Body count for the whole area is over 400 and the brass say that the gooks are split up into little groups now and if we keep pushing them we will destroy them before they have a chance to regroup. We have caught some stuff. I now know what it feels like to be mortared four or five times a day. I like a firefight a hell of a lot more than mortars or mines. In a firefight you can shoot back but mortars you can do nothing but get down in your hole and pray the next one will be farther away instead of up closer.

We would set in on a little hilltop at dusk, dig a shallow hole, break out the c-rats and bang down a can, and when it got dark we would move to a new position and dig a deeper hole. We would then set out Claymores and LPs and establish fields of fire. We had two men to a hole, two hours on, two hours off, all night. The reason for moving was to throw off any NVA mortar team that scouted our first position. Many times I heard the impact of mortars on the hilltop we just left.

If we got mortared at night and someone got hit, the first thing we did was to shut that person up. If the NVA running the mortars could hear someone screaming they knew they were on target and would drop some more on us.

I am drinking a beer now and it tastes good!!!! I went all day on a hump and most of the night on one canteen of water. We have been getting about two meals a day and not enough time to eat any of them — we eat c-rats cold cause we don't have time to heat them. The thing I still like is a cup of coffee....

Well, I must sign off right now because I haven't much time and it is getting dark and we have no candles.

Well, so long for now and I will write when I can.

Love, Rog

P.S. Send me some pictures of home and stuff. Mostly I want to see you people and the house and cars. I haven't much time to read now so hold off on the books, Dad. I can hardly wait to get home. I can taste Mom's cooking right now.

Maybe 8% of the men who went to Vietnam ended up as grunts. The rest we called REMFs, rear echelon mother fuckers. Grunts got the picked-over remains of the gear, and little, if any, support from the REMFs. There was also a drug problem in the ranks of the REMFs and there was a thriving black market. Line outfits never had any drug use that I could see. Grunts had to depend on each other for our lives. The NVA carried small bags of raw opium around their necks. If they were hit they could chew the opium and still fight. We did kill a lot of doped-up NVA soldiers.

When we came back from an operation to rest behind the wire for a day or two we even had a difficult time getting hot chow and using another battalion's outhouses. We usually just stole the food and equipment we needed.

1/9 letter 114
New York, NY
March 6, 1967
March 5

Dear Mom and Dad,

Well, I am staying back in the rear for a couple of days. We were on a march and I passed out along with seven other guys. I was humping a 29 lb. radio plus all my gear and I just passed out — heat exhaustion. They called in choppers and med-evaced us out. We were given some sort of fluid in our arm and I feel a hell of a lot better right about now. I must go out this evening on the resupply chopper but I don't know.

The medevac chopper took us right up to about 8,000 feet and it got real cool. I drank three canteens of water and had that IV in and it was a day before I urinated. I passed out running to get out from under an NVA mortar attack.

We now have a body count of 300 gooks — not bad for three days, is it? This doesn't count the ones we missed or were dragged away or were blown up in artillery and air strikes....

We have really been kickin' tail out here in operation Prairie II. I was on Prairie I and it was a farce. This one we are getting some gooks. I just heard that Delta Co. has a bunch of WIAs and choppers can't get in because a heavy firefight is going on. They are taking out Huey gunships with fifty cal. and rockets plus jets with 250 lb. bombs and napalm plus artillery. There is going to be a hell of a show out there in the next couple of hours.

We are listening to all the fighting on the field-type radio here at Dong Ha.

Well, last night I had a good night's sleep on an air mattress with a poncho liner. A poncho liner is the best thing the Marine Corps has scarfed up from the Army. It is a lightweight quilt-type blanket. It is camouflage, dries quickly and is compact — great. We are supposed to come in from the field tomorrow or the next day and have a couple of days of rest before going back to Operation Chinook II. When we finish Chinook II I don't know where we will go or what we will do but I hope we will have a permanent position for a while and rest up a bit — like till Sept. 15 which is my rotation date. Sure would like to be home for my 21st birthday and I just might make it. But I know a couple of guys who are starting their fourteenth month.

I remember getting that poncho liner. God, it was great. The world I was living in was so small that getting that poncho liner was the best thing that had happened to me in a month.

We have had it pretty hard lately, a lot of humping, not much water and chow and it's been hot!! I have killed my share of gooks. I lost count at nine or ten.

Counting the enemy dead was something our Vietnam strategy was based on. We would have a firefight and when it was over we were supposed to count the enemy bodies. Everyone was shooting machine guns, M-79 rounds and our air support and artillery. We would have to estimate the number of enemy killed by finding the arms, legs, and heads. It was easier to estimate by counting heads. I really didn't know how many I killed in big fights. We would find mass burial sites of NVA soldiers. I once was ordered to dig up a mass grave to count the enemy dead. It was a big pile of dirt with swollen, blackened arms and legs sticking out and it was about a week old. I refused.

Well, how is it going on at home? What is happening around old N.R.? I will be home for part of the football season next year and for most of the squirrel season. I hope to get some good hunting in at something that doesn't shoot back.

I hope to buy a nice handgun when I get back. Maybe a .357 Mag revolver or a heavy cal like a .44 Mag. Wish we could carry personal sidearms. I would be toting a .357 for sure. I carried a .45 and M-79 grenade launcher for a while and a Thompson .45 sub and I am looking forward to the M-16 which we are supposed to get this month. But I know the Marine Corps pretty well and we will probably be lucky to get them in the next three months.

Well, I just heard the news. My old outfit 2/9 is going back to the World (States) pretty soon. Damn!!! I had to get transferred. Well, that's the way it goes.

Maybe we will go somewhere to re-form. We are getting a lot of casualties. Our Company lost 42 men in the last few weeks but the ratio of gooks to us is still 25:1— On Operation Prairie II right here it is 50:1.

Well, I have to sign off now. Lots to do.

> Love,
> Your Son,
> Rog

Our days were spent on the hump. We regularly humped five to ten miles each day in 100-degree-plus humid heat. We humped swamps, mountains, coastal sand dunes, jungle, tree lines, rice paddies, and all kinds of terrain. Everything we owned was on our backs. The load was 50 to 60 pounds. We threw away everything we didn't absolutely need. We never had enough water. Our waists and shoulders were covered with "saddle sores" that were kept raw by sweat and dirt

A Marine in the thick jungle. Quang Tri Province. March 1967.

and cartridge belts and packs. We couldn't wear skivvies as it was too hot. We were so dehydrated that we seldom urinated, and we learned not to stop to pee. If we stopped we would have to run to catch up with our squad's position on the hump. We just peed while we humped. We learned how to get up and get down with all of our gear on our backs. Never sit down, only go to one knee. You might not be able to get back up. We learned economy of motion. We learned to lean forward and take small steps and not to bend our knees climbing a hill. We learned to hit the ground, dump our packs and roll when we were under fire. We learned that when the order to drop our packs was given we were moving into attack formation and blood would soon flow. We would then go into the fight and kill or be killed mode.

Cam Lo Bridge

March 10, 1967 letter 115
U.S. Navy
March 8

Dear Mom and Dad,

Well, I finally got to stop moving around. We are supposed to stay at our present position for a week or so. We are a guard detachment for a place called

Cam Lo. We protect a large bridge that Charlie would love to blow. Our weapons consist of mainly five 90mm tanks. We could really tear some gooks up if they give us a chance.

Not much danger of being hit here because we have a lot of ARVN troops around. You never can tell.

We are sort of resting up. Our unit was put up for a Presidential Unit Citation and Navy Commendation Medal for Prairie II. We counted over 750 hardcore (red star) body count and twice that many wounded. More than likely the figures run up a lot higher. That is all we found. We stopped counting bodies one day and also stopped picking up weapons because we had to move out. We lost a good number of men also. 189 casualties for three companies. We might rest up and get some replacements before going hunting again.

We did get the Presidential Unit Citation, the Republic of Vietnam Gallantry Cross Unit Citation, Vietnam Presidential Unit Citation, RVN Civil Action ribbon and several others. We paid for these ribbons in the blood of friend and foe. While on active duty after Vietnam I never wore my ribbons. It would take 30 years and a good deal of introspection before I wore my war shirt with my ribbons to the Wall. I wore my ribbons to honor all the familiar names carved there in the stone.

Cam Lo bridge, where I was almost cut down by an ARVN manning a machine gun. March 1967.

The boats on the river were probably full of enemy weapons. Cam Lo Bridge. March 1967.

I have been in over a dozen and a half mortar attacks and I know how demoralizing they can be. Especially to a bunch of bearded, filthy, hill crazy Marines.

We don't take prisoners. We only took 9 prisoners during the whole operation. The rest of the captives "disappeared." We found a Corpsman that the gooks had caught alive and tortured to death. After that it was bayonet the wounded or shoot them with a .45. We didn't care. It is surprising how little a human life means in war. I would just as soon swat a fly than bayonet a half-dead gook. When I get out of this stinking hellhole things will change. It is all a frame of mind. I just got sick and tired of seeing my friends getting blown away by gooks who were wounded and who wanted to give up.

We should be getting mail tomorrow. I haven't gotten any for the past couple of weeks and it will be good to hear how things are going back in old N.R.

I have mailed three rolls of film home. They are taken of Operation Chinook II and the first part of Prairie II. The roll I have in the camera I plan on including some of myself as I didn't have time to do self-portraits in the other. When I send home film make sure, Dad, that you sort through them first and take out the ones that you don't want the women to see. Remember those slides are like gold to me.

God, I looked at myself in a mirror a couple of hours ago and I look like a Greek sheep farmer and I still prefer women. (That's a pun.)

I have a couple of hard core VC items that I would like to send home. A canteen and some small personal items. I will probably get a chance if I want to hump them but I will most likely junk them. Humping a 29 lb. radio plus everything else everyone carries isn't my idea of a ball.

Well, I have to do a heck of a lot of getting ready for a patrol tonight. So long for now. I am under 200 days.

Love,
Your Son, Rog

A 1/9 letter 116
March 15, 1967
Part I

Dear Mom and Dad,

March 10

How are all of the nuts back in the States? Us — the nuts over here... We are ok.

I am sitting here eating a loaf of gook bread with c-rat jam. It is pretty good. The bread is like French bread and it is very chewy. Tastes good when you are hungry — wish I had some butter. — Boy, chocolate cake with caramel icing, ice cream, tossed salad, steak, French fries, hamburgers, beer. The list could go on and on forever.

Just came in off a patrol an hour ago. It is 01:00 in the morning. Pretty hairy patrol because I was point and because of its great range. Must have humped for a solid three hours. So dark you could hardly see the men behind me. We expected to get hit tonight but didn't even get sniped at. On the way in through the wire I was walking through the maze that all wire has and the point has to memorize, I heard a fight break out in the bunker on our lines that I was approaching. I heard a machine gun bolt cycle and an ARVN saying, "VC. VC." The bastard was going to cut us down but a Marine was standing watch with him and had to knock him out to keep him from opening up. I had no place to go as I was halfway through the wire. I called, "Coming in" and had shot a green star cluster flare so they would know we were friendly, but the gook tried his best to kill us. When we got in I tried to kill the gook but he was some high-ranking official's son. You can't trust any of them.

Given the chance I would have killed this guy without any remorse what-soever. I think he was an NVA agent. He had protection. At times I dream of being caught in the wire in the dark waiting for death to knock me down. Even today I sure wish I could have killed that bastard.

I hope there are no loud noises like cars backfiring or firecrackers until I can get used to life again when I get back to the States. You may find me picking myself back off the ground.

I hope we got that Presidential Unit Citation that we are up for. Would add another ribbon to my chest and look pretty good in my record book. Doggies are about the only ones who get them — mostly because they have so many men. I guess even with the M-16 they aren't as well-trained as we are. I know they live a hell of a lot better and all in all the living standards of Marine to Army or, as a matter of fact, to any other branch of the service is pretty comparable.

I have had an Air Force captain say to me, "How can you live like that?" — reply, "Got me, Sir, you just have to get used to it." Crazy G. D. Marines. Marines are also the only branch of the service that doesn't get liberty in VN. Who would want to face a company or a squad even after they lived a couple of months in the bush? We would most likely tear the people-to-people program to a million pieces.

We have been chewed out a lot for mistreating P.O.W.'s — Hell, can't a guy have any fun?

Now a gook won't give himself up unless there is an officer around. They beg, "No kill — No kill." We don't take many prisoners, only honchos or high-ranking NVA non-coms.

Boy, if I could hump it all I would have a mess of the "spoils of war." I will start collecting when I get short so I won't have to hump it all over the country of Vietnam.

Take your pick of terrain over here. Endless miles of rice paddies, swamp, thickest jungle you ever saw, elephant grass, rolling hills, mountains, sand dunes and flat lands. On that map, I have been to Da Nang, Phu Bai, Khe Sanh, Dong Ha, Cam Lo, Chu Lai, Hue, Quang Tri, plus innumerable smaller towns. The operations have been held at Quang Tri province plus a couple of other places. I have three operations under my belt and am going out on Phase II of Chinook II most ricky tic.

We have it pretty good now here at Cam Lo Bridge. We guard against the insurgent Communist forces that want to blow it all to pieces. We opened up last night. Tanks had fifty cal. and 90mm firing. We had an M-60 machine gun — myself as Gunner — and we had a couple of ARVNs. Some gook — ARVN — Army of the Republic of Vietnam — had opened up with his Browning Automatic Rifle. They usually put BARs on good men. This fool said something and commenced to fire every last round he had with his eyes closed into the deck about fifteen feet in front of him. Ten magazines in succession cach one, one long burst. Then the S.O.B. started throwing grenades. I fired a belt, 100 rounds, just to get my cookies and then grabbed the ARVN who was preparing to make his bird and everything quieted down. This wasn't the guy who tried to open up on our patrol.

I will continue, late, got to hit the rack now. Bye. See you tomorrow (in my letter, of course).

Part II

Well, here I am on the back of the last page. We got word we are moving out in Chinook II tomorrow. Have to finish up Phase II. Should take about a month. We are going to be in the Toby Ton Ton Valley. Shouldn't run across many Charlies. Strictly "Search and Destroy" with all the weight on "Destroy." Going to burn or destroy (blow up) everything in sight. Going to be fun. May run across booby traps so I will watch my step. I want to be able to dance when I get home.

Well, have lots of stuff to do. Got to close.

> Will write when I can.
> Love,
> Rog.

One day in March we were humping the mountains of Quang Tri and we were caught in a storm. Our company was strung out single file following a footpath up a ridgeline. The sky turned black and we got caught in a cloudburst. It rained so hard that my vision was reduced to a few feet, it became hard to breathe and the pockets of my utilities filled up with water. We hunkered down and kept in contact with the man in front by putting one of our hands on that Marine's haversack. I had a pack of c-rat cigarettes in between my helmet and helmet liner and they got soaked. It grew cold and hailed. In half an hour the sun was shining. Welcome to Vietnam.

Quang Tri

A 1/9 letter 117
March 31, 1967
March 24

Dear Mom and Dad,

Well, I finally had a chance to write. We have been humping the hills and mountains for the past 10 days searching and destroying. I don't know what operation this is but it is in the same general area of Prairie II. We got the hell knocked out of us yesterday by a part of a battalion of NVAs. Alpha Co. lost a full platoon plus some and we were fighting for our lives. Second platoon walked right into an ambush and the gooks gave them hell. A lot of the guys

I knew got it. I was lucky, not a scratch, but they shot holes in my radio and I also pulled a piece of shrapnel out of the radio. One man saved us from being overrun. He went out front with an M-60 machine gun and held them off while we formed a defense position. He killed them until he ran out of ammo. He was then killed himself.

Sgt. Zeke was our company supply sergeant. Zeke didn't have to be in the field with us, as he could have had it good in the rear with the gear. He humped with us because he was a great guy and he took care of his grunts. He got us chow, he got us ammo, and he got us water. He got us everything we had. Zeke made sure we had what we needed.

Alpha Company was moving in column across dry rice paddies toward a tree line. Our lead platoon came under heavy automatic weapons fire from the tree line. Mortars were impacting the center of our column and the enemy plan was to cut us in half with the mortars and kill the front of our column and then leave before we could bring in air strikes to kill the tree line. Several Marines in the lead platoon were hit and more were going down. Zeke ran forward and dragged two wounded Marines out of the kill zone. Zeke then picked up an M-60 machine gun from a wounded gunner and ran forward once again into the kill zone. Sgt. Zeke attacked the ambush that was killing first platoon. Firing his machine gun from the hip, he assaulted an enemy strong point in a tree line and

Flooded rice paddies. The paddy dikes were always mined so we mostly humped the mud. Street Without Joy. March 1967.

A province gate on the Street Without Joy. March 1967.

broke the back of that ambush. Although wounded, Sgt. Zeke continued to kill the enemy until the NVA cut him down. As we carried him in his poncho back down the column to the company CP, a lot of Marines came forward to put their hands on him. We counted 11 dead NVA around him. Zeke saved countless Marine lives that day. Sgt. Zeke was posthumously awarded the Medal of Honor. Semper Fi, Zeke.

I haven't received any packages for the past month and a half so I imagine there will be a few if we *ever* go to the rear. We have a long hump ahead of us today (7000 meters) and I have 35lbs. of radio plus chow, ammo, and stuff to hump....

Radio-humping man. When I carried the radio I put the antenna down my shirt and out my sleeve. I made less of a target without a high antenna. The enemy liked to shoot radiomen. My squad on patrol on the Street Without Joy. March 1967.

Artillery is going over my head hitting the gooks. They are dug in pretty good because air strikes aren't routing them so it looks as if we will have to go in and get them.

We had artillery support from a battleship in the South China Sea. We were told that the shells were the size of Volkswagens. When the shells went overhead and landed a half mile away the shock wave would rock the earth that we were digging our holes in. We waited for a short round.

Air strikes were a common method of support. The jets would come in 50 feet over our heads firing their 20 mm cannons and the hot empty 20 mm brass would rain down on us. The jets would fire rockets, pickle off napalm or drop 500-pound bombs. What a show! We dug our holes deeper after an air strike. A dud 500-pound bomb dropped one day and we were sent out to secure it the next morning. The only thing we found was handcart tracks showing where the NVA picked up the bomb to use in a booby trap.

I will be carrying a pistol pretty soon as I can get one off an KIA or WIA. I have an idea when we come out of the field I will steal an M-16 from someone in the rear. We are supposed to get M-16s around the first of April. Damn — April already. Time is going fast out here in the bush. Most likely get my warrant for Lance Corporal when we get back to the rear. *About time.*

Well, I have to get going. Have to adjust my gear so it doesn't rub me raw. Well, I will write when I can and you know it may not be often until we get out of the bush. Meanwhile there is some fighting I have to do.

Love,
Rog

P.S. April, May, June, July, August, September

A 1/9 letter 118
March 31, 1967
Easter 1967

Part I

Dear Mom and Dad,

Well, I have a little time before we are moving out to our objective. It is only 3000 meters so it shouldn't be a bad hump....

Boy, when I get older and have the coin I want to travel overseas. Nothing like it. Especially the Orient. Might have to try the other shore on a Mediterranean cruise or something before I get out of the Corps.

Resupply choppers coming in now so we will be moving soon. Better sign off for now. I will finish up a little later.

Love, Rog

Part II

Well, it's a little later and I got hold of a pen.

I plan on putting on a party when I get home. Will do quite a bit of drinking. Everyone who comes will bring a six-pack or a bottle and I will have some too.—We will turn on the record player and away we will go.

Boy, is it hot! I wish I had a bathtub full of ice cold fruit salad like Mom makes and a case of cold pop.

We still haven't moved to our new objective yet. Air strikes are going on about 1500 meters away and I sit here with an empty camera sobbing away. Napalm is so nice and burning men make great targets.

We caught two reinforced NVA companies in the open one day. After calling in artillery we hit them with napalm air strikes. We then took them under grazing fire from machine guns set on a hilltop at 600 yards. We grunts moved in under the grazing fire and started killing any enemy we found. The NVA were jumping up on fire and running and screaming and we were shooting them down. Sometimes the ammo they were carrying cooked off and their bodies would explode. It was a turkey shoot and we killed a lot of them that day. I remember thinking how much fun I was having. The NVA were so well trained that those

Napalm strike on NVA troops. Burning men make great targets. The savagery of war got us all. Quang Tri Province. 1967.

who escaped regrouped and started mortaring us while we were collecting their weapons.

Well, we are due to go to the rear soon. At the rate we are going we will have to go. We have lost most of my friends and more than one third of our manpower. We lost them to mortars, mines, and in firefights. So if someone is hit and starts yelling "Corpsman!" or just screaming in pain the gooks know they are on target and will commence to pop thirty or so rounds in on us. When that happens we have to shut up the guy that's hit and then grab our hat. (Move out.)

Speaking of Corpsmen. Those guys really have some gonads. They are where the action is thick. They will run across a mine field to a wounded Marine. I saw one get his foot blown off doing it. We had one that had his Unit I (first aid pack) blown out of his hand by a mortar yesterday. He was untouched except by exhaustion. He worked on the wounded until he collapsed. They are the only part of the Navy the Marine Corps looks up to. The cry, "Corpsman!" is an old one to my ears — eight months old. My heart goes out every time I see these guys running into the middle of a firefight. First aid pouch in their hand, jumping out of their holes during a mortar barrage to help a guy who is hit. We have had four or five killed because they tried to help the wounded. They have more guts than anyone I have ever seen except a grungy Marine. — He doesn't have guts. He's just stupid and kill-crazy.

On the "street" we had a Marine step on a toe popper. A toe popper was a small plastic mine made by the U.S. that was designed to wound and couldn't be found by a metal-reading mine detector. The Marine went down and the cry "Corpsman" went out. The enemy then opened up on us from a tree line about 75 yards away. Corpsman Robert Syler got up under fire and ran towards the downed Marine. Doc Syler was almost there when he hit a toe popper himself. The mine took off the back of Doc's heel, but that didn't stop him from crawling towards the wounded Marine as the enemy fire hit around him. We put enough fire on the tree line to call in a medevac and both Doc Syler and the wounded Marine were loaded up and whisked away. Semper Fi, Doc.

Here I sit hot and dry wondering if the Strough's Beer Co. is still in business. What I wouldn't give for a cold beer or four. A shower, steak, French fries, salad. I could go on

Forever.... Forever.

Well, I have to go now mainly because we are saddling up (pack animals, you know). Each man in addition to regular gear and chow carries demo, machine gun ammo, mortar rounds, etc. adding up to 20 lbs. extra.

Well, here we go.

Love,
Rog.

A 1/9 letter 119
April 1, 1967

Dear Mom and Dad,

Just made up of good hot java to keep the chill off me. Funny climate — cold and damp at night, hot and dry during the day. Oh well.

The way you make coffee is to burn a small ball of C-4 until the coffee or water is really boiling good about thirty seconds. Then add coffee and boil until the cup boils over and puts out the fire. Relight and let it boil a second time and you have java — *strong!*, black and hot. You make a lot of strong coffee with only a small pack of instant c-rat stuff— only way to do it.

Coffee means more to me than the readers of this book will ever know. I

The war was run on c-rat coffee. Dong Ha. April 1967.

could escape for a moment into the black depths; I could wake up my mind and body for the next watch; I could warm my cold hands with coffee. I could taste and smell coffee and become coffee's friend. C-rat coffee took me away from the war for a moment. Simple things meant so much.

Reflections in a can of c-rat coffee:

> *How many times*
> *did you sit up with me?*
> *Kindle my thoughts,*
> *be my only friend.*
> *How many times did I ask you*
> *for an answer?*
>
> *Sitting in my hole at night*
> *waiting together*
> *to die, maybe.*
> *You were my only company,*
> *you kept me going.*
>
> *I forsake the world sometimes,*
> *yes.*
> *But never you.*
> *Don't you see,*
> *you were my friend*
> *and I was yours.*
>
> *I looked into your*
> *black depths*
> *and was nourished*
> *by your warmth.*
>
> *Sometimes you would not*
> *let me rest.*
> *I hated you for that.*
> *But how could a grunt*
> *hate his only friend?*
>
> *A lot of time*
> *has passed now.*
> *But I still have you.*
> *Old friends are the best.*

Not much in the way of action today. Just a few snipes here and there.

We are supposed to go back to the rear pretty soon — not soon enough for me though — all the guys are pretty tired, mentally as well as bodily.

I remember crossing a river while humping back to Dong Ha. We had been on one of the prairie operations and had lost a good number of men. I don't know where he came from or where he got the ice but there was a little Vietnamese boy standing on the riverbank trying to sell a cold Coke for one dollar American. One of the men in my squad pulled out his K-bar and started walking towards the kid. I asked him what he was going to do and he said that he was going to get the Coke and cut the kid's throat. This Marine told me we could push the kid under a bank of the river and hide his body. I had to put my rifle on him to stop him. I told him I would kill him if he touched the kid. That Marine stopped and turned to me and told me not to turn my back as he would get me sooner or later. The savagery of war had taken his soul. That Marine was killed eventually. War is a heartless place where men are willing to kill children for a cold Coca-Cola.

It would be nice to go to the Slop Chute and soak up some suds. Two per man per day, 20 cents each. Not enough maybe but at least some music and a couple of cans can help relax a person. Of course, Army, Navy, Air Force doesn't limit your drinking and they serve hard stuff. Who could contend with a bunch of drunk Marines straight from a couple of months in the bush.

We are more or less a blocking force right now. Maybe we are getting a rest — about time I should say — humping 7000–10,000 meters a day does get tiring. I have done so much humping with a pack on lately I feel as light as a feather when I walk around without my "Combat Gear" on. I swear I will be shorter when I get home. My feet will be all the way up to where my knees were. They have been worn halfway up now.

I have decided that when I get on the way home I will not eat any real good food like ice cream and pies — mmm — until I get home. It will be better then. A lot better.

The gooks sure use mortars a hell of a lot up here. They really must be hurting in a long march with all of that garbage to carry.

We got a new C.O. A 1st Looy. He was attached to our company first off. You know just watching to see how we worked I saw him run up to a bunker, grab a machine gun out of a gook's hands, and bounce a frag off the gook's head before running with the gun. Got some guts. He is a great guy.

> *Our new LT was a Mustang. A Mustang is a Marine who started as an enlisted man and then became an officer. Mustangs usually make great officers. Our new LT was a good one and he wouldn't ask any of his men to do something he wouldn't do himself. He was a Semper Fi Marine.*

Well, we have tanks inside our perimeter now and they make everyone breathe a hell of a lot easier. I have seen them in action and they fire a canister round that does play hell with the gooks.

I hope I make it home for my 21st birthday. Looks like it will be very close. Can't really complain if I don't as my 13th month is up Sept. 10 — Marines serve 13, all other services serve 12 months.

If we go back to the rear soon we will get M-16s. Can't wait to try one out. At paper targets, that is.

I wonder how it is to live out of a foot locker and wall locker instead of a pack. Man, that would be living....

In packages, could you send me one meal with every one? Something novel. Chinese, like that chop suey, chow mein. Man, that was great. Maybe spaghetti and a can of fruit, you know, and a pair of socks would be plenty and every now and then a small can of stewed vegetables. Good God, I could go on for ages. Only five months left — a lot better than thirteen.

Can't wait to go into the Red Eye, sit and order a gin and tonic, light a cigarette, and sit and sip and soak up the atmosphere. Damn, I'll go buggy before I get out of here.

When I get home I will have a lot of living to catch up on in a comparatively short time. I will really be moving all the time and will spend time at *home*! Just sitting, eating garlic chips, drinking Coke, watching "Bonanza" Sunday nights. Mom, have enough stuff to make a cherry pie and an apple pie when I get home, plus some chocolate ice cream. I can taste it now.

Well, got to cut this short, will write again whenever I get a spare moment.

Love,
Your Son,
Rog

I thought at the time that I had it tough. What I experienced was nothing compared to the hardships the NVA grunts suffered. I cannot imagine being strafed, bombed, burnt by napalm, and shelled by battleship artillery. The firepower of the United States of America was focused on killing NVA. Marine grunts fought for 13 months and went home, but the NVA soldiers fought endlessly. In the end, our enemies were willing to die by the millions for their cause. We were not.

Camp Carrol

A 1/9 letter 120
April 1, 1967

Dear Mom and Dad,

Well, we were pulled out of Prairie III after about five or six days of heavy fighting. Good thing, too. Did you know that 1/9 has the highest casualty rate of any Marine battalion in the DMZ? As a matter of fact, the highest casualty rate in Vietnam. One consolation is we kicked more NVAs ass to put it bluntly.

We are now at Camp Carrol, a large artillery base about 6–7 miles from the DMZ. There are Army and Marines here but mostly Army. Being an Army-controlled base means — hot, good chow — hot showers, cots or stretchers to sleep on, tents and plenty of ice. Most times we can have beer and pop, too.

Well, we are on an outpost that takes 1 hour and a half to climb up to. It is rough going with no stopping. We have a river we can take baths in. I have never been so tired or exhausted or dry in my life in these mountains. I spent two hours sitting in a pool among some small rapids in the river just soaking up water and sunshine. Boy, did it feel good. Almost felt normal even though there were about twenty naked, hairy, dirty Marines splashing around.

We regularly went days without food. Sometimes we had one c-rat a day. Sometimes we had two. One time after four days without resupply, I found a small can of dehydrated ham and eggs in the bottom of my pack. Usually c-rat ham and eggs were thought to be pretty bad. I gathered my fire team around my hole and we had two spoonfuls each. That was the best meal I have ever had. Appetite is truly the best sauce.

Well, we finally got the M-16s. They are pretty nice. Glad to get them finally. They are lighter than the M-14s and they put out a round with a higher muzzle velocity.

India Co. 3/9 got massacred last night from the exact place that we left. Hope we don't go back as we are full of short-timers. They hit 3/9 just like they hit us. First automatic weapons and machine guns and then walked 60s in on them — they got the bunch.

We are supposed to get the whole April draft to replace the men that we lost. We are also supposed to get the perimeter duty at Dong Ha or Phu Bai air bases. Would be pretty good duty to put it mildly. Also supposed to go on Chinook II for two weeks before getting the air base.

It was at this time I started to lose hope of surviving. I was just waiting to get hit. I only knew one man serving with the Walking Dead who served his whole 13 months without getting wounded. I knew I was going to get hit. Everybody got hit. It was just a matter of time and luck. Killed or maimed, just a matter of luck. Some guys had already been hit once or twice. If you were hit three times you went home. We made pacts with each other so we knew who got our gear when we went down. My writing of letters slowed down. The world I was living in was all but indescribable. Blood everywhere. This was the time that a corpsman told me he knew about me leaving the corpsman at Kim Lin. That corpsman told me that I was on my own when I went down. I was on my own in a very dangerous, shrinking, savage world. I didn't realize it then, but I was a very lucky man.

Boy, it is a real hot one today, going to get hotter, too. I am glad we aren't out humping. We carry machine gun ammo, 100–200 rounds per man, two blocks of C-4 demo, 60mm mortar rounds, flack jacket 5 lbs., entrenching tool, four grenades, fuse lighters, fuses, blasting caps, chow and cigarettes plus Claymore mines and rifle ammo, poncho liner. God, I could go on forever — three canteens, etc. — it adds up to a heavy weight on your back —

damn heavy. Flack jacket to keep the heat in and you hump about 2 or 3 miles up and down hills. Saddle sores from your gear that never heal. We always seem to run a foot race — heat exhaustion is common. We had about 100 cases of it.

Water was precious. We would lay all the plastic from our cigarette packs around our holes at night. In the morning we licked the condensation off for our morning drink. We kept a c-rat can handy so if it rained we could catch the rain in our ponchos and dip in the can and fill our canteens. For years afterward I would dream of a canteen that never ran out of cool sweet water.

Speaking of heat. Is it getting any hotter in Ohio? Well, by the time the leaves turn green and then red and yellow then brown at the edges I should be getting home.

Well, I really have to be going along.

Hey, that M-16 is something. Delta Co. got a gook last night and shot him in the shoulder. Ripped his arm off and made him do a flip — dead from shock before he hit the ground.

Well, got to go.

Love,
Rog

1/9 saddling up with the new M-16s on Operation Prairie. Phu Bai April 1967.

Cam Lo

A 1/9 letter 121
April 12th, 1967
April Fools Day

Dear Mom and Dad,

Well, we are still here sitting next to that cool, wet river. I sure wish I had some film for my camera. I could get some good pictures of the mountains.

When I was back in the World [States] I used to think that a river was just nice to look at. Over here I see one and I want to jump in and drink....

Sure hope we go back to Chinook II base camp. We would be standing perimeter. We have been in the Cam Lo area for a month or so and it is pretty hard on the men.

Well, I have been on Prairie I, II, III. We really saw some action on those. All of it was at the DMZ fighting NVAs. Chinook II was a firefight involving one platoon against 140 gooks on one side, 60 on the other — crossfire, but they sprang the ambush too early and we had good cover — we just lost a few.

Boy, we sure are due for a rest and we need replacements for all the men we have lost. I hope we get both. I hope also they don't decide to send us back after a couple of weeks. I have saddle sores from my cartridge belt and pack. They won't get a chance to heal as long as we do all this humping. We move out all day and set in and dig a hole at about 6:00. We are ready to start humping the next day at 6:30, hole watch or L.P. so we get at best 4 hours sleep a night. It gets kind of tiring real fast. Well, can't bitch much. There are some guys carrying heavier loads.

I led a charmed existence. I once stepped over a mine and a guy behind me hit it. I had holes shot into my radio. I didn't give a shit about anything and I was getting shot at every day. My total existence was about killing NVA. If I killed all the NVA the war would stop. I remember a machine gunner getting hit with an RPG and getting torn in half. We cleaned the guts and blood off his gun and gave it to someone else and we kept on humping. My squad members became strangers. I slept curled into a ball in the bottom of my hole.

Beautiful morning. Sun shining over the tops of the jungle and mountains. Boy, I thought the Blue Ridge of the U.S. were something. You ought to see this place — Only there you drive around. Here you hump....

How are the slides turning out? I am really anxious to know. I know that I screwed up a couple here and there but I want to know how the rest turned out.

We are, or we were supposed to be, helo-lifted out and in five or six times so far — We got helo-lifted out once. In all the others we humped....

Well, I best be running along. We only have one pen for the whole fire team (4) and some of the other guys want to get a letter off. We don't get much of a chance to write.

Well, got to be going — Got another month under my belt.

Love,
Rog

Cam Lo

A 1/9 letter 122
April 12, 1967

Well, we are off Operation "Big Horn."
The final statistics:

	Us:		Them:	
	20 KIA		5 KIA	
	79 WIA		0 WIA	
	2 MIA		0 MIA	

Boy, we got our ass stomped.

Charlie Company was overrun in an ambush that wiped out one platoon. They even had guys playing dead to avoid being shot. We came to their rescue by running through a mine field losing four guys. The new M-16 jammed. We had to fix bayonets and go in to save Charlie Co. from being completely wiped out. We found guys who had taken apart the rifle to clean it and were shot in the head. We also found a ditch that the Corpsmen had staged the wounded in. The Corpsmen and the wounded were all shot in the head. The M-16s jammed. We are up the river without a paddle. Our new guns don't work.

On April Fool's Day in 1967 we went to an artillery base called Camp Carroll. We had our trusty M-14 rifles taken from us and we were issued the brand new lightweight M-16 rifles and we set out on an operation on the "Street Without Joy." I was humping a squad radio at the time and we had our perimeter set for the night, but we heard a big gunfight break out some distance away. I tuned my radio to battalion net and listened to Charlie Company get wiped out. They were calling for help and I heard the company commander say, "Our weapons are jamming; we cannot defend ourselves." Charlie's CO was then shot in the throat and killed. We saddled up to go to their aid and we ran through the dark into a minefield and lost men trying to get to them. The order was passed to "fix bayonets" on those little black rifles and we attacked into the ambush that was killing Charlie Company. We drove the NVA away and we found what was left of Charlie at first light. I will always remember small groups of Marines that had been executed while trying to clear their jammed M-16s. A ditch had been used to stage the wounded and all the wounded and the corpsmen treating them had been shot in the head. Machine guns had run out of ammo and none of the few survivors had grenades left. The new M-16s didn't work!

We captured one NVA and used him for bayonet practice. After this we took no prisoners. I can still smell the smoke and the blood of the battlefield; I can still taste the metallic blood taste. If we had not arrived when we did, Charlie Company would have been completely wiped out. If the NVA had stayed and fought instead of bugging out, my company would have suffered the same fate as Charlie.

Once our M-14s were taken and we were given M-16s, the NVA had better rifles than we had. The AK-47 is a great weapon. The AK-47 submachine gun was suited to a rough, dirty, close-quarters environment like Vietnam. The U.S. was the most technologically advanced nation on earth and we had inferior grunt rifles. I felt completely abandoned by my country and my Marine Corps. How in the hell could they do this to us? Everyone was the enemy. We lived between a rock and a hard place.

We tried to get our M-14s back but the powers that be wouldn't replace the defective M-16s that cost so many Marines their lives. High command told us that the M-16s failed because the grunts didn't clean them right. They told us it was our fault the weapons were shit.

We felt completely abandoned by the High Command and it got grimmer and grimmer. We now couldn't even defend ourselves. We were the Walking Dead.

We did too much humping and my feet are really beginning to tell. I have blisters from being wet from paddies and then walking a few miles. Ouch!

Well, I have about four rolls of undeveloped film, including two rolls of 36 exposure color slides that I would like to send home. I have no way of sending them. See if you could figure out a way. Well, sometimes we go without mail for two weeks at a time.

I can only write so often because of operations. I will continue writing when I can though. We have pulled more in the last few months than most guys pull in their whole tour over here. It also looks like the 9th Marines aren't going to get any rest for a while, too. We are going to Dong Ha today for something big. Just about the whole 3rd Division is going to be up there — maybe a big push at the good old DMZ. I hope like hell not because it is pretty hairy up there.

Boy, I can count five flies on one sore on my leg and there is one on the hand that I am writing with plus about 20 more all over me. I have stopped trying to chase them away — gave up....

The days are going by pretty fast. September will be here pretty soon and I will be getting on that plane bound for Cleveland — Hopkins. Being in the field makes the time go by a lot faster. We definitely need a rest though. We are all pretty tired.

Love,
Rog

We were fighting in a savage war where no quarter was asked for and no quarter was given. If the NVA caught you they would execute you—if you were lucky. If the NVA had the time they would torture you to death. I had a friend that was caught and tortured and set out on display for us to find. War is man's worst endeavor.

We would just shoot any NVA that tried to give up. The NVA would fight hard and in their attacks they were not afraid to die. The enemy troops opposing us were hard men, well trained, well equipped and heartless.

Dong Ha

A 1/9 letter 123
April 14, 1967
April 12, 1967

Dear Mom and Dad,

[...]

Well, we are back at Dong Ha for a while at least. We are going out tomorrow to guard a bulk fuel depot somewhere and we are going to be there approx. two weeks before we go to another operation. I really do wish we would get a home, or permanent base to operate out of. I would really like to stay in one place for a while and not have to look out for gooks all day and night and live out of a pack and dig a hole every night. I am now packing on my back:

8 magazines 20 rounds each	poncho
180 extra rounds	bayonet
3 frag grenades	cartridge belt
2½ lbs. of C-4 demo	3 canteens
5 lbs. mortar round	poncho liner
100 rounds of MG ammo	radio battery
entrenching tool	and *chow.*

Wow! As you can see I do pack some stuff. When I get a package from home I do eat quite a bit of it right off. It's good to eat while you can for tomorrow is another day.

Well anyway, we are getting a little slack — not much but a little. Everyone really deserves a lot more but what can you do if they think the 9th Marines are the only ones fighting in Vietnam and we *are* fighting.

Home sweet home in the rain for a couple of days, behind the wire at Dong Ha. April 1967.

Operation Big Horn, the one we were on last, we really got whipped. We were tired and miserable and all we wanted to do was drop somewhere dry and sleep. That is why we got hit so bad. The NVA were fresh and dug in and waiting. That's how it goes. The new place is going to be by a beach so we will have a little fun in the sun.

Well, we have hot chow and no hole watch tonight again so it should be OK — until tomorrow. I am really looking forward to the day when I get out of this place.

Well, we are going to chow — got to run — will write from the beach tomorrow or the next day.

Love,
Rog

A 1/9 letter 124
April 21, 1967

Dear Mom and Dad,

Well, here it is night and I am writing the first letter I have written in a long time by candlelight. — Candles you sent — Outstanding.

Boy, that Koolaid and lemonade and ice tea is great. The water here is pretty raunchy so let's get some junk to put in it.

I finally got a bunch of film off to you. I think that the last roll was cracked (the little case that it comes in may have opened slightly under the pressure of my humping it all over Vietnam and may have let some light in). It was heartbreaking news to hear that it was all screwed up. I had some irreplaceable photos on it. Well, that's the way it goes. [...]

We got beer tonight (two per man). I have consumed about ten so far and I am just about on cloud number 9. Can you blame me? We hump (without exaggeration) from dawn till dusk. They give us two meals (c-rats) a day because we never stop for lunch. I mean we hump every time we stop. We get down on one knee whether it be 15 seconds or 15 minutes with about 50–60 pounds on your back with armor vest and all your crap hanging on your waist and neck. It can get pretty tiring. MARINE!!! WOW!!! If only the people back in the World knew. Well, the newspapers, etc. can't ever tell them. In fact, when we are interviewed by civilian reporters, which we are very often, we are told to keep our mouths shut and refer them to a higher authority. My answers to all questions from "How do you like the civilians?" to "What are, in your opinion, our chances in Vietnam?" "IT SUCKS!!"

The NVA are very careful, serious people. They know their job and they do it very well. If you could see some of the captured gear you would be amazed. They have some great modern equipment. Whereas (is that the word?) we might as well go out wearing all white with bells tied all around us.

The NVA never walk into our ambushes (only one). We walk into theirs and when we do we assault them and usually wipe them out. They like to ambush Army units because Army lies down and fires. The gooks then mortar them and throw grenades. When they ambush Marines the grunts get up screaming, all yelling curses, and charge the ambush. This really unnerves the gooks. That is why they don't like to ambush us.

Marines are trained to attack into an ambush as that is the best way to survive. Ambushes usually follow terrain features. Sometimes they are laid where a path makes a bend so we could place an automatic weapon firing down the path. Sometimes we would cover the approach and exit of an ambush with Claymore mines. Sometimes ambushes were four men and sometimes they were 40 men. All the ambushes we did were at night and that meant we would lie on the ground at the ready all night. Sometimes the men covering the approach and exit would signal the rest of us if the enemy was coming. We got used to lying silently in wait in the dark and in the rain while clouds of big tiger mosquitoes and hordes of leeches practically ate us alive. Most ambushes failed because we never saw anybody. You have to remember the land and all that was in it belonged to the NVA. We were just temporary.

I still look for ambushes, trip wires, disturbed earth, and movement whenever I am in the woods.

Well, it is late and I must sleep. So long for now.

Love,

Rog

Quang Tri

A 1/9 letter 125
April 21, 1967

Dear Mom and Dad,

Well, I finally now have a few moments to write. You remember where you read in the papers that the NVA overran a place and set loose a bunch of prisoners. Well, they were supposed to overrun it and hold it for 24 hours. We prevented this. Quang Tri is the place and we humped the hills all around it. Averages about 12,000 meters a day and that means moving out at 6:00 in the morning and walking for 12 hours straight till 6:00 or 6:30 and then digging our hole. Wow. I have some blisters that you won't believe. Well, we ran into them a couple of times and that is that. Four days of pure hell in the hump. Well, our company is back in the rear now for tonight. Tomorrow we are going out again to a place that is somewhat like CoCo Beach. Should be OK.

Don't send any more film!! My camera got soaked from the rain in the last couple of days and isn't opening the shutter. Hope it dries out and works. I will send it home if it doesn't work once I fool with it for a while. I put it in my sea bag and stashed it.

Well, our weapons are cleaned, we have already gotten hot chow and we are now awaiting word for shower call. I have been wearing my clothes until they rot or tear. Well, we have to shave today, that is if we want our beers — we have to buy them of course.

Well, I have been getting some news about the guys from Caroline, Jerry's sister. She writes pretty regular. Nice gal...

Well, I have to shave. I want my beer. I also have to shower. I am beginning to smell myself and that's when you are really bad.

Well, got to be going. I will write from the beach.

Bye for now,

Rog

In our machine gun ammo every fourth round was a phosphorous tipped tracer. The NVA had green tracers and we had red ones. Good machine gunners like Okie could direct fire by tracking their tracers. When our tracers were going out they looked cool as hell. When the green tracers were coming the shock waves made them look as big as basketballs. Tracers were good but they gave away our machine gun positions. Okie always carried 200 rounds with the tracers replaced by regular rounds. The NVA were smart: they tracked their tracers into our helicopters.

Outside Dong Ha

A 1/9 letter 126
April 21, 1967
Part I

Dear Mom and Dad,

Well, here we are at the "beach." Our platoon is out guarding a crane that is dredging a channel in a shallow river for deep-hulled boats. We are running around in cut-off trousers with bare feet and no shirts. Really nice to get out in the sun and do some relaxation for a while.

I have a good hot cup of c-rat coffee going and things couldn't get any better right at the moment. Some of the guys got a hold of a football from one of the Navy personnel and we are going to have a big game later this afternoon.

We are finally going to get some sleep. We put one man on watch, writing letters or something like I am doing now and the other men in the hole are free to do what they want — sleep, ride the gook cows, anything. Riding cows is big around here. We will most likely start patrolling tomorrow but it won't be real bad. Just a few villes and scattered hamlets and the gooks are supposed to be friendly.

I guess there aren't a lot of VC in this area. This is good news. That means we won't be sweeping around here at least. I will try to write once every couple of days to kind of catch up on what I missed but there isn't a whole lot to tell. We got some good men in our squad to replace those we lost. Three in all. That leaves us three short of what we started Chinook II with. The new guys seem pretty good and are nice and strong so we evened out the load and they are humping all the extra stuff now. All I am humping besides grenades and extra M-16 ammo is 10 lbs. of mortar rounds and a Claymore mine.

I didn't even know the names of the guys in my squad that we lost. I didn't want to know the replacements. I still have one day in a fierce battle that I have no memory of. I know we lost half our men but for the life of me I cannot remember the fight.

We are more or less an outpost and are still eating c-rats. What the heck anyhow. We aren't humping all day and we are getting three meals instead of two. We can always get bananas and stuff from the gooks to fill in....

My feet have cleared up pretty good. They are still tender in spots but as a whole they are better.

Well, I must close for now. Will continue later on today.

Sylvester McIntosh in the elephant grass. Quang Tri Province. April 1967.

Part II

Well, here it is 5:00 and I just got up. I slept all day and I feel a little old. Soon as I make myself a cup of brew I will be all set. I will start making that list of food I want to eat on R&R after I finish this letter.

The wind is pretty strong but it didn't blow down any of our hootches as of yet. Kind of hope we don't get pulled out for at least a long while so we can get mail regularly....

Well, I have to close now. I will write in the next couple of days.

Love, Rog

While going through captured NVA gear I found some of their chow. It was a long tubular bag of raw shelled peanuts that was tied together at the ends. The NVA trooper would carry the peanuts draped across one shoulder and across his chest. I carried and ate those peanuts for two weeks and I could feel the difference between c-rats and NVA rations. The NVA chow gave me more staying power and strength.

A 1/9 letter 127
April 22, 1967

Part I

Dear Mom and Dad,

How's everything at home? Fine, I hope. Over here we have it pretty good.

Captured NVA gear. I carried and ate the long bag of raw peanuts at the lower left.

Captured NVA gear including a round tomato can mine and jungle wrapped demo charge.

Still guarding the crane. I had a listening post (L.P.) last night. Got pretty hairy at times. Slept with a .45 in my hand....

When Charlie Co. went into the back of the ville to help Delta out they were ambushed but good. The gooks were dug in and they had everything from an RPG (rocket propelled grenade) to a recoilless rifle. One platoon of Charlie Co. was wiped out and there were 19 KIAs and 42 WIAs. The Marines got overrun. Gooks shot our wounded after the Corpsman had treated them and moved on. KIAs included the C.O. of Charlie Co. I don't know about this one guy in the article who was a hero but I didn't hear anything about it. My knees were knocking that night. I had first watch in a position five hundred yards away and we were pulled out to go help them. We got into a firefight and shot it out. Well, that's the real story.

The real story was that the new M-16s didn't work. I look back on this now and I still get pissed. A bunch of pampered lawyers and bean counters in suits sitting around a table with coffee and cakes decided to give a big-money contract to someone who probably faked the field tests of the M-16s we were issued. These decision makers never send their sons to fight. A lot of Marines died because of these bastards. We became expendable.

Looks at if we might be at this position for a couple of weeks. No one knows what will happen afterwards. We are used to living on a last minute notice anyway. Most of the time we don't even know the name of the operation we are on until we come back.

Here is a list of what I have done so far:

1) Operation Prairie I
2) Operation Prairie II
3) Operation Prairie III
4) Operation Hastings
5) Operation Hastings II
6) Operation Chinook II
7) Operation Big Horn
8) Operations against insurgent communist forces at Da Nang
9) Defense of Khe Sanh
10) Defense of Chu Lai
11) Defense of Dong Ha
12) Liberation of Quang Tri

Phew. I am bushed.

Well, no word on promotions yet. I am really ticked off. Most of the guys I came over with that go in halfway decent units have four or five months in grade as Lance Corporal and are going to go home Corporal. I will probably come home a Lance. If I stayed in 1/3 I would have come home a PFC. Burns me to see ignorant hicks make rank for just being here, not for doing anything. In 1/3 you had to kiss buttocks and that's one thing I would never do and I made that quite clear. Well, mail call is coming up soon. I will continue this later — got to go see who remembered.

Part II

Well, I missed out — better luck next time — maybe tomorrow....

Well, I will chow down then I am going for a swim. Going to wash our clothes and scummy bodies.

Be see'n ya soon

Love, Rog

A 1/9 letter 128
April 29, 1967

Well, here it is the 26th of April. Thought I would write now because if what I heard is true I probably won't be writing for a while.

They moved the Army into Chu Lai, formerly a Marine base. They are moving Marines up north and are more or less stockpiling them around Dong

Ha. In my opinion they are going to form a big offensive or defensive push in the DMZ. We have to stop infiltration from the north.

From what I hear we will be laying barbed wire and running platoon and company-sized outposts. I would say it's about time for 1/9 to settle down somewhere. I have seen more over here in my past four months with this outfit than most guys see during their whole tour of combat duty.

The ARVNs are pulling a sweep operation to our right front. All their rounds are zinging over our heads. I am down at the bottom of my hole, of course. Being up at the DMZ doesn't actually please me. We will be choice targets for both mortar and massed attacks. Have no fear, my hole will be deep. Very. I guess I will dig a semi short-timer's hole. When a couple of months pass it will be a full short-timer's hole. Deep and dark and nothing but a direct hit could get me.

We are supposed to get pulled out of the field approximately 20 days before we leave Vietnam. To get the animals civilized again. Well, this plus a week or two for R&R gives me about 100 days left in the field give or take a week. Going to be the longest 100 days I have ever spent.

Well, the captain is coming down to eyeball our area. (We are still guarding the mud scoop.) So there has to be a great big police call and stuff. I guess I will be going because we have to clean up all around. There go those rounds again. You can hear the snap as they break the sound barrier right over your gourd....

Don't let Debi smack up the fenders too much. I would sure like to drive the MG when I get home. Well, I must di-di (Vietnamese for scram).

Love, Rog

At this time fate intervened and I was allowed R&R. I went to Bangkok, Thailand, and spent $600 in five days. It was one big party. I started the days drinking Bloody Marys and jumping out of the second-story window of the hotel into the swimming pool. There was a corpsman on R&R with us and he made sure everyone had any meds they wanted. I cranked up on my first experience with amphetamines. We were supposed to relax but the combat mindset of not giving a shit stayed with us. We stayed drunk and bought a new woman each night. I returned in worse shape than when I left and was thrown back into heavy combat right away. I didn't get a chance to write a letter until after I got hit.

Dong Ha

A 1/9 letter 129
No postmark May 1
Dear Mom and Dad,

Well, here I am back in the rear on my way to Bangkok for R&R. I had my choice of Singapore, Bangkok or Hawaii. I figured Bangkok, Thailand, is pretty close to Vietnam so I guess the plane won't take long. I am supposed to leave Dong Ha tomorrow for Da Nang. I hope to leave Da Nang the 2nd of May but I hear the flights are all jammed up so I may have to wait a few days. I talked to a guy about a half hour ago that is just coming back from Bangkok and he told me the do's and don'ts and the hotels, bars, etc.

Well, did you hear about the rocket attacks? I had a ringside seat for the one on Dong Ha. We were out guarding that dredge and we saw the rockets launched and we saw them hit. There were one hundred or more launches. You could see them traverse back and forth covering Dong Ha with explosions.

The rocket attacks were because of Tet 1967. The next year, Tet 1968, was the North Vietnamese invasion of the south. On my way back to Dong Ha for R&R we stopped the truck at the city of Hue for some reason. I saw some young Vietnamese men around military age but dressed in civilian clothes. I had my M-16 and the young men looked in my direction. I felt the heat of the liquid hate simmering in their eyes. The first time I felt this emotion was with the women at Kim Lin and that was so far in the past I could barely remember it. I felt that emotion several times from prisoners before we started killing them. I'm sure these guys were NVA troops, officers maybe, reconing the area. The hate just radiated from them and I became a mirror once again reflecting and magnifying the burning hate. I almost cut them down. We soon saddled up and went on to Dong Ha.

We also saw muzzle flashes of two VC rocket positions. It looked like Dong Ha was completely demolished. Destroyed. But we ended up not even getting hit bad at all. I have a rocket fragment I will send home along with some other souvenirs once I get to Da Nang or Thailand.

When they have articles of the missile attacks on Dong Ha in the papers and magazines, please save them for me. I will keep them and the fragment together someday — you know how I mean....

Well, I guess I had better sign off now. I will drop a card or three and a long letter — also film. A lot of film.

Well bye, Rog

Da Nang

A 1/9 letter 130
No postmark
May 3, 1967

Dear Mom and Dad,

Well, here I am at transit awaiting a flight to Bangkok. I have been to the PX and I bought a Nikon Nikormat Camera for $137.95 and it's on its way home. The PX in Da Nang is something else. It is like a department store. They have everything but binoculars. Boy, do they have it. They also have a U.S.O. next to it with a snack bar, pool table, etc. *Hamburgers.* Wow!!

When we get to Bangkok we can choose any hotel for $6.00 a night. This includes room, bath, air conditioner, TV, pool, room service, etc. They also give grunts from line outfits like 1/9 a carton of butts and a fifth of our choice. As you can imagine, there are girls over there — quite a few. I will be frank. They go to the doctor for a checkup every week and carry a shot card on their person. The first thing to do is get a "steady" and live with only one while you are there. This was told to us by a high-ranking officer at R&R briefing.

I have been living for the present. No past, no future. I don't give a damn about anything but me and my buddies' present. You can't give a damn, that would only complicate matters. I guess you are wondering, Good God, what has happened to your son? Don't worry, I'll be ok — completely normal when I reach the States. Maybe not completely, but at least semi-normal.

Well, I have to go — light is fading and all so I will close.

Love,
Rog

P.S. Will drop you a line or two from the mysterious Orient.

A 1/9 letter 131
May 10

May 8, 1967

Well, here I am back in old RVN. We really had a good time in Bangkok. I did a little shopping so you can expect a small package soon and a large one — 49 lbs.!! ...

Boy, R&R sold me on the Orient. I hope to live in the Orient for a couple of years once I get out of school. The people are so nice — everything is different. You can do anything you please and you don't feel pushed. When you say "thank you" you really mean it. You know the bored "thank yous" you receive in the States — could be "nuts to you!" ...

I do believe Bangkok is a modern architectural paradise. The buildings are modern, even the poorer sections of town. The styling of houses is beautiful, each and every one looks like a little hideaway. Every bar, restaurant, shop, store, hotel, every place you go has a doorman. The guy will do everything you want to please your every whim. You can go swimming, bowling, dancing, to a show, drag races, just about anything you can do back in the States. Also there is cock fighting, king cobras, temples, all kinds of stuff....

Well, I will tell you more in a day or so.

Love,

Rog

A 1/9 letter 132
May 12, 1967
Dear Mom and Dad,

Well, here I am still back at Da Nang. Seems as if it is really hard to get a hop to Dong Ha. Most of the incoming flights to Dong Ha are from Chu Lai or Phu Bai. Really not anxious to get back because 1/9 is out on an operation right now and I have no urge to get into the field. May be the platoon radio operator when I get back. Yep, the platoon commanders only link with air and ground support and all that rot. Usually they make a Corporal a radio operator but this time *maybe* a lowly P.F.C. will make it. This would mean no more squad-sized patrols, night ambushes, or listening posts. Makes life less exciting but a lot safer. Of course, our looy goes where the action is and I go right behind him wherever he goes. This is just a maybe. I will send you a note on how I make out. [...]

Our Mustang LT got a Dear John letter while in the field in late April 1967. He went stateside on emergency leave and patched it up with his wife. Two weeks after returning to combat the LT was with the point fire team and we got into a well-camouflaged NVA bunker complex. I was right on his tail as I was fire team leader. The NVA waited until they had a 25-yard shot and they opened up on us with an automatic weapon. The LT caught a round under his arm into his chest and went down. I hit the deck and dragged him behind a tree while firing back at the bunker. LT called out for his wife. Doc Terry Rudolph was there and he looked at me and shook his head. After a few moments LT became quiet, pale and translucent and just faded away softly, calling out for his wife. Damn, damn, damn, I put a grenade on the bunker and Doc Rudolph, and our platoon sergeant, Sgt. Kent, and I pulled him back and carried him to the company CP. LT wouldn't order any of his men to do something he wouldn't do himself, so he took the lead and that got him killed.

Sgt. Kent took over the platoon and he was killed the next day. Sgt. Kent ran out from behind a tank to attempt to drag two wounded Marines to safety and an NVA machine gun got them all. The men Sgt. Kent were trying to save were buddies. One had been wounded before and they both had only two weeks left in their tours. I was medevaced out with their bodies a day later. Damn, damn, damn.

I have some pretty nice stuff on the way home, people. Take care of it for me until I get there. I have several of one thing and I hope to start a collection pretty soon. With what I have it is a fair start. Not good but fair. I plan on staining some of the wood and maybe cutting it over a little to make it more distinct.

Haven't had any mail for 10 days now. I am looking forward to getting back and finding what the postmaster has for me.

How did the rolls of film turn out that I sent home in that package? That hat I sent home was a dead gooks. See the shrapnel holes in the side? I am going to see if I can pick up some camouflage utilities for squirrel hunting. Old bush tails ought to just be coming into season when I get home.

Boy, I came back from Bangkok in worse shape than when I left. High living and no sleep — boy, I am really glad to be getting these days of slack back here in the rear before I go out in the field again. If I ever had the chance to go back to Bangkok I would go again. I know now the places to go and the people to meet. The next time it would be more of a "tourist" R&R. I didn't go to all the places I would have liked to because of the limited time. Believe me, it went by just like a dream. I did have a very, very good time though and I guess that's what matters. It wouldn't seem right to me if I was a civilian but since I am in the Corps and I have been facing death and destruction so long it was really the only way I could relax.

When I get home we will sit, mix up a batch of gin and tonics and talk about what I have missed, not my experiences.

Gosh, my stomach is still all mixed up. I can feel fine one minute and the next cramps and nausea and yech!! Well, it should straighten itself out with a couple of days of c-rat meals in it.

The PX wasn't open today — I was going to get a carton of smokes and a case of peaches (canned) to take out in the field for the guys. Oh well, sorry about that. When I go to Dong Ha I would like to take *something* back with me.

Well, I have to finish this up. Chow is going. Well, be seeing you in 4 months.

Love,
Rog

No one wanted to go back to Phu An, but we attacked that place for the second time in the middle of May 1967, just after I got back from R&R. The NVA had rebuilt the defenses and were waiting for us. My platoon and my squad were point-attacking the NVA bunker complex. We were not allowed any supporting arms other than a platoon of six Marine tanks. The NVA were set up in a gigantic X so that any Marines inside the X would be in crossfire. The bunkers had tunnels connecting them with strong points of heavy machine guns and RPG positions.

We had to sacrifice Marines to find the well-camouflaged bunkers. Most of the fighting was grenade range, 25–35 yards. The first day my platoon commander was shot three feet in front of me. I pulled him behind a tree but he was gone in a couple of minutes. I was heartsick, as he was a good man. In four days we attacked three times. We lost our second in command, Platoon Sgt. Kent, in the next attack and then we lost all of our squad leaders. After three days our platoon was down to one under-strength squad. At the end of the battle there were two Marines in my platoon that were not wounded. The rest of our men were 14 KIA and 29 WIA.

We had to load all our wounded up on tanks to get them out of the kill zone crossfire. I was covered with blood from three days of fighting and humping the wounded up on those tanks. One day the dead on the tanks started to cook in the sun and the NVA were shouting and laughing from their bunkers and shooting the dead Marines into pieces. Trees were flying through the air and the ground was hot.

We got up on line with tanks for a fourth frontal assault on the bunkers. I was carrying an M-79 with 36 rounds. We tried to hide behind the tanks while the NVA were hitting them with RPGs. I remember shooting NVA that were crawling up on the tanks with burning satchel charges. The tanks outdistanced us and rolled across the bunkers, and the bunkers opened up on us. Everyone hit the deck and a machine gun 30 yards away stitched our squad. I was shot through my left hip and the guys on either side of me were hit also. The guy on my right was killed and I dragged his body around and used it for cover. To this day I don't remember his name. I was lying on about 30 rounds of M-79 grenades like a hen with her eggs and I was waiting for a bullet to strike them and blow me in half. Two of my fire team were down, hit about 15 feet in front of me and calling out my name for help. My left side and leg didn't work. We were pinned down with rounds snapping and popping off leaves right over our heads. Anyone who rose up to shoot was shot. I was too close to the bunkers to use the M-79. It turned into a hand grenade duel then. I remember the NVA Chi Com grenades flipping end over end in arcs towards us. I threw all the grenades I had and I got hit with shrapnel from an NVA grenade. I pulled a hot chunk of shrapnel out of the guy on my left's back. After some time I received friendly fire shrapnel from another M-79 gunner trying to hit the bunker and get us out of the crossfire. We managed to withdraw after being pinned down tight for a couple of hours. The only thing that saved me was the fact I was lying behind a dead Marine in a tank trail and I was four inches lower than most of the guys that were killed. I was being dragged out and I looked to my right and saw our corpsman, Doc Terry Rudolph, working on the wounded he had staged in a ditch about 70 yards back from where we had been pinned. Rudolph was covered with blood and he was cutting and tearing strips of cloth from the utilities of dead Marines and using those strips of cloth to bind up the wounds on those of us still alive. The only medical supplies he had left after four days were his scissors.

I had a big hole in me and Doc Rudolph looked at my wound, stuffed a sock in it and got two other lightly wounded Marines to drag me back to where the majority of the wounded were being staged. Another corpsman looked at my wound and then he went over to a couple of wounded Marines who just crawled out of a tree line. As that doc was working on those wounded a tank loaded with dead Marines backed out of the tree line and ran over them and crushed them. Right in front of me, and I couldn't do anything. The tank was streaked with blood and guts and I think I emptied my pistol into that tank. I passed out then because the next thing I remember I was being dragged aboard a large Chinook helicopter. The Chinook had two motors and had space in the center with two rows of fold-down seats on either side. There was a bloody pile of dead Marines in the center with about seven or eight wounded on either side. The door gunners were hammering away with 50-caliber machine guns on either side and we took fire pulling out. The pile of bodies was three feet deep and I knew most of them. Some had been out in the sun for two days. The guy across from me took a round in the chest while we were pulling out and we covered up the hole with a cigarette pack so his lung wouldn't collapse. The blood in the chopper was half way up my legs and we were all sliding around in it. The blood was sloshing around and covering everything. The dead were sliding around in the blood and the guts and I was completely covered with blood.

At Dong Ha medical station they had to cut my blood-soaked clothes and boots off to see where I was wounded. My fingers were stuck together and I couldn't untie my boots. I was fucked up big time. I still dream of that charnel house of a helicopter ride. Blood everywhere.

The doctors, who had been working for four straight days and nights, were cleaning out my wounds and they nicked an artery. I had blood spurting over my shoulder from their mistake. They put a compress on it and I woke up on a stretcher lying in a pool of my own blood. One guy said, "He's still alive," and I was taken back into the OR where they stopped the bleeding, and then I was shipped off to a hospital at Clark Air Force Base in the Philippines.

My last memory of Vietnam was lying in a pool of my own blood on a stretcher in a dark hallway. I knew I had survived and that I was fucked up but I knew I was out of the hump and I was going home to the World.

A 1/9 letter 133
No postmark
American Red Cross
May 18

Dear Mom and Dad,

I was a lucky man. The very first thing I asked the Red Cross for when I awoke from surgery was paper, pen, and an envelope.

Well, here I am back at Da Nang. I am *OK*. Don't worry. I tried to stop the telegram saying I was W.I.A. but there was no way I could do it. They just don't let you stop it at all.

After I was hit I got medevaced to Dong Ha, from there to Phu Bai, then to Da Nang and I now am going to Clark Air Force Base in the Philippines for recovery.

If it all works out I won't be in the field again. I will do anything to keep out of the field — anything. I was shot with a machine gun in the left hip. The bullet went through and came out my buttock. It felt like someone hit me with a sledgehammer. It got numb pretty fast so I wasn't in a whole lot of pain. I got hit a second time by grenade fragments an hour later and a third time by friendly fire from an M-79 trying to take out the bunker that had us pinned down.

There are two guys left in my platoon. We went in with about sixty. Lost our looy, our Plt sergeant, all the squad leaders, 13 KIA, 42 WIA. I was lucky to make it out. Things were getting pretty hairy there.

It all happened at Phu An, a small fortified hamlet in the DMZ. The NVAs were so well camouflaged and dug in even the tanks we had rolled right over them. There was so much fire that the ground was hot.

I am in an air-conditioned ward in Da Nang right now. We are supposed to get out of here in about 4–5 hours to go to Clark.

Well, I have a Purple Heart now. I guess I will be proud to wear it when I come home. Should lay me up for at least four months. After that, light duty for another month and I will just about be on my way home.

I would like to know just what that telephone or telegram said.

I was lucky. Really lucky yesterday not to get hit bad. Since my wounds are not slight ones, it doesn't hurt much and I will be perfectly all right except for a few big scars.

Well, I will write a longer one when I get more time.

Don't worry.

Love, Rog

WESTERN UNION TELEGRAM: WASHINGTON DC MAY 24 1967
DR. AND MRS. R. E. JACOBS
7487 JULIA DR NORTH ROYALTON OHIO:

THIS LETTER IS TO CONFIRM THAT YOUR SON PRIVATE FIRST CLASS ROGER E. JACOBS USMC WAS INJURED ON 16 MAY IN THE VICINITY OF QUANG TRI REPUBLIC OF VIETNAM. HE SUSTAINED GUN SHOT WOUNDS TO THE LEFT LEG AND LEFT SIDE OF BACK FROM SNIPER FIRE WHILE ENGAGED IN ACTION AGAINST HOSTILE FORCES. HE IS

BEING TREATED AT THE THIRD MEDICAL BATTALION. HIS CONDITION AND PROGNOSIS WERE GOOD. YOUR ANXIETY IS REALIZED AND YOU ARE ASSURED THAT HE IS RECEIVING THE BEST OF CARE. HIS MAILING ADDRESSS REMAINS THE SAME

WALLACE M GREENE JR GENERAL USMC COMMANDANT OF THE MARINE CORPS

5

Japan: 106th General Hospital, Ward F-4, Yokohama: Letters 134 to 146

Introduction: May 1967–June 1967

In these letters from May to June I describe my convalescence at 106th General Hospital, Yokohama, Japan. I was medevaced from Dong Ha, Vietnam, to Clark Air Force Base in the Philippines first, and then to Japan. The 106th is an Army hospital and I was there because all the naval hospitals were full as a result of increasing casualties coming from the war.

I arrived in good spirits; I was out of that motherfucker. Against all odds I survived, I was out, I was safe, I was finished with the hump.

My new surroundings were wonderful. I had a clean bed, I had all the water I wanted to drink, I had hot chow, I had clean clothes, and I had time that was mine and mine alone. Gone were the patrols, the ambushes, the hole watches, the mortar attacks, and the listening posts. I wasn't walking point and there were no mines and booby traps. I was no longer the hunted and no longer the hunter. I could sleep as long as I wanted but I found no matter how many meds I took I could only sleep two hours at a time. All in all it was heaven for a grunt like me, and there were round-eyed women in the form of Army nurses and Red Cross "Doughnut Dollys" asking me if I needed anything.

At first I couldn't get out of bed. After a time I graduated to a wheelchair, then to crutches and finally a cane.

The other wounded guys were in worse shape. There were young men without arms and legs, without genitals, without faces, with tubes draining out of them and without hope. My wounds were serious but I lucked out— no bones or organs were hit. Another quarter inch and I would have lost the ball-and-socket joint in my hip. I went into the burn unit by mistake and saw men whose faces and fingers were melted and I thanked whatever God there was for my wound.

The pain was constant and I was receiving Demerol around the clock. This was my first exposure to narcotics and the feeling was somewhat like the aftermath of a combat high. I felt a sense of invincibility, well-being, peace, and a general sense of calm. I liked it, and hard drugs would continue to haunt me for the rest of my life.

I didn't know if they would send me back. I had another three months to do, and if they sent me back I was sure I would be killed. The last months before Phu An I had lost all hope of surviving. The thought of returning to the meat grinder of war just ate me up. The thought of returning to war is still in me after all these years and it still eats me up.

Japan

106 General Hospital letter 134
Yokohama
May 22, 1967

Well, here I am at Japan. I talked to the doctor today and he said I might not be back in the field. Most likely not. I am coming along pretty good, getting a shot every eight hours. My tail is getting more sore from the shots than from the gook bullet.

Well, our radio man was hit with the same gun I was. They dug a .51 cal. slug out of his hip. It was a heavy machine gun.

They (here at the hospital) think I am coming along pretty fair.

Well, I have been to the Philippines and then here to Japan. Yokohama to be exact. I guess they are going to work on me a bit. They want to slice it open from entrance to exit hole, leave it open, clean it out, and then sew it up. If they do that it shouldn't take too long to heal up. The doctor said that I could write you and say my tour of duty was almost up. They *might* send me home.

If I could get convalescent leave it would be great because that isn't counted on your regular leave. They said they might send me back to the States. You know from my letters as well as I that the Marines could send me right back into the field, never can tell.

My wound is just kind of a dull ache right now. They have been giving me Darvon pretty regularly and I don't feel much.

I guess you can read from the papers we all caught hell because of Ho Chi Minh's birthday. In the DMZ it was pure hell, dissolute hell. That's all I will say about it.

The hospital is very nice. It has air-conditioning, single racks. They have our ward walled off into four bed cubicles. The chow is good. There are guys always ready to do things for you. Pretty nice.

Of course, I am among the chosen. I can't walk or anything yet. The guys who can walk are usually helping do all kinds of stuff. Tomorrow I guess they will cut me up. They removed the drain today. That kind of smarted.

Well, I will try to get any word I can out of the doctor about going home. I don't think he was too confident, so don't count on it. It could be a chance though...

Well, got to run. Chow is on the way — also shots!!

Love,

Rog

106th General Hospital letter 135
Yokohama
May 23, 1967

Dear Mom and Dad,

Well, I have been here a few days now and I am feeling a little better. They have me scheduled for surgery Wednesday. Just going to sew me up — clean out the wound. They normally use a spinal from what I have been told.

Well, they are changing the dressings about every four hours. The doctor wants it kept wet and moist so he can sew it up. They call surgery "Where going to get some of your blood." This place is a nut house. Most of the corpsmen should be in a psychopathic ward. One guy laughs a high-pitched giggle when he plunges the needle in.

It is an Army hospital and they say they are going to use leather for stitching up Marines instead of stainless steel. If they shave the hair off your legs or arms so the tape won't pull, they use a scalpel rather than a razor. Just to practice. We also have Army nurses. Ugly captains and majors but every now and then a pretty Lt. gives me a shot. Really not much to tell, pretty boring laying here. I am going to get a couple of model car outfits or a paint-by-number set to pass the time.

Putting together model cars was surreal after the hump. I had a difficult time believing that I was safe. My hands would shake. The pain meds took the edge off the pain and they dumbed me down enough to get some sleep. The world of the hospital was a complete contrast to the World of Hurt that is a grunt's life. I stole a table knife from my food tray and kept it under my pillow.

The Red Cross woman came along and took orders for the PX. They pick up things that you order. Pretty nice. We also have a library. Going to read up on a little photography. Left my camera at the company office before Phu An with my name tag on it. I will try and have it shipped to me.

Well, did you get the Nikormat and how do you like it? Could have bought a Nikon "F" but I figured I had better wait — see how I develop in the wide world of photography. Get my packages from Bangkok yet? I am busting to know how you like the large one, Dad. I plan on using the items to decorate a future home. I also mailed a third package right after I got back containing film and a couple of gook items. I was wearing that M-14 magazine when I was down at Da Nang.—Remember Kim Lin? Been in my seabag since.

I don't know what I am going to do about my gear. I guess I will have it shipped home. I wish I knew for sure if I am going home.

If and when, maybe 6 weeks or two months. Maybe next week, who knows?

I hope if I come home I can get convalescent leave at home. Should give me some more time to stay there. They only give you twenty days' leave now when you return from Vietnam.

I am supposed to get my Purple Heart from some high-ranking officer pretty soon. I will wear it home. I guess I will be proud of it. I rate three of them. Two for small shrapnel wounds I said nothing about before. If I had all three I would be coming home for sure, not just hoping. I guess I got shot in the most uncomfortable place I know. I can't sit, can't lay on my back, and I can't walk too well. When I lay on my stomach my back hurts. Boy, am I in a bind. Didn't take a sleeping pill last night. Had a hard time sleeping but I want to try to stay off the "pill."

Some of the guys here are a lot worse than me   some are minor—I guess I am in the middle range. I get a shot every twelve hours now. Penicillin. My tail is getting sore, better than every three hours.

Three guys from my squad are here in the ward (F-3). We usually get together and shoot the breeze although it has to be at my rack. (Can't get out for long because of pain.)

[...]

Well, I will finish this one up for now. Sorry if it's hard to read. I am laying on my side and I am all cramped up.

Well, bye for now—will write again soon.

Love,
Rog

P.S. Notify my friends of change of address. I would like some mail.

106th General Hospital letter 136
Yokohama
May 24, 1967
Part I
Dear Mom, Dad, Sis

Well, how's the family? Still no word on if I am going back to Vietnam or coming home. Any way you look at it, it will probably be a month or two.

Still haven't sewed me up! I don't know when they are going to get around to it. Of course, they are swamped down in surgery because of all the Marines coming in from the DMZ area. I guess I can wait. Sure would like to get sewed up and on the way to recovery though. I can even sit down now. I hobble almost pigeon-toed and all bent over limping to the john and stuff. When I get there it is a different story. I have to hang onto a trapeze over the seat. Quite awkward let me tell you.

Still getting good Army chow in bed. I can order what I want now from a sheet of paper. They have the menu and choices. Not really much to choose from but it is OK. Can't wait for some good home cooking. Steak, salad, and french fries. Stuff like that.

If I do come home I will go to a military hospital closest around Cleveland and acquire convalescent leave from there.

I would be in and out of Great Lakes Naval Hospital in Chicago for 11 months. I had three 30-day convalescent leaves in a row. After 90 days at home I was a civilian, not a Marine.

In today's Marine Corps they have a Wounded Warrior Barracks. I visited one at Camp Lejeune a couple of years ago. The WWB keeps recovering wounded in three platoons. The first platoon is ambulatory Marines still on pain meds and under doctors' care. The second platoon is Marines who are recovering and going back into duty. The third platoon is Marines who still need medical care and are being discharged because of wounds. All Marines in the WWB have their own room, computer station, and bathroom. All these comforts are paid for by private donations, mainly from retired officers. The Marine Corps figured, and rightly so, that keeping these wounded warriors in the company of other wounded warriors was a good move. All these Marines have a similar combat experience, and staying together in support of each other is just what the Marine Corps is about. Semper Fi.

If I could sit down I would get in a wheelchair and go sit out in the sun a while because the weather is beautiful. Smells and feels like Spring back home. I haven't felt those sensations for almost a year. God, almost too good to be true. I guess they thought I was depleting the world's supply of penicillin because I missed shots last night and this morning. Not complaining. Maybe they are just giving my sore tail a rest.

Did you get my packages? They are awful important to me. I lost the insurance stubs I had with me and I lost all of my stuff the 16th of May when I got hit.

In this hospital I was counting my lucky stars. I was there in this place of healing instead of lying wrapped up in a bloody poncho somewhere. I'm alive, I'm alive, I'm alive.

They have been changing my dressing pretty regularly every four hours. Right now I have a piece of gauze stuck up the large exit hole and it has dried and stuck to the wound. Going to smart when they yank it out!!! They know what they are doing though. Sometimes I wonder if it is good for me. I can hack it.

After my hump in Vietnam I can hack any hardship. I ignore discomfort. The only reason I stop to put a dressing on a cut is because I don't want to get blood on my work. Even today when it rains and everyone around me scurries for cover I stand outside and look up into the rain and laugh. When those around me are tired, cold, wet, and hungry, I make sure they are ok because I'm a warrior, and then I laugh. Most people don't know a damn thing. Grunts who make it on the hump know all about sacrifice and suffering.

We have a 19 year-old Red Cross girl that comes in and sits and talks to hardened killers like me. She is studying psychology and she wants everyone to bring their experiences and hidden stuff out into the open. Funny. She gets sick every time we start talking about firefights and stuff. We don't make fun of the poor girl or anything but it is a source of enjoyment on our part. She asks for it.

Some Full Bird Colonel is supposed to come by and give me my Purple Heart today. I was wondering when I was going to get it. I haven't even seen a Purple Heart medal up close. I guess I will wear it home whenever I get there.

Well, they want to rip out the old gauze and stuff some new gauze in so I will continue after the "blood-letting session" is over. If I still have the strength to write.

Part II

Well, it's over now and I am jammed with some more gauze. Guess what? It's infected — OK — Joy — Well it will just take some more time. Nothing to worry about. No deep abscess or gangrene. Should be cleaned up soon with the help of shots.

The docs opened my wound up, cleaned it out and dealt with the infection I contracted as a result of the nicked bleeder I received at Dong Ha.

I was in Japan for a little over a month, and during that time I slowly got better. I started to get around OK but I was afraid that if I recovered they would send me back. I cheated death so many times in combat I was sure it would catch up to me if I went back to Vietnam.

I just talked to a Red Cross volunteer and learned the condition of miniskirts. Wow. Makes me want to come home to the States even more. Does Debi wear them? I guess so. She is sweet sixteen. I remember when I was that age. Seems so long ago.

Well, I got to slide, Clyde, go Joe, and talk that "soul" talk. Chow's on the way. Finish after I eat.

Rog

Part III

Well, I have to finish for good now. So long and bye! ...

> Love,
> Rog

With a hole in his gluteus maximus

106th General Hospital letter 137
Yokohama
May 29, 1967
Part I

May 24, 1967

Dear Mom and Dad,

Well, they awarded me my Purple Heart today. Full Bird Colonel came around "In the name of the President of the United States," etc. They also took a picture of me getting it pinned on. I will try to get the picture but I am not promising anything.

I ended up giving my Purple Heart to a girl who ended up breaking my heart. She told me she needed more of me than I was willing to give. After that I stayed alone for many years. At the time I didn't want or need anyone. I was a grunt on the hump.

They are going to super clean my wound tomorrow and sew me up Monday morning. They will give me a spinal in both cases I hope!! The doctor came in today and stuck his finger all the way up to the knuckle in the exit hole. I almost climbed the wall behind my rack. Quite painful. Quite. I guessed I cussed a little because the nurse, a Captain, blushed and left. I patched up things with her later though.

I really would like to get sewed up so I can start recovering. You know, like walking around and stuff. My wound will pinch and be sore as hell for a while but at least I know I will get better and in time I will be doing squat jumps.(I shudder every time I think of it.)

Still no word on if I am coming home or not. I have a better than average chance. Keep pulling for me and I may just make it. If I have convalescent leave I will pull about twenty days and save the rest for Christmas.

When I get back to the States I will try to get into a field that offers some training. Maybe public relations like photography or something. Pretty hard to get into that but I have a good record. No rank, but a good record. I was up for Lance for the 9th time last month. May have made it but I don't know. Doesn't matter to me that much anyhow. I was holding down a

Corporal's job for the past three months. Fire team leader. Now everyone in my team is dead or in the hospital. Some will be going back to Nam for sure.

Boy, I don't know what I would feel like if I had to go back. For sure kind of rotten I guess. My surviving men (2) should be OK. With a lot of luck they should get home safe and sound.

I guess you read about Ann Thoug and Con Thien in the papers. I got hit at Phu An moving behind tanks during a frontal assault on dug-in NVAs. The tanks rolled over the NVA bunkers and the gooks just waited till the tanks were past them before opening up on us grunts. We killed 137 on the third day including a gook that was 6' 4" and quite a few over 6' tall. Built like Charles Atlas, too. Kind of made us think who in the hell are we fighting — Red China? They were Chinese we think, under wraps as of yet though.

Well, Operation "Hickory Nut" may have turned out to be my last. Here are all the rest:

Prairie I	Big Horn
Prairie II	Chinook II
Prairie III	Cheyenne
Prairie IV	North Carolina
Hastings I	Hickory Nut
Hastings II	Quang Tri (Liberation)

We lost men in all of them. We were in the DMZ in eight of them and every one we did humping that would make normal American young men shudder. I wish I knew how many patrols or ambushes I have gone on. How many times I sat in a hole at night with a cupped cigarette under my helmet.

I still wonder how many times I hunkered down in my hole. I still wonder how many times I set my grenades and my rifle on the edge of my hole and waited for death to appear. The strange part about all this was that I wanted death to come so I could light him up with my rifle and throw my grenades and blow my Claymores and kill the son of a bitch. Again and again and again. I never was so alive as when I fought and defeated death.

Part II

Well, there has been a 36-hour break in between the last sentence and now. They sewed me up finally. I am now closed. I have an IV tube in my arm and it makes it kind of hard to write. The only bad thing about surgery is no smoking because of the use of oxygen in the room.

I am on complete bed rest again. They have this tube in my arm so I can't go anywhere. Boy, does my rear hurt!!

Well, in a couple of days it ought to get better — can't get worse.

Well, I will sign off now.

Bye for now, write in a day or so.

Love,

Rog

106th General Hospital letter 138

Yokohama

May 31, 1967

Part I

Dear Mom and Dad,

Well, they yanked the IV out and I am on shots again. I was on IV for a couple of days and that needle was driving me nuts.

My wound is coming along nicely. It hasn't really hurt for the past few hours. It just burns now and then. Boy, is it tight! I have to keep one leg flexed so there is no tension at all on it in order to keep it from hurting. They have it sewn up with stainless steel wire and catgut, silk, I mean. Quite a network of stitches where the bullet went in and came out. Over a hundred stitches.

I just read the "Stars & Stripes" KIA list. A lot of guys who were good friends names were on it. Most of my friends from 1/3 including Stan Godwin and Machine Gun Okie were killed. I lost count of the guys who I was with every day, friends that talked about home, girls, parents, and stuff like that.

They are all dead now. You can't kill enough gooks to avenge their deaths. Isn't much compared to the suffering those guys' families are going through. Damn, it is not worth it!

My buddy Machine Gun Okie was killed in action at Quang Tri in May 1967. Okie sacrificed his life by willingly, single-handedly manning his machine gun to allow several wounded Marines to escape a devastating ambush. He was wounded himself, but he kept on firing his M-60 and sent his gun team back to safety one by one until he was alone. He got flanked and the NVA killed him with grenades. Machine Gun Okie was posthumously awarded the Navy Cross. Okie was a stand-up Marine and I was proud to call him my friend. Semper Fi.

I guess I didn't mean that really, but our forefathers died. Now we die. And our sons are going to die. Makes me so mad to think of a people too ignorant to rule themselves causing all this. If we do anything we ought to either move out or take complete control until the time comes when the people can govern themselves.

North Vietnam is never going to stop lying and infiltrating into the south — Solution — Destroy every living thing including women and children north of the DMZ — Everything.

Do you know what they do to VC prisoners? They put them through a rehabilitation course and then set them free to join the VC again. — Most of them do and they take the weapons we gave them. We Marines have stopped taking prisoners. It just means something extra to guard and that takes men which we need in the front. The VC have learned not to surrender to us because we simply destroy them. Makes no difference if a man has a submachine gun blazing away at ya when you zap him or has his hands up and yelling, "Chi Hoi," the open arms program for VC defectors.

I have lost friends to "Chi Hoi." Sure their arms are up in the air — a grenade. Boom! One dead loyal gook along with a couple of hometown boys. No good. Hands up? Good, means he can't shoot back — He may not be faking — Gook-lovers don't last long over here.

Well, I had better get off that subject before my pen burns through the paper.

Chow just arrived so I will postpone until after chow.

Hate and rage controlled my heart. War had a hot grip on my soul. I had developed a bottomless reservoir of heartless rage. That rage was a shield for my heart in a war of savagery. Letting go of the rage and lowering the shield was the hardest thing I have ever done. I had to start all over and learn how to care about things. My shield still comes up at times. I find now that being of service to others allows me to heal myself. I hope this book will allow readers to find some way to help those on the hump lower their shields and learn how to care for themselves and others.

Part II

Hey, I just got *mail*! First I have received. I don't know what to say. I had hoped that you would get my letter first. Well, I'm glad you did. Great about Debi making cheerleader. I hope all the gears in the (horse) Mustang stay in one piece! I know females and stick trannys. Sometimes they don't mix. Of course, there are a few females who do handsprings in front of a football crowd. If she has much trouble learning to drive a stick she will be getting pretty bad. Well, I am sure everything will turn out fine....

I read that article in *The Recorder* and phew! Didn't really want it printed but it's ok. Maybe people will want to know more or maybe they do know more about the war now. The war needs knowing about. True, it doesn't affect that many people personally. Not everyone, but quite a few, have sons and husbands and want to know what they are fighting for.

I received a card from Kay and Grant and will write them a letter as soon as I finish this one. Amazing how many friends you get all of a sudden. I guess people are like that though — human nature....

Well, I will sign off. I have to figure out a way of making my bed without getting out of it. ??? I don't know either.

Love, Rog

106th General Hospital letter 139
Yokohama
Memorial Day 1967
Part I

Dear Mom and Dad,

Well, here I am again. Really not much to write about. One thing when I got hit I lost my wallet that has my driver's license in it along with all my cards. My license isn't due to be renewed until my 21st or 22nd birthday but I'd still like to know what can be done about it while I am over here if anything....

I bought a Sony AM–FM solid state radio for $35.00 portable. Get real decent sounds from it. I am now catching up on all the songs and keeping up with world affairs and the war. It really keeps me going because it gives me something to do because I can't get out of bed....

Memorial Day today. So many guys are gone. Well, it isn't me so no use worrying about it — honor them in memory.

Excuse me please — chow — and I am hungry.

Love, Rog

In doing research for this book I found that my buddy Stan Godwin was buried on Memorial Day 1967 in Silver Hill Cemetery in Frostproof, Florida. He never did get to see snow.

"Remember Me" is for Stan and all the rest. I remember them.

> *Remember me is the fire that I light,*
> *Remember me hold me close against the night.*
> *Remember me the flame of memory,*
> *when I am gone remember me.*
>
> *Remember me the fallen say*
> *Remember me night and day.*
> *Remember me in your memory,*
> *on the hump remember me.*
>
> *Remember me as not died in vain.*
> *Remember me to ease the pain.*
> *Remember me keep your memory*
> *Strong and true remember me.*

Remember me as you grow old.
Remember me in story told.
Remember me deep in memory,
forever young remember me.

Remember me you know I cannot stay,
you light the fire I move away.
Remember me, search your memory.
Warmth and love remember me.

Remember me as a bridge between two worlds,
remember me when our flags are furled.
Remember me, the light of memory,
burn bright into the night, remember me.

Part II

Chow was pretty good — roast pork. Can't wait to taste real home cooking. Going to be great after so long.

Well, a pop music program should be coming on. Some of the new songs are pretty good. We have the nurse on duty wake us up at 3:00 in the morning so we can listen to the oldies but goodies. We can sleep in the daytime so we lose no sleep. As a matter of fact, that's what we mostly do — sleep.

I know I have some packages back at 1/9. I hope they send them on to me. Sure would like to dig into a package from home.

Well, I could ramble on but then there wouldn't be anything to say in my next letter.

Bye.

Love,
Rog

106th General Hospital letter 140
Yokohama
June 2, 1967

Dear Mom and Dad,

Hey! Two letters today. One of them was only dated three days ago.

I am going to start monkeying around with snakes. I had two separate times that I was almost bitten, once by a bamboo viper and one by a fer-de-lance. Anyway, I chopped the viper's head off with a machete and shot the fer-de-lance with a .45.

The corpsmen called the fer-de-lance the "two step" because two steps is all you get after being bitten. My fer-de-lance came at me in the moonlight when I was on a listening post on the second night of the battle at Phu An. I was sitting in a position in a thick tree line in the dark with another Marine. The snake slithered down a tree and stopped two feet from my head. The moon was full and I could see that the snake was a six-foot "two step." The other Marine and I were sitting back to back with only a radio, grenades and pistols. Every 15 minutes we would key the radio three times to let headquarters know the NVA were not massing for an attack. We had to be completely quiet and hidden because of the enemy that was probing our lines. The other Marine didn't know the snake was there, and we could not talk or make a sound. After a time I finally fired my .45 from about a foot away at the snake's head and we jumped up and ran 75 yards in the open back to our lines. We had to run in front of a dug-in tank that was loaded with canister rounds. We called "LP coming in" so the tank did not open up on us. I ran into the tank in the dark and knocked myself out for a few minutes. We were then told to go back out and I said no. I didn't care what they would do to me. We stayed in the perimeter the rest of the night. In the morning we attacked.

Those articles you received I was using that M-14 magazine for a support for my rifle as I held in and banged them off. It was in my cartridge belt. That automatic rifle magazine is from a Red Chinese assault AK-47 rifle. It holds thirty rounds and I just so happened to plug the owner of it. That was the one that was in his rifle. Same number of rounds also. It was during the fight at Kim Lin.

They started me on crutches today. Boy, do my legs smart. The muscles have sharp pains shooting down the back of my legs. I haven't walked since the day I got hit on the 16th. Boy, I was surprised to find I was so weak. I guess I lost a little weight too. I'll work a little each day and find some extra stuff to do. Maybe in a week or so I will be off crutches and on a cane.

Boy, my stitches itch! I don't fool with them because if I do it would probably go all screwy again and the doctor would find some excuse to stick a drain in it. The stitches catch on my clothes. I have wire and silk all crossed and stuff. I have a sneaking suspicion that it isn't going to be pleasant when he takes the stitches out. Ouch!!

Well, I have it pretty good now. Take my nap in the afternoon and I am set to face the rest of the day. The high point of the day is mail call, chow, and the different music hours of rock 'n' roll 3:30–4:00 and 8:00–9:00. All the rest is big band, classical. Some is pretty but hillbilly I can't stand.

I am going to have a little get-together when I get home. Sort of a beer bash. We are also going to get together and sit up at the Red Eye until closing time like we did before (maybe a couple of times). I also will ride a motorcycle. I have had the itch for almost a year and I haven't even seen one.

Well, just finished noon chow. We had hamburgers, fries, and stewed tomatoes.

One more shot to go! Tonight's my last shot and I will have no more from now on.— They wore out my tail and have been giving me the shots in my thigh. No more shots! Just piles of pills. I should be learning my destination pretty soon. I sure hope it's back to the good old USA. Can't ever tell though.

I guess I will go to the movies tonight. I heard the last one they had was really good. Had Woody Allen in it and I guess he made everyone laugh so hard they almost broke their stitches.

I heard my doctor has two weeks left in the Army. He hates it and is sending guys home with a lot less time under their belts than I. Good news I hope. Still have my fingers crossed.

Boy, they have a cute nurse! She was just talking to us. Real nice and easy to converse to. They also have a couple of bulldogs. The bulldogs slap your fanny before smacking the needle in. The good-looking one kind of caresses it. Ahhh! Doesn't even hurt. Woman's touch, ya know. Makes me wish I was home even more than I do regularly.

I hope to go outside pretty soon. If I can go to the movie tonight I will go out and get some sun tomorrow. My tan has somewhat paled. Darned shame. I looked like an Indian. Of course if I put on a pair of shorts it would look quite odd. White legs with sores and leech bites and other assorted scars all over them and tanned arms and face. Actually, my face wasn't that tan. A helmet doesn't let too much sunshine through and if it does you had better watch it.

Well, time is flying by and time for exercises (again).

I must close. Will write again soon.

Love,
Rog

106th General Hospital letter 141
Yokohama
June 5, 1967

Part 1

Sunday, June 4, 1967

Dear Mom and Dad,

Well, hi folks. Wanted to drop you a line to tell you I'm doing fine. Still on crutches for walks of over fifty meters or more.

Pretty soon they will have me going to the mess hall for my meals. Should strengthen my legs. I am also on the list for air evac. I don't know where I may be going as of yet but I am pretty sure I should be out of here in a month. If they did send me back to Vietnam I would be in the rear quite a while before I could go into the woods again. I am not worried. I spent 10 months in that hell-hole. I doubt if they will send me back — I hope that is. Well, chow is here now so I will go. I have to eat — looks good — fried chicken.

Bye for now,
Rog

Part II

Well, that was pretty good. The only thing wrong is the milk. They have stuff they call reconstituted milk. Not unlike powdered milk back in the States. Kind of sweet. Yeech! Well, I got a letter from Steve Phillips yesterday. Also from Gram and Grandpa and Aunt Mary. I answered all. I hope I get some more mail tomorrow. So far I haven't missed a mail call. Sure keeps a guy's morale up....

I can't wait to climb into the car and drive! More than a year since I have driven but I assure you I haven't forgotten how. I sure would like to take a ride on a bike also. Maybe I can manage it with some of my motorcycle friends.

I have 47 stitches in my hip. Counted them yesterday. Feels like it every once in a while, too. I have P.T. tomorrow. They tie weights on my legs and I do all kinds of exercises. Some are quite difficult. I can't touch my toes at all. My hands get about two feet from the floor and that's all.

Boy, are we giving them hell in Vietnam now. First time I have heard the Marines mentioned so much. Our KIAs almost equal to the Army's every night. We are doing a good job. The enemy is finally fighting in full force. I don't know if we are forcing their hand or if they have orders to try and hold their ground instead of disappearing into the woods. My guess is that they will hit a big base like the Khe Sanh or Dong Ha soon before they are all cleared out of the DMZ. Last ditch fanatic effort to gain some kind of victory. Ho Chi threw those extra men in so this is what can be expected.

Well, getting late and I am tired. Not much of a letter yet. Will finish tomorrow before mail call.

Love, Rog

Part III

Here I am back again. They changed my address again, darn it. It seems whenever I get somewhere and everyone finds out my address they put me somewhere else. Well, this ward is OK. Most of the people on it are ones with their arms damaged or something like that. That means they get around pretty good. I guess about all of them are either going to be here a long while or are awaiting transportation somewhere.

Today I am going to ask and find out where I am going — probably won't know any more than when I started.

Well, I just found out they won't know where I am going until they receive the orders on me. In other words until about a day before I leave. With that it should be a month at the most before I know what is going on.

Boy, my nerve endings must be repairing themselves. My side is really hurting. More like a burning than a dull, deep throb I had before. I have P.T. at 3:30 in the afternoon. Going to hurt! If I try hard I will bust a scab and it will start bleeding again. The doctor says it's not bad and nothing to get all bent out of shape about. Naturally. Got to admit it does kind of bother me when I feel blood trickling down my leg after P.T. or when I am sitting at the PX snack shop.

It's raining now and the sky looks sort of dull gray. Even light, perfect for taking pictures. Sure hope that supply sergeant sends me my camera and film. I know I had some packages back in the rear also. I staged them when I came from R&R because I went into the field the same day I got back and I couldn't hump them. In fact, I didn't even have time to read my letters. I did read them later on in the field. I stuffed them into my helmet to stay dry. During a 45-minute rain I collected a whole helmet full of rainwater and filled three canteens from rainwater caught in my poncho. You just put it on, spread your knees and form a pocket. Then take a c-rat can and scoop out the water and fill the canteens. It rained every day without fail. The heat would be a steam box so hot you could hardly breathe. You couldn't find any shade at all so you sat and the c-rat chewing gum in your mouth would crumble up because of the lack of moisture. Then maybe an hour later around 3:00 it would rain for almost an hour. Just enough to get your pack wet all through. It then would get cold and stiff and would stay wet all night — including your clothes.

Those jungle utilities are great. They will dry out twice as fast as regular. They are lighter also. I sweat some as you know, but never like I did in Vietnam. Every inch of my clothes would be wrung out. I'd get a canteen full of water out of my shirt alone. It looked like I just jumped out of a stream. My clothes would actually be running with water. Sweat would drip from my shirt. That's how we get the term salty or faded out utilities. It was possible to put on a brand new set and come off the field with a faded (salty) set a month later or sometimes two weeks without taking them off. Just let the rain or the streams wash them while you hump.

Boy, I had better hold off before I write a book or something. — What can I say? I am hoping I can come home. I have a pretty good chance of doing so. I have an equally good chance of going back. If I do go back I probably won't see combat again. I hope not. I will most likely do a job in the rear for a while until I come home — that is if, if, if, if — damn. It's tearing my guts up.

Bye, Love, Rog

Life is strange. Forty-five years after writing this letter, my letters and photos and memories would be combined to become this book.

106th General Hospital letter 142
Yokohama
June 10th, 1967

Part I

Dear Mom and Dad,

Well, here I am on my stomach again. My wound got infected but they are pretty sure they can catch it with penicillin and streptomycin.

I was in the chow line and I passed out. They had to move me back into bed rest.

I had the deep sutures get infected. The ones about two inches deep. They cut into my skin and sank down about ½ inch. They caused open cuts and that's what screwed me up. They are going to grab the stainless steel, pull up, snip the wire, then yank them out! Boy, when he goes digging I commence to yelling. I have been on Darvon for the past three days plus Demerol shots. I swear it hurts like nothing I have ever felt before. I can't walk at all. In fact, I can't even go moving around in bed without just about yelling. Boy, am I sore. The pain does make me shudder and seems to take every bit of strength from me. I have a small temperature also. Nothing to worry about — maybe a little more pain and time. [...]

We had one ugly nurse come into the ward and give out pain shots while we were asleep. That nurse would just stick the needle through our sheets into our thighs without warning. One of the Army guys was waiting for her and waited until she was poised to stick him. He grabbed her arm, took away the syringe, pulled her across his rack and stuck her buttock with the shot. She started yelling, the lights came on and by the time the orderlies arrived she was drunk with Demerol. Everybody was laughing and she was pissed. She woke us up and asked permission after that.

Well, I will finish tomorrow.

Bye, Rog

Part II

I have a hot water bottle on my wound. It has drawn some of the pain and soreness out but it still hurts. The swelling in my lymph gland in my abdomen has gone down considerably also. I guess the only real pain I have to go through is when he takes the stitches out. After that it should be over. Until that — ouch — I don't look forward to it. It is definitely going to make me yell again and they will not give me a local or anything. After yanking them out I maybe could get a shot of joy juice. I hope so. It cuts the pain.

Well, I just got through with P.T. Took the soreness right out. Made the wound drain and took some of the blood and junk out. That hot water bottle is bringing a lot of pus to the surface. All I do is wipe it off, pour some high-test sodium hydroxide on it and I am all set. It bubbles all the pus out and cleans it pretty good.

I feel better. In fact, I think I feel good enough to roll over and let him give me my shot in my rear instead of my thigh. My leg is kind of sore. I guess it bites a little more in the leg. I still am real sore. Boy, I can hardly touch it. I hope when he pulls the stitches out that he gives me something for the pain. He will most likely give me Demerol—100 cc's. After he gets done instead of before he takes the S.S. stitches out....

Well, I better sign off now. Chow should be coming along pretty soon. I am really getting back my appetite.

Love,
Rog

106th General Hospital letter 143
Yokohama
June 10, 1967
Friday, June 9th

Part I

Dear Mom and Dad,

Well, I feel better about fifty percent. They pulled the stitches out last night. I didn't yell at all. I had a towel stuffed in my mouth. God, did that smart. Wow. It was worse than when I got hit. Well, anyway, I am feeling better now by a long shot. I even got up and was walking around and it didn't hurt too much. Before, whenever I moved, those stainless steel stitches would sink or cut deeper into the soft flesh and it would send *pain*! through my entire left hip and abdomen and tail. Well, now all that has been cut down a few degrees....

No news yet of coming home. Seems a good chance as always. Will let you know the first chance I get pen and paper in my paws after I know who, when, where, and what....

Well, chow coming and I must go and eat to regain some of my lost weight (142 lbs.). I look like a tree....

Part II

Got some mail today. Four packages no less. I guess my mail from 1/9 is starting to catch up. I also got a couple of letters. Funny, we will never know how much mail is in the dead letter office or was lost or something. I remember the bottle of vodka Steve sent me was kind of special because it was once in a chopper shot down and then recovered.

The doctor poked and probed and dug some more "hard pus" out of my wound. Wow, that was not pleasant. Whenever he comes around I always end up on the short end of things....

Being in the hospital, and if I am sent home, I get another three months of combat pay. This is pretty good because it will keep my pay up around $170.00 per month....

Thank Debi for her letter. I will write one to her tomorrow. I have decided to buy myself a handgun when I get home. I want to plink with yours for a while before deciding if I should go small or large. A .357 or a .41 mag — sure sounds sweet. I had a .38 Red Star Hanoi officer's pistol, but I lost it when I was hit. I really hated losing it. It was a beauty.

Well, I have to go before I write enough pages of this letter to fill a big brown envelope.

Love,
Rog

106th General Hospital letter 144
Yokohama
June 12, 1967

Dear Mom, Dad, and Debi,

Part I

There is a — well, a lot more chance of me going to Vietnam than the States right now. They just took over a hundred guys out and sent them to the States. From what I hear they are sending guys to Vietnam hand-over-fist because they need the manpower over there. Especially the Marines. Damn, I wish my swollen lymph gland had been a hernia. Do you realize that if I stayed here another 20 days I would be coming home for sure? If you have 60 days or less to do they can't send you back. If I do go back I won't be out in the field until I have about 20–40 days left and then I would be getting awful short. I am afraid that I will be scared as hell. Right now I am a bundle of nerves. I wish to hell they would tell me one way or the other. If I have to go back I am going to go to the club and get DRUNK so bad they will have to carry me back to my rack in a stretcher. I know it won't prove anything at all and it will make me feel bad, but how many foolish things did you people do in your lives?

The uncertainty of my future was a holdover from combat. In the hospital I saw only danger ahead of me. People around me were not dying every day, but I felt that that was only temporary. I never thought I would live to be 21.

When I was 21 I thought I would never live to be 22. When I was 22 in the Virgin Islands I forgot how old I was for a good number of years. I never thought I would live to be the age I am now. A lot of combat veterans live their lives of uncertainty within a cycle of self-destructive behavior with no thought of the future. I used drugs and alcohol to change my perception of reality for many years. I didn't take care of myself well. On the hump after war I ignored my teeth and my appearance, and when I needed stitches I used duct tape. I have felt I have lived on borrowed time since Vietnam. I realize now that the borrowed time that I have been given has really been a rare and precious gift. It took me a long time to figure that out but I finally did. I'm a lucky man.

Well, how is it on the home front? Did Debi start driving stick? She ought to start on that since she is pretty coordinated. She had better not crinkle any fenders on the Buick before I get home. I'm going to be wanting the car for dates and things. I have been writing the guys and there have been a lot of promises made of some good times. I am glad because I have a lot of living to catch up on. There are quite a few things I have missed. Boy, do I want to come home....

If I go back I guess 1/9 will not be doing much because we lost so many guys last time we were out. I sure hope we don't go out, but I don't want to be sitting in Dong Ha getting mortared every night. Boy, there I go again. I am probably scaring the hell out of you. I am doing the same to myself.

I sure hope you get that large package from Bangkok soon. [...]

Part II

Sunday is about the dullest day of the week around here. Everything's closed and there is no mail call. I guess I will take a walk this evening and take in some more flicks.

I hate to go long distances because my armpits are getting sore as hell from the crutches.

Well, I have just about talked myself out for this letter. No word from my old outfit as of yet.

> Be seeing you soon (I hope),
> Keep pulling for me.
> Love, Rog

106th General Hospital letter 145
Yokohama
June 16, 1967

Part I

Dear Mom and Dad,

Well, here it is Tuesday the 13th. I still don't know where I'm going or when

I am supposed to go. I hope I find out soon because I am all tied up inside. Boy, I have been getting mail hand-over-fist. I have gotten letters and cards from people who haven't written me in months. At least it is a way of finding out what's going on back home.

I was living a nightmare about going back into combat. I had stuffed back any feelings of camaraderie or friendship with anyone for so long that I felt completely alone. The corpsman at Kim Lin, our platoon getting wiped out at Phu An, saving the child at Quang Tri, the screams of burning men on the DMZ, the mines on the Street Without Joy, and the constant months of fighting to survive had reduced me to an animal. I truly know the meaning of the word grunt and I truly know the hump. The one thing that I wanted was to be somewhere different than where I was.

I have to go down to the gym for P.T. again today at 3:30. It is right across from the PX. I will go down after mail call at 1:15 and sit around the snack bar and have a Coke or something. It does a guy good to get out of the ward and get some fresh air. Every night I go out on the porch (outside steps) and sit for about an hour by myself. It's really nice and the air smells kind of like back home and there is that Spring breeze that North Royalton has.

I got Debi's picture and the ones of the house and cars in my wallet now. They, as all the pictures you send me, are priceless. I only wish I had not lost my wallet when I got hit. (I bought a new one at the PX.)

Well, I am getting around pretty good now. My leg, more like my tail, is stiff. Seems like it is getting better day-by-day. I am off crutches now and I have a definite limp that will go away in time. Should take about two weeks for the limp to disappear and another two weeks or a month before I am OK for duty. But if I go back I will be in the rear so long that I will most likely get a job back there. Then I hope I will be short enough to maybe stay out of the field.

Gee, I wish I had heard something from the guys of my old platoon. I wrote the platoon, but I have received no word on how anyone is doing. Most likely what happened is someone opened it up and read it and then lost it or something before passing it around. Well, anyway, I just might get something from them in the form of my camera....

I took one roll of film already with the Nikon "F" and I have another roll in it to take. I will finish up these rolls and see if I can get them developed somewhere. If I can I will, but if I don't have enough time or something I will send them home.

With my cameras I was trying to engage my mind in something that would chase the thoughts of the hump of war away. I would find my salvation years later by finally realizing I was supposed to make things. Things like this book.

I guess I will go over to the Marine Corps Liaison Office today and get some boots and utilities. Maybe I won't because if they send me back to Vietnam they will see that I already have utilities and won't issue me jungle boots and jungle utilities. If I go back in hospital PJs they will have to issue me jungles. If I come home in PJs they will issue me a leave uniform most likely before I get to my next hospital. I can't go wrong by not getting them.

I could buy some civilian clothes and spend my evenings at the club getting stoned. If I received orders for the Nam ... that night I will be at the club — you can bet on it.

Most of the guys here at the hospital are Army. You ought to hear when we compare "notes." They have it made. They get *hot chow* out in the field. Helos bring it in for them. They don't hump half as much as we do. They don't carry as much as we do on their backs. They don't stay out as long as we do. They have a twelve-month tour — this includes putting a man out of the field on his eleventh month. They get liberty in towns, whereas we get nothing. They don't believe some of the stuff we have to do. They are amazed because of the way we live and the way we are treated. Makes their mouths drop open when I tell them how many months I have in grade.

I think they respect the Corps mostly because they think all jarheads are crazy. Well, we might be crazy, but if I don't get out of here soon I will be crazy.

Love, Rog

P.S. Excuse the sloppy writing of this letter

Part II

Chow was pretty good tonight. Hamburgers and french fries. Since I have a cane they have a Mama-san help me with my tray. I can really get along without the cane but with it my leg doesn't tire so quickly. I am doing P.T. daily for my leg and for my entire body. I am starting to gain back the weight I have lost. I weigh now around 150. I hope to put on about ten more pounds. Of course I will lose it if I have to go back to Vietnam. I guess I had better keep in shape. Don't want to be sucking wind when I start humping again.

I guess I'll go down and get my dressing changed. They want to keep a wet dressing on my wound so it will stay draining.

Well, I had better be going.

See you soon by chance. I hope.
But I am not very confident.
Love,
Rog

106th General Hospital letter 146
Yokohama
No postmark
June 16, 1967

Well, it's been one month since I got shot. I am getting around OK. I use a cane for anything that involves walking other than around the ward. The cane helps quite a bit.

Well, no word on where I am going yet. I will let you know as soon as I get the word. I guess I will call you on the telephone. I don't really want to do it because it's four dollars a minute and it really costs a lot of coin.

Boy, do I like eating in the mess hall better than getting a tray sent up to your ward. The mess hall offers a choice of salads, hot food, and coffee and it is pretty good. I ate in the club today. I had two BLTs and a large Italian village salad. So damn good I ordered another salad. Doesn't even compare to the ones at home though. I want to make a meal of a salad and maybe cheese and sausage pizza on the side when I get home. That is a must.

I have been going to the show every night for the past week and a half. That's how long they let me up and around. Well, they have some real decent flicks showing. A lot of them are recent, popular, and sexy. Whenever they show a flick at a military base you can count on the guys screaming and yelling suggestions when a certain part comes on. I feel sorry if there are any women in the audiences. I never had time for any shows and stuff back in the States. Now all I have is time and the shows really fill in and complete a day.

Can't sleep at night for some reason. Probably because I am a bundle of nerves. Sure wish I knew where, what, when, and how. Well, I guess I better go to chow before my stomach acids eat my body up. Bye for now and will continue later.

One morning I was told to get my shit together—I was getting shipped out. It wasn't until we got on the bus to the airport that they told us were going to the World. We were going back to the World! They gave everyone a knockout shot and loaded us in a transport plane on stretchers like bunk beds, only six high, and we were off. We went to Alaska first, and while we were refueling the guy across from me started coughing up blood. He turned translucent white and then he died. He almost made it home. The nurses were really torn up by his death. They covered him up with a blanket. Then we all went home.

6

USA, Afterword: 1969 to 2012

Introduction

I thought I was done with my hump when I survived Vietnam but I brought my hump home with me. I didn't know it, but a hump started in combat is never, ever over. Grunts carry the hump for the rest of their lives. Every year, every month, every day, every minute, and every second, the hump lives on and on. Many veterans take their own lives to end their hump. I damn near did. I'm a lucky man. I found a way to live with my hump.

The Hump

The hump separates the men from the boys
on the hump you have no toys.
The hump will make you love the dirt
the hump is a World of Hurt.

On the hump through sharp elephant grass,
on the hump through solid jungle mass.
On the hump vines pluck and pull
on the hump the World of Hurt is full.

On the hump down jungle tracks,
on the hump with loaded backs.
On the hump men fall and die,
on the hump you never see the sky.

I've been on the hump my whole life long.
My hump started with the Viet Cong.
Jobs, women, towns on the hump, I pass them by
on the hump I slowly die.

On the hump the pain blocks what is real,
on the hump I cannot feel.
The hump ate my life, I know that now,
I want off the hump but I don't know how.

I need off this hump to feel my soul
oh God the hump has taken its toll.
On the hump my life has been
oh God I need this hump to end.

May 1967–January 26, 2012
"will continue later"

So ends my last letter home from the war and the last overseas letter my father numbered and kept. In Vietnam I could not stop writing and break the connection to home. Writing these letters in every spare moment I had gave me the hope that I would survive and make it home. The small spark of hope I had grew into a reality and I made it. I was going home.

I arrived at Great Lakes Naval Hospital in Chicago on a Friday afternoon. I could hardly believe I was back in the U.S. I was told that I could go home on a 30-day convalescent leave starting the following Monday. I said, "OK" and thought, "Screw this." I picked up my cane and my seabag, went down to the lobby, caught a cab, and went over the hill straight to the airport. I got a flight to Cleveland, got in another cab and went another 20 miles to North Royalton. I had the cab drop me off up the street from my home.

Home was my safe place. Home was a canteen that never ran out of good sweet water. Home was a place in my head I could escape into and live with cherished memories. Home was a place where you were never in danger, a place where you were never hungry, thirsty, exhausted, scared, alone, full of rage, abandoned. The memory of home eased the World of Hurt that was the hump. Home was warmth and love in a sea of pain and home was the end of the hump. I was finally going home.

I limped the last 100 yards, breathing in the air of home and came upon our house in the woods. It was just like I pictured it all those nights sitting in my hole. No one was there so I went in a basement window that I used to go in when I was a little kid. I went through the house slowly. Everything was as I had imagined it, my room, my bed, and my books. My clothes were still in my closet and all the things that I had collected as a boy were there. My guns were still in my gun rack. I touched everything to make sure it was real. The kitchen, the living room, the basement, and the MG was still in the garage. All was as if I had been gone for only a few days instead of a lifetime. Home was just as I had remembered. I had made it, I had finally made it home. I was at the end of my hump. I went into the bathroom and looked at myself in the mirror and I saw a stranger, a skinny old man. The only thing that had changed was me. I heard the garage door open so I stepped out to see Mom and Debi driving in. The car screeched to a halt and we had a tearful reunion. Mom called Dad and he came home from work and my family was together and I was home! I don't remember what we had for supper, but what I do remember was taking my shotgun and .22 down, loading them and putting the shotgun between my mattress and box springs and the .22 behind the door.

I called Great Lakes on Monday and got a chewing out for going "over the hill." I was told to report back in 30 days. My first convalescent leave was a blur. I drove a car for the first time in a year and a half. My large package arrived from Bangkok with a heavy cast bronze Buddha statue among other things. I went out to a local nightspot to meet girls and dance and ended up backed into a corner drinking beer after beer. I used to like to go to this place and dance but I felt overwhelmed by the noise and all the people. They were all bunched up. I had a profound sense of impending danger. I had to get away and be by myself. I went outside into the parking lot and took up a position and stood guard. Someone had to stand sentinel.

I found I wasn't wearing my uniform like I had planned so very long ago and I couldn't relate to my childhood friends. They all seemed so young and innocent; they had no idea of the hump. I was carrying groceries for my Mom and a car backfired and I ended up on the deck under our station wagon with the groceries all over the parking lot.

I had two more 30-day convalescent leaves after my first one.

I was home but I had changed and things were different. Looking back now I can see that Mom and Dad were splitting up and within a year they would go their separate ways. My home would be gone.

I always had girlfriends before going to war but now I couldn't relate to any of them. I wouldn't let them get close to me, except that I met one young woman and fell in love and had my heart broken.

My buddies kept asking me about combat and when I started to tell them about it they recoiled and tried to change the subject. How do you explain what it feels like to kill someone with a bayonet?

I received orders to Quantico, Virginia, where I was assigned to a military police position. Still carrying a gun, still on the hump. Most of 1968 was a blur as I was doing every drug imaginable to try to get away from my hump. I was put on mess duty and I stayed in the kitchen and figured out how to change my MOS [military operational specialty] out of the grunts and into the cooks. I received two quick promotions and ended up becoming a corporal and head cook at the bachelor officers' quarters. The BOQ was situated off the main base and I had my own private room in the basement. I kept a motorcycle behind the building. I was the only cook with a Purple Heart. After a little less than a year my enlistment was up and I was honorably discharged from the United States Marine Corps in March 1969. My home was gone, my parents living states apart, I was out of the Marine Corps and I still had my hump.

I walked out of the main gate at Quantico and changed into civvies in the bushes. I left my uniform on the ground and hitchhiked to the airport in D.C. I got a ticket to the island of St. Croix and started a new life as "Crazy Jake." I bought a really fast motorcycle, got a cut-down shotgun and a 1911 Colt like the one I carried in Vietnam and lived on the beach for the next six years. I fathered two children at this time. I couldn't let the women get close to me and I moved on. Rum was cheap, pot was plentiful and there was very little law. I bathed in the ocean just like I bathed in the rivers in Vietnam. My hump led me to set up a fighting hole on an out-of-the-way beach for maybe two or three nights and then saddle up and move my hole to a new spot. I did this week after week, month after month, and year after year, and in the end I became feral. I got by fishing off the beach at night with hand lines, diving alone, and selling my catch at a native market. I risked my life by doing hard, dangerous jobs that few would do. I figured they couldn't kill me in Vietnam so I just didn't give a damn. My hump drove me hard. I was approached two times by people who wanted me to kill someone for them but I backed off because I could smell a set-up. All this time I was always by myself and I still lived out of a pack. I was always armed and my only possessions were those I could carry. I was fully on the hump. I really liked going fast on my motorcycle. If I scared myself hard enough it was almost like a post-combat languor.

I met some folks in a bar one night and got offered a job in the rock music business so I came stateside. I worked as a roadie and road manager for a couple of small-time bands, carrying the petty cash and a gun, scoring drugs for the bands and providing security. I spent two years sleeping in or under our stolen equipment truck. The band went hungry more than once and in Atlanta all that seven of us had to eat for two weeks was 20 lbs of potatoes and a half-gallon of oil. Fried taters two times a day like c-rats. We played roadhouses all over the South and ended up playing large concert halls in New Orleans and Atlanta. The road life wore thin. Some folks died because of the drugs and I got out. My hump continued.

I don't remember why, but I moved to Aspen and became a ski bum. Being a beach bum in St. Croix was easier because of the weather but skiing was fun. I worked summers as a ranch hand cleaning out and repairing irrigation ditches. Winters I skied. All this time I lived out of a '62 Chevy station wagon. I was essentially homeless, with no regular meals, sleeping on the ground, still on the hump.

I went back to the beach at St. Croix for a time and my father found me and convinced me to come stateside and check into a VA psych ward. While in the hospital I met a World War II vet who got me a job working in a custom van factory in Indiana.

I worked the production line at all the travel trailer, van, and motor home factories in northern Indiana for a couple of years, always changing jobs when I became bored. I was always alone and had a growing gun collection and I was still on the hump. I was living on the edge of civilization but I was not civilized.

I started shooting black powder muzzle-loaders in competition and was soon running the woods wearing buckskins and moccasins that I handmade from deer that I killed. I started to study and do research about American history. My area of interest centered around the time period 1754 to 1806, the French and Indian War to the Lewis and Clark expedition. All my clothes, weapons, and gear were carefully researched, handmade by me, and historically correct. My hump and I built a library of reference books. I found myself intellectually engaged for the first time since boot camp and my hump started to change. Others desired the historically correct objects that I had made to the point that they wanted to trade money for the things I made! What a revelation. I enjoyed making the objects and I was being financially rewarded for doing something I actually enjoyed. I found a Native American–based spiritual path and was given the name Lone Wolf in a ceremony, as I was truly a lone wolf. I was engaged on all levels, physically, intellectually and spiritually. This is the time when I started to realize I was a maker. I was asked to join a group called the American Mountain Men, and I spent a couple of years working on my membership requirements. I found myself writing a journal just like my letters home from the war. I was still on the hump but my hump was changing.

Hunting log entry November 28–29–30 1982 Penn mountains

Set up camp just in time for freezing rain. It started around 3.00 and continued all night.

4:00 A.M. up and cooked breakfast. I took my .50 cal flintlock, loaded her, wrapped up the lock and lit out. I heard deer in the darkness, saw nothing. About noon I struck a fire with my flint and steel and made coffee. Good fire after freezing rain and drizzle for 12 hours.

I moved into the swamp to still hunt in the afternoon. Big hemlocks, low area. Dips and holes, tough walking with mocks. I saw three does, had one twenty feet away. My danger sense started tingling like it did in the war. Saw him, the deer had a head full of horns and he was coming right at me slowly. I couldn't move or pull down on him. Finally he was fifty feet away and dipped his head behind a tree. I pulled down and touched her off. My rifle sparked and the charge started burning slowly, a long hangfire. The sound of the flint dropping into the lock alerted the buck and he looked right at me. My rifle fired and all I could think of was sight, sight, sight. The ball went through his chest, blew up his liver, and came out the rear leg. He went thirty yards and lay down.

I nearly shit trying to watch him and load at the same time. I finished loading and went to where I hit him and put my hat down and followed the blood. I jumped him up but his tail was down tight, the sign of a good hard hit. I ran him down and finished him with my war club. I made it quick; it was easier than the doe last year but dealing death is never easy.

After putting some tobacco down and giving thanks to the deer's spirit. I field dressed him and started back. The drag back to my camp was tough. Big deer and a swamp and then a big hill. Rubber legs when I got back. Ate the heart and tenderloin with potatoes and corn. I was probably the only flintlock hunter crazy enough to hunt in the freezing rain. Enough said, 8 point rack, about 110lbs dressed.

I will always treat the critters and their surroundings with the respect they deserve. They are truly gifts of the Great Spirit, deserve honor and respect and help whenever they need it. I will tan the hide and eat the meat and give thanks for the deer's sacrifice so I may live.

Lone Wolf

After working for some folks sewing tipis for a year in the early 1980s I got a call from my dad. He had settled in the North Carolina mountains and wanted to see me. I went to visit. I pulled up my tipi stakes and moved yet again in my endeavor to find an end to my hump. When I first visited Dad he took me aside and handed me a shoebox. In the box were these letters and photographs that I had sent home from Vietnam. He told me that I was grown now and these letters and photographs belonged to me. His hump with these valuable mementos was over. Now they were back where they started. They were my hump now.

In the North Carolina mountains I got a job building log cabins and started to collect tools. Still risking my life, I took a bad fall that left me in a back brace for a year. The first thing I did after the injury was pay my rent for six months in advance. During my recovery I found myself keeping the lights on and food on the table by selling small wood-turned lathe work I made from pieces of firewood. I could stand up for maybe an hour or hour and a half a day, and I spent that time at my small lathe. My Marine Corps training kicked in and I ignored the World of Hurt my back put me into and I slowly recovered and learned more and more about woodturning. My work improved as my health improved. I looked for a way to sell the things I was making and found a varied and rich history of crafts and craftspeople here in the Appalachian Mountains. I juried into a craft co-op and started to focus on making vessel forms. As I learned, I constantly upgraded my equipment and I was again intellectually and physically engaged and my hump changed once again. I became a full-time professional maker.

I met Lucy and finally had someone to share my life with. She is a maker too. With her help I stopped my self-destructive habits of smoking and doing the drugs that I had done for so many years trying to manage my hump.

I juried into two major craft guilds that provided many opportunities to show and sell my work. In 1986 I started to design and build my studio. I took my hand-made graph paper design and laid out the building on a hillside with a military compass and a string. I then cut the trees, hauled the logs to a mill and had them sawed into framing. It took me two years to build my studio, working a half day seven days a week. The other half day I would work on my lathe, learning more and more. *My work matured to the point that I was included in a great many national invitational shows. At this time I started to tell some of my fellow craftsmen that I was a Vietnam veteran. For many years I had to hide the fact that I had fought in Vietnam. Most of my professional craftsmen colleagues were in college when I was fighting for my life in Vietnam. Most of these folks demonstrated against the war and did not separate the warrior from the war. Two events of disrespect give me pause. The first event came when an artist known for being an outspoken elitist got me aside and with a smile told me he was a conscientious objector to the Vietnam War. My reply to him was not to worry, that "I had killed enough gooks for both of us." That*

reply shut the man up. The other event came when a fellow wood artist and his wife adopted an Asian baby. We were at a craft show and they had their new baby in their booth. I was walking past and stopped in to see the little one. The craftsman stepped towards me and blocked my attempt to see their new baby. They wouldn't let me near the child. That hurt me terribly. I saved a child's life in Vietnam but I was a "baby killer" in their eyes. I bear no ill will toward these ignorant folks.

I addressed my hump directly in some of my work. I made a series of narrative pieces that told Vietnam stories. Five narrative pieces are in the collection of the National Vietnam Veterans Art Museum in Chicago. The museum also has one of my Sentinel Series sculptures. My Sentinels are guardians and protectors. Every one who has been through the fire of war is a Sentinel in their heart. I am. Sometimes I sell Sentinels and sometimes I give them to folks that need protection.

All this time my hump and Marine Corps training sustained me. It gave me the strength to keep learning and doing. I became a

Three Sentinels. Black locust with metal elements, turned and carved. Every person who has been through the fire of war is a sentinel in their heart. We watch over and protect the innocent. I have made about twenty of these sculptures (courtesy Tim Barnwell).

teacher, a mentor, and a respected member of the large crafts community. My hump prevented me from making friends, but I sure knew enough folks.

Lucy and I together discovered kayaking and we now paddle whenever we get a chance. I keep a kayak journal.

Dec 24, 2006 Lake James NC

Lucy and I headed for Lake James this A.M. Saw a Redtail in his hunting grounds and a Turkey vulture spiraling over the road. Put in at Cannel Bridge and met Jack and Nancy. Jack is 70 and races kayaks. We all went together. Saw an Osprey with a Crow diving on the Osprey at the put in. Saw Herons, Kingfishers, Ducks, Loons, and Gulls. Had a good six hour paddle. Made coffee on a beach and took out at 3:30 and headed home. Saw a young Eagle right over our truck while loading up the boats. Good trip. Had Steak and potatoes at home.

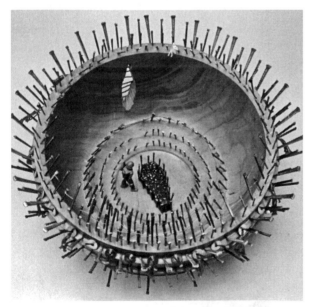

Memorial Bowl. Cherry with nails, wire, figurines. One of a series of eight pieces produced over a 25-year period. This narrative work is one of a series that I did around the turn of the century. Creating this series allowed me to use my art skills to work on my personal demons. After I made these and retired them to boxes in my studio I found there existed a place for art about Vietnam. All of this series found its way into the permanent collection of the National Vietnam Veterans Art Museum in Chicago, Illinois.

After my hump manifested itself by creating some major health problems, I hit the wall in 2000. With my partner's urging I sought help from the Veterans Administration. I first had to have lifesaving surgery and then I addressed my hump directly. The VA then told me that my hump had a name: they called it post-traumatic stress disorder. I started the medication and therapy that I continue to this day. The therapy is good and I finally have made some friends. My friends are mostly other veterans.

I was still lacking an important element in my life. I was engaged physically and intellectually but not spiritually. I thought back to when I was Lone Wolf and I started to find my Native American Spiritual path once again.

Walking the Red Road is difficult at times. The best way I can describe it is that it requires a cultural shift. For example, I now base my decisions in life on how those decisions will affect the children generations from now. I also live in a spiritual world where all things are treated with respect. Healing is always available on the Red Road. I was the recipient of an old Lakota ceremony that contributed greatly to my healing from war.

The Warriors Welcome Home Ceremony has been used for centuries to allow the transformation from a war-fighting warrior into a peaceful warrior but a warrior still. The traditional ceremony takes a number of hours and has many elements. As part of the ceremony I was awarded an eagle feather and I was given a new name, Akicita Tokala, First Warrior. At the end of my ceremony I was welcomed back into a village with the women trilling. The support of all the people filled my heart. I'm a lucky man.

In the spring recently I had an appointment at the Asheville Veterans Administration Hospital. I was early so I went outside and walked to a great spreading grove of old large oaks trees to wait. I sat at the base of one of the oaks and leaned back. I put some tobacco down as an offering, thanked the trees for all the healing they provided to the patients of the hospital and I just soaked in the beauty that surrounded me.

I noticed that every time I had come to the VA there were always one or two veterans sitting and enjoying the peace and solitude that the oaks provided.

Perhaps veterans could design and build a landscaping project that would protect the trees and encourage more veterans to use the space. During my appointment I spoke to a social worker and he encouraged me to design and submit a plan to the VA.

I came up with a design for a circular cairn that could be built in the center of the grove of oaks. Stone cairns have been used by humans all over the world to memorialize significant places or events. Stones endure; all else is temporary; stones are forever. The cairn would be six feet in diameter and have a two-foot tall wall constructed of block and faced and topped with stone. Folks could place stones in honor of veterans, each stone a prayer for healing. I paced off the distances, drew up a rough plan and submitted to the VA for approval. I heard back from the director of the hospital within three days and was given the green light.

I went to a group of veterans and asked for help in building the cairn. The group, mostly Marines, was enthusiastic and in eight weeks and with generous donations of time, materials, outdoor furniture, trackhoes, and backhoes, and sweat we had the Warriors Path Project built. Most of the donations came from veteran-owned businesses. The Warriors Path and Cairn would not have been possible without the help of these hard-working veterans: Steve Genetti, Jerry Hyatt, Charlie Johnson, John Cowart, Bobby Knight, Jesse Jones and Guy Wells.

During the excavation something wonderful happened. One of the crew, a three-times-wounded Vietnam Marine, spotted something in the newly turned earth. He reached down and picked up a four-inch-long rose quartz spear point. We stopped working and sat on the ground and passed the sacred object around. We had received a message from the warriors of the past to the warriors of the present in that 7500-year-old artifact. Right then we changed the name of the site from the Veterans Cairn to the Warriors Cairn. When we finished the construction in 2010, we had a dedication ceremony with over 100 veterans in attendance. We placed the spear point into a time capsule and the capsule into the cairn. The Warriors Cairn at the Asheville VAMC is a strong spiritual place of beauty and healing for many veterans. I've seen stones with three generations of veterans on them. There are stones honoring veterans from WWI, WWII, Korea, Vietnam, Iraq and Afghanistan. There are stones for nurses and pilots. One veteran of the combat heavy Iraq war humped a backpack full of stones to the cairn and, in a moving ceremony with other veterans, he placed the stones in the Warriors Cairn one at a time. The Warriors Cairn has opened hearts and has fostered healing. I am truly grateful that I could play a small part in that. If you do things for the right reasons the things that you do will be good.

The finished Warriors Cairn.

In 2006 I still had the box of my letters and photographs that my dad had given me years before. I felt the haunting burden of the memory of Vietnam when going through the letters and the photographs. I felt the full weight of my hump in these letters. I took a few letters out one day and read them. My response at first was to write some poetry. Some of the poems I wrote are included in this book. When in the presence of that box of letters I felt compelled to do something, but I wasn't sure what I was supposed to do. After several weeks my thoughts became clear. I was supposed to use these letters so others could learn what happens when we send our young to war. It was simple: my hump and my inclination to be a teacher and a healer would combine in a book. I started to create this manuscript. Reading each letter was hard and it was the hump. All the memories of war came back in a flood that threatened to overwhelm me. All those men I rolled up in their bloody ponchos still haunted me. If I had tried to deal with the grief in Vietnam I would have never survived. I had to stuff that grief into those bloody ponchos with those men and hump it for all these years. I've had to set this manuscript down and walk away several times because unrolling those ponchos became just too painful. The Marine Corps taught me tenacity so I toughed out the hump and dealt with my pain. This book came to life, but it has been a long hard road.

Today I am once again engaged on the physical, intellectual, and spiritual levels. I work out at our local gym and practice Tai Chi. As a result of traveling the Native American path of the Red Road my relationship with the natural world around me is rich and full. I greet each sunrise and each sunset with a small gift of tobacco and a prayer of thanks. I spend a lot of time making new objects in my studio. I'm just glad and thankful to be here. I want to leave this world in better shape than I found it. As I reflect on my life now I can see that my letters home from war were as much about me talking to myself as they were me talking to my parents and keeping the connection to home. As long as I could keep writing and not break the chain of letters I would live and I did.

In October 2009 I made the decision to move on from my past. I spent a day with my letters. I carefully handled each one. Some of the letters still had the mud of Khe Sanh and the blood of the Street Without Joy, Kim Lin, and Phu An on them. I purified each and every one with a prayer and sage, cedar, sweetgrass, and tobacco. I put them all in a painted red box with rubbings of the names of 14 friends I had taken from the Vietnam Memorial. I put some photographs, newspaper articles, poems, and tears into the box. I put a flag under the lid and I wrapped the box with a black ribbon. I then humped that box of cherished letters, memories, and emotions to Washington, D.C. and I humped it to the Wall. It was raining a bit and I could not make out the names so well because the Wall was wet. It was as if all the names on the Wall were all mixed together, but it was OK. I've been there before so I knew just where to go. I got to my knees and set the red box down at panel 47W line 21 under the name of my drill instructor, Sgt. Good, because he was the one who made me a Marine and he was the one who started me writing these letters that saved my life. I said a prayer of thanks and I asked Sgt. Good to take care of my letters, and he will. The letters don't belong to me now. My letters and this book and the hump that goes with them now belong to the thousands of children, women, and men, friend and foe, that died in the Vietnam War. This book is for all of those children, women, and men, humping, humping, humping, their endless hump.

> *Semper Fi,*
> *Rodger Jacobs*
> *Jake*
> *Jacques*
> *Crazy Jake*
> *Lone Wolf*
> *Akicita Tokala, First Warrior*
> *Rodger Jacobs*

Appendix 1: A Letter from Colonel Albert Slater

Letter from Col. Slater, October 2009. Col. Slater was my company commander Alpha Company 1/9 Vietnam. He wrote in response to reading my letters. (Printed with permission.)

Dear Rodger,

I really enjoyed our phone conversation and reading the rough on your future book "The Hump." Your letters home from the moment you entered MCRD Parris Island, throughout Vietnam, and through your recovery in the Naval Medical system constitute a very special and precious diary that so many will enjoy reading. I respect your tactful restraint in your Vietnam letters, realizing they would be read by tender family loved ones in addition to your father. Those of us who survived shared with you the hump of exhaustion and extreme emotions of fear, hate, anger, sorrow, disgust and the love of killing those rotten no good bastards — etc. This combat was so intense that I don't believe anyone can adequately describe it verbally. Only those who were there and survived can grasp the extent of it and then suffer the aftermath upon our return to the World [USA].

Your follow up post Nam troubled hump is touching, well written and also shared by our combat survivors. Too many of our warriors who returned never found peace, happiness, spouse, family support, help or work. Your biographical sketch is excellent as are all of your writings.

A very important quality in your forth-coming book is your perspective. Most Vietnam combat publishing seems to be written from a higher echelon viewpoint experience. It is so important that you continue to write with detailed honesty from the refreshing perspective of a true Marine PFC combat warrior. The casual reader can get a good feel for what you saw.

In the world of today and the scheme of things I've managed to put aside the detailed remembrances of our combat so as to maintain an attempt at normalcy and serenity. For years those memories permeated my mind driving me crazy and hurting those around me. Having read your book, I'm excited for you and I'm, aroused with all the details of our combat with A 1/9. I've enclosed some new publishing involving us that you may not have. I've also gone off the deep end talking about viewpoints and experiences that I obtained from my company level [3] echelons higher than your platoon. While I could see and feel [sense] your dilemmas, I wasn't in the fighting holes with you. I tried to remain where I could lead our Marines, influence the action and get support from above. There were times when our ranks were so depleted and combat so close and intense I felt a part of you, such as when I killed an NVA warrior at Phu An with my .45 handgun. This closeness to you, at a fire team level, in combat, was my most precious experience. Nothing else ever lived up to it and to some extent it hurt my career thereafter in the peacetime Marine Corps. So please tolerate my writings and ramblings. Perhaps something within can be used in the book. My writing may be bulky, hard to read and my spelling poor but I'm giving it my best shot.

Your first encounter at the Street Without Joy was in late December 1966 when the famous French author Bernard Fall was killed after tripping a Bouncing Betty land mine. This was before I came aboard. His death was world news. Later our Marines stated they had shown Fall the mine triggering devise, but he activated it while seeking cover from incoming. This also killed the Gy Sgt accompanying Mr. Fall. This area was a virtual minefield that only the locals and farmers knew how to safely navigate. Marines related to me that they required a farmer to lead them on patrol. When a Marine was killed by a landmine they took turns beating the farmer until he died. These happenings reported to me later by Marines in their leisure were my first indicators of the irrational rage and hate that permeated our Marines.

Your first encounter at Phu An was on March 24, 1967, when Sgt. Singleton was killed (MOH). This was probably the toughest and costliest combat A Co. had seen to date. You were met by ambushes, heavy machine gun fire, and a well-entrenched bunkered NVA stronghold similar to what we would encounter in May. After your CO, Capt. Festa, med evacuated due to mortar concussion injuries, I replaced him. I found "A" Co needing replacements, replenishments and a physical and psychological break after this encounter but they never got it.

In early April 67 after independent patrolling, we were called to our forward combat base at Con Thien, where we provided base security and where our trusty M-14 rifles were taken and replaced by M-16s. We were given classes and allowed to familure fire our new rifles. During a stay at Con Thien we were hit by artillery from a single NVA pack howster. It was a low trajectory weapon and the incoming noise gave us time to get down before impact. I required our Marines to always wear their helmets and flack jackets outside of fortified bunkers plus get down during incoming. This brought laughter from a contingent of South Vietnamese soldiers who sat in the open without protection. One pack howitzer round chanced to land on top of their group killing and injuring many. I heard follow up snickering from some of our Marines.

Later in April our company led the battalion in a night approach to the Street Without Joy. Some Marines tripped new plastic landmines (Toe Poppers) that would mangle feet and legs but would not kill. Charlie Company went into attack after receiving fire but the attack failed with numerous casualties. The company commander was killed and C Company was decimated and unable to function. We were ordered to go to their aid and relief. We traveled in the dark en route, walking in the tracks made by a tracked vehicle to avoid mines. We found most of C company to be dead and wounded lying in an open field in front of the enemy position. Expecting the worst, we formed into an attack formation moving through the remains of C Company. To my relief the NVA had pulled out. We established a perimeter of security within which we cared for and evacuated C company WIA/KIA. To our horror we found that in the attack their new M-16 rifles had jammed. As the Marines helplessly fell to try and clear their rifle jams, the NVA walked among them shooting them in their heads at point blank. Luck was on Alpha company's side for had the NVA remained in place we would have met the same fate as C Company. We carried the same new M16s and the same lot of ammunition. All Marines present were infuriated over the failure of our new weapons and the indiscriminate killing of helpless unarmed Marines. A lone NVA POW being escorted to BN for interrogation was found dead (bayoneted) on the side of the trail. This was the first of multiple NVA POW killings during my tenure.

I notified the Bn immediately of these circumstances, saying it was imperative that we get our M-14 rifles back. How could my Marines continue to seek contact with our enemy with a rifle they couldn't trust to fire? We all carried images of those defenseless Marines killed as they tried to clear their jammed weapons.

Bn called back with a forced-standard absolute reply. We would not get our trusty M-14 rifles back. "The M-16 was proven to be an effective rifle through all extensive field conditions." Bn's only conclusion is the jams were Marine caused — most probably the failure to properly clean the rifle. Shortly thereafter a Marine Colonel was helilifted to our field patrol base, where he again reiterated DOD and military position that the M-16 was problem free and we were to blame for its malfunction.

I felt totally abandoned in our dilemma. When we received the M-16s we were told they were self-cleaning. Cleaning kits were issued one per four-man fire team. DOD did not want us writing home that this multi-billion dollar contact was defective and killing our servicemen. In later months the 1/9 armorer wrote a paper saying he had stacks of jammed M-16 rifles in his armory at this time in which the fired cartridge casing had expanded and sealed in the chambers. Unlike today's effective M-16 rifles, our first-issued weapons did not have chromed chambers, a DOD money-saving measure. Further published analyses claim we were issued faulty ammunition with a wrong powder that caused cartridge-casing expansion upon firing. At the time no one would listen nor analyse the problem. Marines died needlessly.

After the "C" Co incident and while on patrol, a Marine stepped on a three-prong Bouncing Betty mine activator without activation. It was a dud and we managed to get him off without incident. There was a God.

In early May we were sent to a village south of Dong Ha where we were prebriefed that a village sentry would fire a round alarming all the villagers who would then take us under fire. We were ordered not to return fire. The sequence of village offensive took place exactly as predicted. This was one of multiple examples of when some unknown higher headquarters designated a hands-off safe haven for an enemy stronghold.

We then were ordered to proceed to and attack Phu An. Remembering our last costly March encounter with NVA at Phu An, our Marines were troubled to be ordered back there. The promise of heavy fire support prep before the attack and the attachment of Marine tanks boosted our morale.

Phu An was a village on the map located south of the DMZ and SW of Con Thien. On the ground it was barren with no indication that a village ever existed. We waited for the prep fire of artillery and air strikes. One attack aircraft went down due to engine failure or ground fire, but the pilot ejected and was saved. As we moved thru Phu An, there was no fire nor enemy presence. We moved north toward Con Thien. The noisy tanks took away our stealth and preannounced our presence, but we were glad to have their additional firepower.

It was 13 May 1967. Our lead platoon sighted NVA and aggressively pressed the attack by an attempted envelopment around the NVA left flank. The Plt commander, Lt. Gorney, was hit and killed. As we worked to extract our wounded, we received heavy mortar and machine gun fire. I requested our power ace in the hole — artillery and air support. This was promptly denied by Bn because of close danger. We were ordered by radio to "cease fire" because we were shooting at friendlies. We were taking casualties and I personally identified an enemy NVA dead. I replied we would not cease fire. I again felt we were totally abandoned from outside resources during this critical moment of need. The tanks were on line firing their main guns, and machine guns were in the heavy firefight. They were taking hits by RPG's that blistered their armament. Our Corpsman was pulling a wounded Marine behind a tank for cover from heavy incoming fire. We saw the tank start up and we tried to warn the tank of the friendlies behind him. Our new radio comm. was not compatable with the older tank comm. and we failed to reach it. To our horror we saw the tank back up, crushing the Corpsman and multiple injured Marines.

I thought, "How can so many things go wrong?" We fought this battle for three days. On the fourth day the entire 1/9 Bn came in, saturated the enemy with the heavy artillery and air support that was denied us and the Bn attacked. The few remaining live NVA had pulled out, leaving behind their extensive dead along with heavy weapons.

Major Fullham, the Bn Co gave Aco a verbal "well done." In the end I was hit with a gunshot wound to my upper arm, evacuated to the medical Bn at Dong Ha, where they cut and sewed, and was then given the opportunity to evacuate to the World (USA). Since my EAS was in July I opted to return to finish my tour as A Co commander.

The NVA at Phu An had simply moved and re-established elaborate defenses to the north. They again dug extensively, building large, camouflaged, multiple and mutually supporting bunkers that were connected by trench lines. We had approximately 20 KIA and over 39 WIA in this fight. Afterward we were a battered, depleted and exhausted company. We then provided perimeter defense at Con Thien while we attempted to recuperate. We resumed patrolling and engaged in two heavy combats in early July. When B Co became overrun and decimated by NVA, we fought to join and help them, finding only a Staff SGT and 26 Marines alive on July 2, 1967. Before my EAS I was replaced by Cap. Ryan. He was killed within two months. All of my fellow 1/9 company commanders were killed. A Co with 1/9 later went to Khe Sanh, where they fought in the siege.

While we were always provided the necessities of ammunition, food, water and medevac, A Co Marines were filthy from repeated sweat and constant living in the field. Our clothing uniforms and boots were worn, ripped, and dirty. We were the last in the distribution chain for uniform replacement. We saw rear echelon Marines, visitors, dignitaries and black marketers with the new uniforms first. When the new uniforms finally reached us in the field, they were picked over, with a lot of extra large and extra small. The few times we were given a few days to rest and replenish at Dong Ha, we were not well received. Our promised beer and soda were never there for us. There was drug use, heavy drinking, gambling, and an unfriendly, ungrateful attitude that greeted us. We saw a fragging at a SNCO club. We termed the non-combat Marines as "rear echelon poges" After two days in the rear I was aggressive in getting our Marines back into the field, where we regained our combat conditioning and attitude.

With the M-16 jam incident, the failure on support of resupply, the negative response for help at Phu An, the overall negative attitude we encountered in the rear and, with our providers, etc., I felt we had to be a self-sufficient entity within ourselves in A Co.

Rodger, you are a rare breed, an experienced Marine combat warrior who saw the most severe of combat. There is a distinct difference between the combat warrior who meets the enemy face to face in battle and the majority of support servicemen, who never were in harm's way in a combat zone. Our public and government see no difference and label all servicemen that served in a war zone as war vets.

The combat warrior suffer the WIA/KIA casualties and fight to survive and kill enemy in an existence others can never know. Warrior survivors return to CONUS with postwar combat stress that is devastating. There are the names of over 58,000 servicemen, mostly warriors, that gave their lives in Vietnam. It is outrageous to realize that more than 58,000 warriors who survived Vietnam combat have since committed suicide.

Additionally, thinking of the pain they suffered and the family members who took a beating before their deaths along the way is atrocious. A combat warrior is a special breed who is proud, self sufficient, resistant to accepting help and is in need of recognition and special VA help. Rodger, I hope you can mention the identity and plight of the combat warrior in the hump.

While our combat was tough [and] costly, we never backed off and we fought our tough NVA foes until they withdrew to their safe haven north of the DMZ. It's apparent we were beating our enemy in combat but the war was lost in the minds of the American people.

With so many things against us and what went wrong while A Co fought the NVA, our saving grace (virtue) was the tough dedication and fighting spirit of our individual fighting Marines. Rodger, you and the members of your combat team learned to do without and to face life and death situations repeatedly, aggressively, without hesitation and with unusual courage, dedication and endurance. You repeatedly refused to be defeated. I will never forget and always be grateful for your dedication and combat heroics.

I hope you can look beyond the painful combat memories and the awful, ungrateful welcome we received upon our return to CONUS. No doubt you will always join A Co. survivors in cherishing the pride in having served among brothers who repeatedly gave their lives for one another.

I'm thankful that you've found a loving, understanding wife, a somewhat peaceful existence, and your artistic talents to divert all toward the positive. May your forthcoming book bring you a sense of peace and success. May you enjoy well-deserved happiness.

> Semper Fidelis
> Love
> Albert Slater

As his letter states, Captain Slater went back into action as Alpha's CO shortly after recovering from the gunshot wound he suffered at Phu An.

In the action in July 1967 that he describes in his letter Captain Slater took Alpha Company into heavy combat to rescue Charlie Company. Charlie Company was being overrun and Alpha Company, under the leadership of Captain Slater, saved many Marine lives that day.

For this action Captain Slater was awarded the Navy Cross for valor, our nation's second highest award.

Semper Fi, Captain Contact

Appendix 2: The Woodturner

Selected Exhibitions

Collectors Choice 2007, The Greenhill Center for NC Art, Greensboro, NC, 2007

A Vision Realized, Blue Spiral 1, Asheville, NC, 2006

First in Fight: The Marine Corps in Vietnam, National Veterans Art Museum, Chicago, IL, 2005

Art in Embassies: Crafts from the Carolinas, Guatemala City, Guatemala, 2003

The Birthday Party, Brand Library and Art Center, Glendale, CA, 2001

Family Legacies, The Art Cellar Gallery, Banner Elk, NC, 2001

Two for 2000, Blue Spiral 1, Asheville, NC, 2000

Select 2000, Green Hill Center for NC Art, Greensboro, NC, 2000

Rodger Jacobs, Woodturner, Blue Spiral 1, Asheville, NC 1999

Small Treasurers, Del Mano Gallery, Los Angeles, CA, 1999

Beyond Tradition, Masterworks of Contemporary Wood, Heller Gallery, NY, NY, 1998

Spotlight 98: American Crafts Council, Arrowmont School, Gatlinburg, TN, 1998

Fanciful & Functional, Hickory Museum of Art, Hickory, NC, 1998

Up Against the Wall, Piedmont Craftsmen, Inc., Winston-Salem, NC, 1998

Turned Wood Now, Redefining the Lathe-Turned Object, Arizona Art Museum, Tempe, AZ, 1997–1998

Artistry in Wood, Hanson Artsource, Knoxville, TN, 1997

30th Annual Centerpiece Project, NC Arts Council, Raleigh, NC, 1997

Design & Narrative, Arrowmont School, Gatlinburg, TN, 1997

Turned Askew, Piedmont Craftsmen, Winston-Salem, NC, 1995

The Spirited Vessel, Sawtooth Center for Visual Art, Winston-Salem, NC, 1995

Treenware, Yale-Smithsonian Symposium on Material Culture, Yale University, NewHaven, CT, 1994

The American Craft, Trinity Arts Group, Atlanta, GA, April 1994

Crafts of the Carolinas, November 1993 through June 1994

Gibbes Museum of Art, Charleston, SC; Rudolph E. Lee Gallery, Clemson University, Clemson, SC; Folk Art Center, Asheville, NC; Spirit Square Center for the Arts, Charlotte, NC; Green Hill Art Center, Greensboro, NC

Vessels '92, The Upper Gallery, Milwaukee, WI, 1992

Small Craft Warnings, Gallery G, Pittsburgh, PA, 1991

Visions & Concepts, Arrowmont School, Gatlinburg, TN, 1990

Wood & Glass, Bascom-Louise Gallery, Highlands, NC, 1990

Private Collections

Arrowmont School
Asheville Art Museum
Jerry Drown
Cora Lee duPont
Elon College Permanent Collection

John C. Campbell Folk School Permanent Collection
National Vietnam Veterans Art Museum Permanent Collection
Norman Lear
Nancy Mangum
Hugh Morton, Grandfather Mountain Nature Museum
National Vietnam Veterans Art Museum Permanent Collection
Southern Highland Craft Guild Permanent Collection
General & Mrs. William Westmoreland
Oprah Winfrey
Ron Wornick
Mr. & Mrs. Robert Zimmerman

Teaching Experience

Arrowmont School, Gatlinburg, Tennessee
Woodturning Instructor August 2001, June 2000, April 1998, April 1997, September 1994, April 1994, March 1993, April 1991
Workshop Assistant, Al Stirt March 1990; Liam O'Neil June 1989; David Ellsworth March 1989
Pi Phi Weekend, All-Woman Woodturning Class, 1998, 1997, 1996
Appalachian Center for Crafts, Smithville, TN

Woodturning Instructor, October 1995
John C Campbell Folk School, Brasstown, NC
Masters Classes in Woodturning January 1996, January 1995, January 1994, January 1993
Woodturning Instructor March 1997, November 1992, August 1991
Private one and two day studio workshops 1988–1999. Approved by the American Association of Woodturners for their scholarship program.

Publications

American Woodturner, American Association of Woodturners
Get a Grip: Woodturning Hand Grips, June 1998
Book Review: "Practice of Woodturning" by Mike Darlow, September 1996
Design at Arrowmont, March 1996
Sneaky Bowls, March 1995
Video Review: "Practice of Woodturning" by Mike Darlow, February 1994
Controlling the Bite with a Back Stand, March 1993
Dust Extraction, March 1992
The Sanding of Turned Wood Objects, March 1989

Index

Page numbers in **_bold italics_** indicate illustrations.